Bound 1968

Voltaire

Voltaire by Nicolas de Largillière
Musée Carnavalet (Paris)—Photo-Hachette

VOLTAIRE

1561

BY GUSTAVE LANSON

English Translation by Robert A. Wagoner

WITH AN INTRODUCTION BY PETER GAY

JOHN WILEY & SONS, INC.

New York · London · Sydney

Library of Congress Catalog Card Number: 66–14137
Printed in the United States of America

TRANSLATOR'S FOREWORD

ALTHOUGH WIDELY RECOGNIZED as the best introduction to Voltaire to appear in any language since its publication sixty years ago (1906), this biography by Gustave Lanson, the famed French literary historian (1857–1934), has been unavailable in English until now. My own enthusiasm for the work was reinforced by the judgments of eminent authorities on Voltaire and eighteenth-century France. One of these, George R. Havens of the Ohio State University, writing in the *Cabeen Critical Bibliography of French Literature* (Syracuse University Press, 1951), made the following comment on Lanson's biography:

"Probably the best brief survey of Voltaire's life and work in any language—accurate, intelligent, succinct, written with a verve worthy of Voltaire himself. No doubt the best book for the general reader or student to begin his acquaintance with Voltaire."

And in a letter of July, 1964, Mr. Havens wrote: "I see no reason to change a word of this evaluation today." (The reader will also note in the pages of the *Introduction* the high esteem accorded Lanson and this biographical study by Peter Gay, an American historian internationally known for his cogent studies of Voltaire and the French Enlightenment.)

Undaunted by the truth in the old adage *traduttore, traditore,* I set myself the task of capturing and recreating the remarkable qualities inherent in the original. The challenge has been an exciting one, comparable, I think, to the experience of an actor or musician who recreates someone else's thoughts and emotions yet cannot do so in any creditable fashion without investing the material with a certain creative force of his own. We perhaps tend to overlook the fact that instrumentalists, actors, singers, and dancers are not the only practitioners of the performing arts. And like his fellow performers, a translator welcomes a challenging part, "a juicy role"—not necessarily a long one, but a good one. Such a one presented itself in Lanson's biography.

Just why this opportunity has been overlooked for so many years in the English-speaking world remains something of a mystery. For during the last two decades there has been an unprecedented output of fine, often superb, English translations of French works old and new: plays, novels, poetry, philosophy, etc. Since the Lanson study is a staple in any Voltaire bibliography, one might have expected an English version sooner, particularly in the United States where the Age of Enlightenment and its brilliant French luminaries have long enjoyed a revered place in American intellectual life—a tradition dating back to pre-Revolutionary days. Lanson's biographical study deserves a wider audience in this country than the relatively few who can read him with ease in the original. It is therefore gratifying to see this project become a reality.

In his own lifetime, and for generations thereafter, Voltaire was a highly controversial figure. For some he will always remain such. As the most representative writer of his age, an age that witnessed a vast movement of political, social, scientific, and philosophical thought affecting both the Old World and the New, Voltaire was, more than any other single writer, the clearing house of those ideas, their disseminator and popularizer. He was like a nonstop tape recorder registering all the intellectual vibrations of his time and, like a playback, amplifying those vibrations for everyone to hear.

Of Voltaire's writings, the average reader is familiar only with *Candide,* that devastating satire on fatuous optimism, on the uncritical acceptance of the view that "God's in his heaven; all's right with the world," or, in eighteenth-century terms, the popular maxim of Alexander Pope: "Whatever is, is right," an attitude echoed in the public's misconception of Leibnitzian philosophy and its doctrine of a "pre-established harmony" in the universe. Voltaire compressed these views into a composite caricature tailor-made for the slings and arrows of outrageous satire: "All is for the best in this best of all possible worlds." Peter Gay, in his bilingual edition of the work (see bibliography), notes that *"Candide* is read everywhere . . . [it] is that rare literary phenomenon, a classic in active cultural circulation." Now the reading of *Candide* alone leaves many with the impression that Voltaire was a rather heartless cynic, devilishly cunning and hilariously clever at puncturing the follies of man and society. We see a world peopled mainly by puppets, irrational creatures with one-track minds, each driven by some relentless passion, mania, or desire and, oftener than not, headed on a collision course with other puppets of opposite persuasion. These animated robots blithely ignore objective truths and scientific facts unless, of course, such truths or facts can be twisted and enlisted in support of one's preconceived notions and prejudices. Their "reasoning" often consists of a series of ludicrous *non sequiturs*. Dr. Pangloss, the incurable optimist, is the epitome of this human propensity. Though caught in a chain of horrendous calamities and dire misfortunes, he is never for a moment tempted to revise his original rosy premise, his unfissionable conviction that all that happens necessarily happens for the best.

Like present-day existentialists, Voltaire recognized the predominance of the absurd in human behavior. His intellectual reaction expressed itself in mockery and irony. To hold men's foibles up to laughter and ridicule is essentially a cerebral activity, a rational response to life's absurdities. In the words of Horace Walpole (who befriended Voltaire): "The world is a comedy to those that think, a tragedy to those who feel." Satire is an escape hatch for one's rationality in the face of heart-rending tragedy. Beaumarchais, a kindred spirit and contemporary of Voltaire, put the same thought into the words of his immortal Figaro: "I make haste to laugh at everything for fear of being obliged to weep." For Voltaire was by no means insensitive to the tragedies of life. He was a man with a heart and with a consuming desire to improve the lot of mankind. He shared the prevailing view of most eighteenth-century *philosophes* that society can be improved and that man can take immediate, practical steps toward that end. Lanson illuminates the positive side of Voltaire's work, particularly in Chapter 9, which presents a concise summary of the philosopher's contributions to the political, historical, religious, and social questions of the eighteenth century and spells out many of the constructive measures Voltaire advocated and acted upon in a spirit of personal commitment, in the *engagé* manner so dear to a Camus or a Sartre.

Like any responsible "conservative" or "liberal," Voltaire wanted gradual and peaceful reforms, not revolutionary violence. He distrusted dogmas of any sort—religious, political, or philosophical. As the foremost historian of his age (and the first great historian of modern times), he was painfully aware of the ease with which dogma leads to fanaticism, and fanaticism, for Voltaire, was the ever-present evil in all the dreadful chronicles of man's inhumanity to man.

In Voltaire's day (as in the sixteenth and seventeenth centuries) perhaps the most intolerant and vehement attitudes were those taken by religious dogmatists. Voltaire waged an all-out war on religious bigotry, eventually assailing organized Christianity in general and the Roman Catholic Church in particular. The virulence of his attacks, often ludicrously irresponsible, inevitably antagonized many who were not bigots. But Voltaire was horrified by the seemingly endless accounts of violence and cruelty committed over the centuries in the name of religion, and he was infuriated that such conduct was often condoned, and even encouraged, by those who professed a religion of love. During his lifetime, Voltaire came to the aid of more than one victim of religious persecution, arousing public opinion and the conscience of all Europe. If today we live in a world where men respect, or at least tolerate, each other's religious views, it is because of men like Voltaire, who succeeded in pulling the poisoned fangs of religious intolerance.

In our day mankind is bedeviled above all by political and ideological *idées fixes,* by doctrinaire rigidities of the right and of the left. And the peril to society is immeasurably greater now than in the eighteenth century, for not only can the new fanaticisms control and manipulate mass media of communications (propaganda machines and methods of thought control have surpassed anything dreamed of in Voltaire's day), but such forces now have potential access to weapons of destruction capable of annihilating the entire human race, not to mention all other forms of terrestrial life. There seems little doubt that, were Voltaire alive today, he would be sorely dismayed by the failure of "enlightenment" to produce a more rational and humane world order. He would, one suspects, ruefully concede the truth in the old French proverb: *Plus ça change, plus c'est la même chose*. Yet one cannot imagine Voltaire withdrawing from the struggle to establish the rule of reason. It was not in his nature to despair. Nor was it in his nature to live the purely contemplative life, a life of spiritual or philosophical detachment. More often than not he felt compelled to get into the act, to fight the good fight.

He would surely be the first to applaud the enormous technological, medical, and scientific advances of our era. He would rejoice over the very real prospect of eliminating poverty, disease, and illiteracy from the face of the earth. But as for the militant proponents of different political and social systems, it seems to this observer that Voltaire would still adhere to his stated policy of *tolerance and test* (the principle Lanson notes as characteristic of

Voltaire's attitude toward political régimes and religious bodies during the last twenty years of his life). It is hard to believe that Voltaire would depart from that principle even in these perilous times when his policy might be formulated as "peaceful and competitive coexistence."

To his everlasting credit, Voltaire (like all the great *philosophes*) placed human dignity, intellectual freedom, and the individual conscience of man over and above all other considerations. He offered no blueprint for a Utopia. He favored what we today would call "a mixed economy." He strongly endorsed capitalism, free enterprise, and the sanctity of private property. He became a landed proprietor and a man of great wealth. And though he lived in an age not yet transformed by the Industrial Revolution, he did not hesitate to advocate and press for numerous socialistic measures, for public welfare programs, public utilities, a state-supported educational system, homes for the aged and infirm, and other humanitarian services to be provided for by the state from taxes levied on all its citizens according to their ability to pay. One can imagine him satirizing the doctrinaire views of ideological zealots of the twentieth century with the same fiendish delight he took in deflating certain *faiseurs de systèmes* in the eighteenth century.

Voltaire disturbed a great many people (and delighted an even greater number) because he insisted on thinking for himself and because he dared to think out loud. His influence, as Lanson observes, defies measurement by conventional criteria. It was enormous in the eighteenth century; it persisted, if mainly in its anticlerical aspects, during the nineteenth century; and it continues, however elusive and attenuated, in our own era. Probably no other writer did so much as Voltaire to instill an attitude of skepticism—an *esprit critique*—in French society as a whole, an attitude that has managed to survive all periods of temporal or spiritual repression. Pierre Daninos amusingly satirized this state of mind when he declared that a Frenchman is born, lives, and dies *méfiant* (suspicious, distrustful). Voltaire helped to create that indefinable thing we call "public opinion." Indeed, public opinion, as we know it, came into being in the eighteenth century. Voltaire persuaded the public that it was competent to pass judgment on any and all questions in the light of "reason" and common sense. Broadly speaking, Voltaire captured the mind of pre-Revolutionary France much as Rousseau was to capture its heart.

In his best-known work *Science and the Modern World* (1925),

Alfred North Whitehead offered the following judgment on Voltaire and the Age of Enlightenment:

"We cannot overrate the debt of gratitude which we owe to these men [the *philosophes*]. For a thousand years Europe had been a prey to intolerant, intolerable visionaries. The common sense of the eighteenth century, its grasp of the obvious facts of human suffering, and of the obvious demands of human nature, acted on the world like a bath of moral cleansing. Voltaire must have the credit that he hated injustice, he hated cruelty, and he hated hocus-pocus. Furthermore, when he saw them, he knew them. In these supreme virtues, he was typical of his century on its better side." (Chapt. IV)

Encouragement for this endeavor came from so many friends and colleagues that it would be difficult to name them all. I wish, however, to express special appreciation to the following: George R. Havens of the Ohio State University, who patiently read the entire typescript and offered innumerable suggestions, notes, and corrections: my debt to him is a large one; also Peter Gay of Columbia University, who kindly offered to write the *Introduction* to this translation, a contribution all readers will welcome; Donald M. Frame and Leon S. Roudiez of Columbia University; Sidney A. Burrell of Barnard College, Columbia, without whose initial help this project might never have got off the ground; Seymour Rudin of the University of Massachusetts, who helped resolve certain stylistic difficulties; Carl E. Jennings and Samuel M. Wagoner of the State Industrial School, Sheridan, Illinois; and colleagues at the State University of New York Maritime College, especially Joel J. Belson, Oscar B. Goodman, and Frederic C. Genzmer. A special word of gratitude is due William L. Gum of John Wiley and Sons for his unfailing patience and reassurance through numerous trials and vexations. And I would be remiss not to mention the invaluable services of Mr. Gum's secretary, Evelyn O'Neil, and Mrs. Harriet McDougal, also of John Wiley and Sons. But I hasten to add that the responsibility for any inadequacies or shortcomings falls on me and not on any of the aforementioned.

R. A. WAGONER

New York City
December 1965

AUTHOR'S FOREWORD

I HAVE ENDEAVORED in this book to speak about Voltaire precisely and historically, without glorification or caricature, without regard for current events or contemporary concerns, seeking always to relate Voltaire's idea or expression to the relevant topics of his own time.

I have tried to bring out the principal directions of his mobile thoughts. The reader who sets out to explore Voltaire's vast and varied literary output is soon lost in a maze of contradictions, which can be partially resolved if care is taken to date each text and ascertain the proper, precise, and relative meaning of each item with respect to the circumstances surrounding its composition. One must distinguish what was written for the public from what was written for private correspondence. One must distinguish his reflective, philosophical views from his purely whimsical outbursts, and his general views of the social order from those occasional wiles motivated by self-interest. One must evaluate all the editorial changes dictated by the intended audience for each work in question, determining whether the changes resulted from some specific event or were directed against a certain individual. Care must be taken to judge from the literary style whether Voltaire was serious or jesting, whether he was speaking for himself or had donned a mask that required a given accent and thoughts or opinions of a particular nature. On encountering statements that appear contradictory, we must try to discover what was actually the author's view and what was simply a concession to popular opinion. Different values must be assigned to his ideas depending on whether they deal with the actual topic under discussion or only with corollary subject matter growing out of his general train of thought. In the latter case, Voltaire, ever anxious to limit the area of controversy, used noncontroversial thoughts and ideas as much as possible, keeping ready to resume the battle on other terrain at the first opportunity.

These indispensable judgments are often delicate matters, difficult to evaluate. One cannot be too careful or too scrupulous in steering a middle course and avoiding the intrusion of one's personal feelings and prejudices. I dare not claim that my efforts in this respect have always been successful.

I would like to thank the librarians of the *Bibliothèque Nationale* and the *Bibliothèque de l'Arsenal,* who have been most patient and obliging throughout the period of my studies on Voltaire these past few years. I wish also to express my gratitude to M. and Mme de Salignac-Fénelon, who so graciously accorded me the opportunity to visit their château in Cirey, less frequented than Ferney, yet no less deserving of attention by those with an interest in Voltaire. Its charming location, which once seemed wild and remote, Voltaire's long room with its ornate doorway, the theatre with its tiny loge and hidden staircase leading to the bedroom of "la belle Emilie"—the entire setting of ten years in Voltaire's life still stands and reinforces with its concrete details the imagination of anyone who has read the correspondence of Voltaire, of Mme du Châtelet, and of Mme de Graffigny.

GUSTAVE LANSON

CONTENTS

INTRODUCTION

by Peter Gay

GUSTAVE LANSON's *Voltaire* is now sixty years old—it was first published in 1906—but it remains the best short biographical study of Voltaire in any language, certainly any language that I know. It is therefore good to have the book available in English, especially in Robert A. Wagoner's faithful and fluent version: I can think of no work to which I would rather send the beginning student, and even the seasoned professional, than this. Lanson's *Voltaire* is, in a word, a classic, and a classic that does not show its age.

To say this much in a field in which scholars are active, numerous, and often contentious is to offer high praise, and it is high praise I intend to offer: in his rich career, Gustave Lanson wrote indefatigably, but he did more than scribble. He transformed the study of French literary history and—what is even more important —he changed men's minds. Born at Orléans in 1857, he attended the *Ecole Normale Supérieure,* which produced so many of the best minds in France, taught at several *lycées,* and was called, in 1903, to the Sorbonne, to the prestigious chair of French literature. He was not an impressive lecturer; histrionics were always beyond, or beneath him. But he had many pupils and almost as many disciples. No one took more trouble to guide students than he; no one was, in his quiet way, more provocative. It is true, he collected detractors, and when he died in 1934, at seventy-seven, romantic souls impatient with his severe method breathed a sigh of relief: there were many who could not share his enthusiasm for sound, well-informed, *scientific* literary history. But his admirers outnumbered, and outweighed, his critics, and the admirers were in the right; perhaps we have less faith in scientific literary history than Lanson, the spiritual follower of Renan and Taine, could muster, but his faith in painstaking research, and his magnificent honesty with himself—his willingness to confess mistakes and change his mind—remain priceless legacies.

Lanson embodied both his honesty and his industry in his schol-

1

arly articles, which invariably addressed themselves to important questions,[1] in his influential bibliographical manual, in his celebrated and immensely popular *Histoire de la littérature française* first published in 1894 and often revised, and in his lively, insightful biographies (which the French call *vulgarisation* but which we would do well not to call vulgar): books like his *Bossuet,* his *Corneille,* and above all his *Voltaire.* That *Voltaire,* the book in our hands, demonstrates his capacity for growth, even in middle life and at the height of his fame, when other, lesser men, rigid with prestige and affluence, would disdain to learn. As a younger man, in the early editions of his *Histoire de la littérature française,* he had thought rather little of Voltaire (and very little indeed of Rousseau), but then, not long before he embarked upon his *Voltaire,* he undertook a strenuous course of reading the classics of the French Enlightenment, and found that his judgments had been shallow and half-informed.[2] The *Voltaire* (like his famous article on Rousseau, published six years later to celebrate the bicentennial of Rousseau's birth[3]) was designed to make, and triumphantly did make, amends.

Lanson's *Voltaire* still breathes the fresh air of new discovery matched with solid learning, and it is this combination that keeps the book alive for us, and keeps it useful. But, inevitably, time has passed; Lanson himself, had he the opportunity, would rewrite the book—although he would have to withdraw few judgments and make few alterations. And he would rewrite it, I think, in the light of source materials that have come to light since 1906, in the light of a new, more detailed understanding of the environment in which Voltaire worked, and finally, in the light of some recent interpretations.

I

When Lanson wrote his *Voltaire,* the standard edition of Voltaire's works for all serious students, including Lanson himself, was that of Louis Moland.[4] For its day it was a respectable edition which intelligently used the scholarship of earlier researchers and added some new discoveries. But it had serious deficiencies. It printed all the letters then known, but, while it was richer than any collection printed before, many letters were still to be discovered, and quite a few were to be redated. Moland also took the trouble of printing Voltaire's revealing notebooks, but what he printed was sadly incomplete. In addition, a number of Voltaire's shorter works had been indiscriminately thrown together into an alphabetical compendium that he called, arbitrarily enough, the *Dictionnaire philosophique*. The real *Philosophical Dictionary* had first been published in 1764, and enlarged several times;[5] but the alphabetical mess that went under this title in Moland's edition included Voltaire's *Lettres philosophiques* (his important book on England first published in 1733 and 1734)[6] and his *Questions sur l'Encyclopédie,* a work of his old age which repeated and enlarged many of the articles in the original *Dictionnaire philosophique*. This was the edition with which Lanson had to work in 1906.

We are more fortunate today. Beginning in the 1930's, volume after volume of new letters have appeared to enrich Voltaire's already vast correspondence: letters to the Tronchins, a family of Genevan patricians—physicians, lawyers, bankers, and magistrates; letters to the brothers Cramer, who published many of Voltaire's later works; letters to his niece, madame Denis. And these collections shed much new light on Voltaire's social life and political ideas, his strategies with publishers and even his erotic experience. Lanson's Voltaire was a complicated man; the man we are glimpsing today is more complicated still.

Fortunately, the scattered treasures of his correspondence are being gathered together into one magnificent whole. In 1953, Theodore Besterman published the first volumes of what will become the definitive edition of Voltaire's correspondence—all the letters he wrote, all the letters he received, and many letters that concern him.[7] In addition, Besterman is publishing corrections and additions in his periodical, *Studies on Voltaire and the Eighteenth Century.*[8] And Mr. Besterman has put us in his debt in still another way: in 1952 he brought out a complete and impressive edition of *Voltaire's Notebooks* that supersedes all earlier versions. It is fascinating to speculate what Lanson, always alert to the nuances of style, would have done with this fine version of the notebooks: here are, in germ, and often in several forms, some of Voltaire's best ideas and most provocative formulations. They show conclusively what Lanson hinted at: that Voltaire, the facile wit, was also a deliberate, hard-working literary craftsman.[9]

The accumulation of new material is one advantage the Voltaire scholar of the 1960s has over the Voltaire scholar of sixty years ago. The ordering of old material is another. Here Lanson himself took a hand. In 1909, he brought out a correct, fully annotated edition of Voltaire's *Lettres philosophiques*—the book he had called, in his *Voltaire,* vividly but accurately, "the first bomb dropped on the

Old Regime."[10] Other scholars have followed Lanson's lead, as they followed him so often: we now have useful editions of Voltaire's *Dictionnaire philosophique*,[11] his *Essai sur les moeurs*,[12] and other books, and we can now see, better than Lanson ever could, just what Voltaire wrote, and when. It is a great help in sorting out a complicated career.

II

For there can be no question: Voltaire's career was as complicated as it was long—and it was very long. Voltaire lived from 1694 to 1778, and was in turn light society poet, half political exile half tourist in England, author of immensely successful neoclassical tragedies, amateur scientist and well-informed popularizer of Newton, a meddler in French and Genevan politics, a friend—and enemy—of the great, a wealthy speculator, a pioneering historian, an innovator in the short story, an influential literary critic, and, in his later years, an indefatigable polemicist in behalf of the victims of French justice, in behalf of toleration and free speech, and against what he called *l'infâme*, against "superstition," "fanaticism" as much as against Christianity and all other organized religions. In addition to all this he was constantly engaged with life—with literary adversaries, with crowned heads, with publishers, with other *philosophes*, with physicists and bankers and physicians (for Voltaire, despite his long life was always just a little ill) —and he was engaged, always, as a wit. Inevitably, innumerable anecdotes arose around him; and some of them were true.

The danger with such a man is that he will not be taken seriously. His admirers will adulate and his detractors denigrate him. Lanson did take him seriously, and announced at the very beginning of his book that he intended to speak of Voltaire with precision, as a historical person, "without glorification or caricature." But just as there were some things about Voltaire that he could not know, there were studies of Voltaire's environment—his social, intellectual, political, and emotional world—that had not been made when he wrote his book. Lanson was therefore reduced to making guesses, often inspired, usually sound, but guesses none the less.

There are three areas particularly in which we now have as complete a view of Voltaire as we are likely to have, but in which Lanson was seriously handicapped. They are his life with madame du Châtelet, his affair with his niece, and his involvement in the politics of Geneva.

Madame du Châtelet—an amorous bluestocking, as intelligent as Voltaire if not as witty, as competent as Voltaire in languages and more competent than he in the sciences—madame du Châtelet was Voltaire's mistress for over fifteen years, from about 1733 to 1749, the year of her untimely death. She died shortly after giving birth to a child that was neither Voltaire's nor her husband's, but Saint-Lambert's—a minor poet whose main claim to distinction seems to have been his success with women. Voltaire lived with madame du Châtelet at her château in Cirey for many years, interrupting his stays there mainly for visits to the Prussian or the French court. Most biographers, almost inevitably, have treated these years as an amorous episode; they allude to the couple's experiments in physics, and their heavy reading, mainly as amusing embroidery on a rococo tale. Lanson himself, however, calls Cirey a place of rest, study, security (it was in Champagne, far from the police of Paris), and love. It was all that, to be sure, and, as Lanson's list suggests, study loomed large: physics and metaphysics occupied Voltaire as they occupied his mistress, and often their labors merged. But it was not until the 1940s that Ira O. Wade examined these years—the decade and a half from 1734 to 1749—with real care, and made transparent what had been opaque before: Cirey was indeed the place for serious study, and what the pair studied even more seriously than Newton's physics and Newton's metaphysics was the Bible, both the Old and the New Testaments.[13] Painstakingly, with grave hostility and alert intelligence, Voltaire and madame du Châtelet studied every verse of Holy Writ, using commentaries, higher criticism, deist propaganda, and their own secular common sense to single out the cruelty of the Chosen People, the inanity of the miracles related in the New Testament, the contradictions and incoherences that mark many of the books of the Old Testament. It is clear today, as it was not sixty years ago, that much of the anticlerical and antireligious propaganda which Voltaire threw into the world beginning in the 1750s, and at an ever-increasing tempo in the 1760s, had been thought out, and even written down, much earlier at Cirey. Love mattered, but work mattered more.

But love mattered too, to Voltaire, although in a way that Lanson could not have guessed. We know today what Lanson did not know: just as madame du Châtelet had consoled herself for her neglect —her lover, Voltaire, was aging—by taking other lovers, usually scientists or poets, so Voltaire consoled himself for the infidelity of his mistress by conducting a long, often interrupted and often resumed, stealthy love affair with madame Denis, the daughter of his sister. This was an extraordinary affair, not only because of the peculiar personage on whom Voltaire chose to bestow his affections and with whom he chose to satisfy his erotic needs, but also because it was kept secret so successfully—this in a world in which private affairs were rarely kept private. The secret indeed was not revealed until 1938, when the first batch of Voltaire's love letters to his niece became public.[14] One wonders just what Lanson would have made of *that:* his sympathetic and discriminating portrait of Voltaire would have become even more discriminating, if perhaps not more sympathetic. It is clear now from these letters that behind Voltaire's proverbial grin, behind his fervent humanitarianism, his incessant activity and tireless sociability, there hid a lonely man.

In his lifetime this loneliness was anything but apparent. When Voltaire finally settled down in the neighborhood of Geneva in the late 1750s, to cultivate his garden, act his plays, and broadcast his views, his country houses—first in Geneva, at *Les Délices;* later nearby on French soil, at Ferney—were always filled with guests. Many of these guests were Genevans talking Genevan politics. From the beginning of the eighteenth century, the little republic had undergone considerable inner turmoil, breaking out more than once in outright civil war. The Genevan patriciate, the old families which conveniently forgot that they were the offspring of immigrants—of Huguenots hunted out of France early in the sixteenth century—had engrossed political power in its hands, and secured it by circumventing the constitution, intermarrying, and keeping the lower orders from any significant share in political life. Voltaire, sensing rightly enough at the end of the '50s and the beginning of the '60s that more serious trouble was brewing, acquainted himself with the Genevan constitution and Genevan political history and intervened cheerfully for years. This intervention, much of it private and some of it highly secret, appears rather obliquely in the correspondence available to Lanson in 1906, but is quite palpable to us now. In consequence, we have some illuminating volumes on Voltaire and Geneva, volumes that enrich our conception and compel us to rethink our judgment of Voltaire's political ideas.[15]

III

Thus knowledge leads to reinterpretation. But, as I have said before, Lanson would hardly resist such reinterpretation, and in any event he would have little to withdraw. His pages on Voltaire's political and philosophical ideas are few, but his judgments are perspicacious and, in light of later discoveries, positively prescient.

The literature on Voltaire has become so vast that it seems to defy summary. But the most important conclusions we can draw from it—conclusions implied or pithily anticipated in the book before us—seem to me to be four: to begin with, Voltaire was serious rather than frivolous, a real philosopher if an informal one. Alfred North Whitehead's phrase, *"Les philosophes* were not philosophers,"[16] has become all too popular. One can see what he meant when he said it: while there were technical philosophers among the men of the Enlightenment—epistemologists like Hume, metaphysicians like Kant—most of the *philosophes* did their philosophizing in essays, in dialogues, even in short stories, and, far from troubling themselves with the refinements of formal logic or subtle points of metaphysical doctrines, they preached a program of humanitarianism, cosmopolitanism, and secularism. But if to think seriously and consistently about problems of society and problems of the relations of man to the universe, if to criticize freely, boldly, and intelligently, the conclusions and assumptions of one's philosophical predecessors is to be a philosopher, then the *philosophes* were indeed philosophers, and Voltaire, the most amusing among them, was a philosopher as well, in his own way.

But what kind of a philosopher? This question brings me to my second point: his religious views. Here recent literature has produced no surprises. It has confirmed what Voltaire himself always said: that he was a deist, or, as he sometimes liked to put it, meaning the same thing, a "Theist." Now a Voltairian deist was a freethinker convinced that there was a God who had created the universe as a rational, orderly, lovely, and moral whole, and had then withdrawn from it to allow men to discover its rules and make their own. Any positive religion exacting belief in miracles, prayers, expiations, saints, or similar excrescences, was simply a superstition. Now there have always been pious admirers of Voltaire anxious to claim him for Christianity, especially Catholicism; they have argued that *écrasez l'infâme* simply meant "destroy fanaticism" —of a kind abhorrent to rational Christians too. But this will not do: Voltaire's entire career testifies against it, and what such careful students as René Pomeau have shown in impressive detail is precisely what Voltaire himself had always said. He was not a Christian but a deist, and indeed a virulently anti-Christian deist.[17]

On the other hand, recent studies have done much to clarify the relation of Voltaire's religious ideas to his politics. Like all other *philosophes,* Voltaire was troubled over the masses, the great un-washed, the *canaille:* if philosophers could live with the truth that God, having created the universe and its physical and moral laws, had withdrawn from it, that did not mean that ordinary men, espe-cially uneducated men, might not be able to bear so hard a truth—it might make them feel lost, irresponsible, and turn them into anti-social beings. Voltaire had no final solution—his philosophizing was too informal and too continuously alive to permit any finalities—but he did have a suggestion: do not lie to the *canaille* more than you have to, or longer than you have to. Give it a noble concep-tion of the Deity, adding to the truth only the single, if important, improbability (that is, improbability for the philosopher) that God supervises man's actions, and rewards or punishes him after death. But even this lie—which I have called a "noble white lie"[18]—need not be carried on forever. As men advance in reason and enlighten-ment, slowly and uncertainly yet over the long run measurably, even the noble white lie will be relegated to the museum of out-worn political devices.

In politics—to come to the third point—the situation is rather different. In some of his best pages, Lanson sketches Voltaire's relativism: constitutional and representative governments are good governments, but there are some states, like France, where such institutions would simply keep the survivals of feudal anarchy alive, where, therefore, a strong king is a necessity.[19] In recent years, this insight has been systematically extended to show that Voltaire was indeed extremely flexible. He was not flexible about goals: he wanted humane government, lenient punishment of criminals, free speech and press, and as much public responsibility as the subjects could take. But he was flexible about methods: England had proved the viability of parliamentary institutions; the Dutch Re-public had proved the possibility of relative equality; Geneva was proving, before Voltaire's eyes, the possibility that even poor craftsmen might be allowed to participate in making public de-cisions. France was different for the reasons I mentioned a moment ago; and so were Prussia and Russia: the historic development of these countries demanded the weakening of privileged bodies in the states—that is, the nobility and the clergy needed to be stripped of their power and their exemptions before good government could succeed. And so, as a political theorist, Voltaire leavened his principles with a strong dash of sociological realism and historical insight.

For Voltaire—and this is the final point—had a strong sense of history, a sense that has often been denied to him. It is true, of course, that he lacked what the historicists of the nineteenth century, great historians like Ranke and his pupils, regarded as the essential historian's virtue: the capacity to appreciate, and to enter into, all ages equally, loving all and judging none. Voltaire loved few, and judged all. It is not that he was a simple-minded Whig, seeing history as a vast theater in which heroes fought unceasingly against villains. But it remains true that he chose sides, praising philosophers, skeptics, rationalists, and denigrating ages of faith. Hence his history has relevance to his political concerns; hence it is often myopic.

But, even if this is granted, recent scholarship has made plain that Voltaire understood the past rather better than many of his critics have been ready to grant. He could even, on occasion, appreciate the virtues, the cultivation, of Christians. Besides, his conception of history as a total view of culture, in which the arts and sciences deserved a place as prominent as the reigns of kings and the battles of generals, and his conception of historical causation as wholly secular—as a sequence of events in which men clashed with men, and sought to master nature—meant a powerful advance in the historical profession.[20] Voltaire was not as detached as Ranke, not as serenely wise—he was in the midst, not above, the battle. But Ranke would have been unthinkable without Voltaire's great histories, without the *Siècle de Louis XIV* or his comprehensive and ambitious *Essai sur les moeurs*.

It is this formula, I think, that will serve us to place Lanson's book in the stream of Voltairian scholarship: recent writers on Voltaire's life and ideas have gone beyond Lanson, but they would be unthinkable without Lanson. And just as historians still read Voltaire with pleasure and great profit, so students of Voltaire should continue to read Lanson, for the same reasons, and with the same effects. We may not end with Lanson—one is never wholly finished, as René Pomeau so well says, with Voltaire—but there is no one with whom it would be better to begin.

NOTES

1. Of special relevance for the Enlightenment are "Origines et premières manifestations de l'esprit philosophique dans la littérature française de 1675 à 1748," *Revue des cours et conférences* (December 26, 1907–April 21, 1910); and "Le rôle de l'expérience dans la formation de la philosophie du XVIIIᵉ siècle," *La revue du mois*, IX

(January, April 1910), 1–28, 409–429. A collection of these two and similar articles would make a most stimulating book.

2. In the *"Avertissement"* to the eleventh and twelfth editions of his *Histoire de la littérature française* (dated July 30, 1909–June 14, 1912), Lanson announces that he has come to see sympathetically, and to appreciate, Voltaire's *intelligence.*

3. "L'Unité de la pensée de Jean-Jacques Rousseau," *Annales de la société Jean-Jacques Rousseau,* VIII (1912), 1–18—an epoch-making article. For an appreciation of its place in the Rousseau literature, see my *The Party of Humanity* (1964), "Reading About Rousseau," 211–261.

4. 52 volumes (1877–1885).

5. See Voltaire, *Philosophical Dictionary,* translated with an Introduction by Peter Gay, 2 vols. (1962), 29–32.

6. The history of this work, which first appeared in an English translation and only a year later in its original French, is well told by Lanson. See below, Chapter 2.

7. This magnificent edition has just been completed—in 103 volumes.

8. There are at present more than thirty volumes of this valuable occasional journal. Each of these volumes repays careful study: some contain special studies on the world of Voltaire and on such *philosophes* as Holbach; others, important articles on all aspects of Voltaire.

9. This is one book that could still profitably be written: a book on Voltaire as stylist. There is Raymond Naves' interesting survey of his taste, *Le goût de Voltaire* (1938); and there are some penetrating but rather brief remarks by Erich Auerbach, in *Mimesis* (English transl. 1953), 401–13; and by Leo Spitzer: "Einige Voltaire-Interpretationen," *Romanische Stil- und Literaturstudien,* 2 vols. (1930), 211–243. I have tried my hand at a brief examination at Voltaire's literary strategies (see Introduction to Voltaire's *Philosophical Dictionary,* 43–47), but more needs to be done.

10. See below, p. 48.

11. The best is the one-volume edition by Raymond Naves and Julien Benda (1954 and often reprinted), which I used as a basis for my translation. But a really critical edition, following all the variants through year by year, remains a desideratum.

12. Edited by René Pomeau, 2 vols. (1963).

13. Ira O. Wade, *Voltaire and Madame du Châtelet* (1941); *Studies on*

Voltaire, with Some Unpublished Papers of Madame Châtelet (1947); and *Voltaire's "Micromégas"* (1950).

14. See G. F. Aubry, ed., *Lettres d'Alsace à Madame Denis* (1938); and Theodore Besterman, *Lettres d'amour de Voltaire à sa nièce* (1957). Mr. Besterman has carefully considered these letters in "Voltaire's Love-Letters," *Times Literary Supplement* (August 30, 1957), 524.

15. The most important contributions to our knowledge are: Paul Chaponnière, *Voltaire chez les Calvinistes* (2nd ed., 1936), Fernand Caussy, *Voltaire, seigneur du village* (1912), and, for Voltaire's sympathetic attitude toward the disfranchised lower orders, see Jane Ceitac, *Voltaire et l'affaire des Natifs* (1956). I have tried to sort out the various strands of Voltaire's political action, and its relevance to his political thought, in my *Voltaire's Politics: The Poet as Realist* (1959), especially chapter IV, "Geneva: Calvin's Three Cities."

16. *Science and the Modern World* (1925), 86.

17. The crucial work in this area is René Pomeau, *La religion de Voltaire* (1956), fair, illuminating, and exhaustive. I have dealt with the controversy in my *Voltaire's Politics,* Chapter V, "Ferney: The Poisonous Tree."

18. *Voltaire's Politics,* 267.

19. See *Voltaire's Politics,* where I treat this relativism in detail.

20. The best book is J. H. Brumfitt, *Voltaire Historian* (1958); there are some intelligent observations in J. B. Black, *The Art of History: A Study of Four Great Historians of the 18th Century* (1926). René Pomeau has edited a large volume, containing most of Voltaire's *œuvres historiques* (1957), and provided it with a fine Introduction.

1

Voltaire's Youth[*,a]

FRANÇOIS-MARIE AROUET, later known as Voltaire, was born in Paris, November 21, 1694, in the parish of Saint-André-des-Arcs. There is little reason to doubt any longer either the date or place of his birth. He was seven years old when his father, a former notary at the Châtelet,[1] became the "payer of spices and collector of fines in the Chamber of Accounts"[2] and, in this capacity, had lodgings in the old court of the Palais de Justice facing the Sainte-Chapelle. He was also seven years old when he lost his mother, Marguerite Daumard. The absence of a mother during his formative years invites speculation as to its effect on Voltaire's character development.

Of the five children of the Arouet household, only three survived: Armand, who succeeded to his father's post; a daughter, who became Mme Mignot; and this last-born, puny and sickly in appearance yet of a fundamentally robust constitution as subsequent events were to prove, and endowed with a magnificent

[*] *Alphabetized* footnotes are those of the author; *numbered* items refer to the translator's notes appearing in the Appendix; notes by René Pomeau are identified: (R.P.)

[a] G. Desnoiresterres, *la Jeunesse de Voltaire, Voltairiana, Œuvres complètes de Voltaire,* Moland ed., V. I; Alexis Pierron, *Voltaire et ses maîtres;* H. Beaune, *Voltaire au collège.* For quotations from Voltaire I refer to the Moland edition.

appetite for living. The Arouets and the Daumards came from Poitou. The former—merchants, tanners, and drapers—were eventually elevated to the liberal professions in the person of the notary and "payer of spices." The latter—farther along the ascent of the social ladder—had recently become members of the lesser nobility, a family of *petite robe*. On both sides Voltaire was completely bourgeois. He emerged from virtually the same social level as Boileau.[3]

From this unpretentious background he received a certain type of conscience and a certain outlook on life. At the end of the seventeenth century the bourgeoisie was beginning to question the privileges of birth, but with the intent to invade, not destroy, those privileges. It considered that personal merit, work, and the evidence of both merit and work—wealth—should share the social advantages enjoyed by the nobility. The middle class was not revolutionary. Any successful bourgeois wanted to be ennobled and to give his children nobility, either *noblesse de robe* or *noblesse d'épée* ("nobility of the robe" or "nobility of the sword"), which is to say, careers in the legal or military professions. Two of Corneille's sons were officers. The eldest son of Racine entered the diplomatic service. The son of a businessman in Rouen married the daughter of police lieutenant d'Argenson and became a field marshal. The son of a bookseller became a *fermier général* [chief tax collector] who, in turn, made his son a councillor in the *Parlement,* later to become Presiding Judge (*président*) Hénault who ended his career with a court appointment as Superintendent of the Queen's Household.

It is not at all surprising, then, that father Arouet, a lesser official in the Chamber of Accounts, wanted to make his son a king's attorney. That would have been a normal advancement for the family. If the young man refused, he at least never forgot the middle-class maxim that among the bourgeoisie it was only fools who remained bourgeois. He also retained the middle-class notion that one must expand the distance separating his class from the lower bourgeoisie, from common tradesmen and artisans. This explains the superior air with which he recalled that the father of Jean-Baptiste Rousseau,[4] the poet, was but a shoemaker who had made shoes for his own father, Arouet. It is the same hauteur with which the duc de Saint-Simon[5] remarked that this Voltaire, having become a personage of some note, was merely the son of a notary.

It was becoming easier for the astute individual to move out of his class now that all ranks were mingling in social life and the marks of one's profession were being discarded. Despite edicts to the contrary, magistrates were abandoning their black garb, cloaks, and collars to appear at theaters and balls and to assume the airs of courtiers. Doctors were becoming men of the world. Even merchants were growing refined, introducing touches of elegance and luxury into their lives and tasting the pleasures of society.[a]

The love of literature is an element of refinement. The Jourdains and Turcarets[6] were acquiring polish. Men of letters frequented their homes as equals, as friends, neither patronized nor patronizing. Poets, philosophers, and scholars, having cast off or learned to conceal arrogant, ill-bred pedantry and being less exclusively attached to the service of grandees, were moving about in the world and becoming the leaven of good company.

Father Arouet was not an old-fashioned notary. He had been married to a charming person of whom we need believe no ill merely because of a bit of slanderous talk. Arouet senior maintained excellent relations with his very noble clients, the Saint-Simons and the Richelieus, doubtless more intimate with the latter since the notary's son and the duke's son remained life-long friends. Caumartin de Saint-Ange, Ninon de Lenclos, the abbé de Châteauneuf (Voltaire's godfather), the abbé Gedoyn, the song-writer Rochebrune, all came to his home as friends. He had known Corneille[7] and Boileau[3] and frequented the Comédie Française. Thus, without leaving his father's house, the child destined to become Voltaire was already setting foot into three worlds: that of the great lords, that of the parliamentary nobility, and that of men of letters. A confused and complex awareness was beginning to take shape.

At the age of ten, François-Marie was placed in the Jesuit *collège*[8] of Louis-le-Grand. Nine years before, his father had given his eldest son to the Jansenists[9] of Saint-Magloire. This apparent contradiction is perhaps simply explained by the bad

[a] *La Bruyère,* chapt. III and VII. *Siècle de Louis XIV,* chapt. XXIX.

state of Jansenist affairs in 1704 following the *cas de conscience*.[10]
The amiable and slightly fickle parent was not one to resist prevailing currents of opinion. In confiding his youngest son to the
care of the Jesuits he no doubt thought he would assure him
thereby a future with fine connections. And indeed Voltaire did
meet at the *collège* the nephews of Cardinal de Tencin, d'Argental, and Pont de Veyle; Cideville, who was to become councillor
to the *Parlement* of Rouen; Fyot de la Marche, later Presiding
Judge of the *Parlement* of Burgundy; the two d'Argensons, sons
of the police lieutenant, both of whom were to become cabinet
ministers.

He had as teachers Father Thoulié, the supervisor of studies
(later the abbé d'Olivet), and Fathers Lejay, Tournemine, Porée,
and Carteron. It is difficult to ascertain the truth in anecdotes
associated with his years at school, but we can hardly doubt the
essential facts they contain, reducible to two points: Voltaire's
precocious intelligence and his precocious impertinence. Either
the Jesuits could not or did not know how to instill in their
pupil a sense of deep religious fervor or piety. Nor did they
succeed any better in giving him firm moral principles. I do not
know what the Jansenists might have done with a nature like his,
but the good Jesuit Fathers of Louis-le-Grand could form moral
people only by turning them into devoutly submissive souls.
Where they were unable to inculcate an obedient, unreasoning
faith, the moral foundation was lacking. What remained were
merely compliant habits, compromises with the manners, morals,
and temptations of the age, and all that easy-going conduct
which their adroit religion made such pious use of to the glory
of God and the profit of the Church. Whoever did not leave their
hands a good Catholic could not come forth with deep and
serious moral principles. Certain weaknesses of Voltaire may have
had their origin in the inability of his teachers to separate
morality from the catechism. We must note, moreover, that at
the beginning of the eighteenth century the Reverend Fathers,
who were polished rhetoricians and excellent humanists, applied
themselves more diligently (although very pious themselves) to
the task of forming good taste rather than religious piety. They
seemed to be satisfied with turning out men of letters, free from

any trace of Jansenism, who would present an appearance of outward obedience to the Church.

Hence the smiling indulgence with which they saw Voltaire
budding under their care. One of their record books characterized
him as "a bright boy but an arrant rogue" (*puer ingeniosus, sed
insignis nebulo*). The precocious signs of his talent delighted
them: an epigram, an improvisation, a translation in French
verse of one of the Fathers' Latin odes. At their distribution of
prizes in 1710, one of them pointed out to Jean-Baptiste Rousseau "a little boy who showed remarkable aptitude for poetry,"
and the established poet looked curiously at this "young student
of rather unattractive features but with an alert and lively expression."

For more than thirty years, down to the feverish hours of the
battle of the Encyclopedia, relations were never broken between
Voltaire and the Jesuits. The latter were reluctant to despair of
winning over to their side such a dazzling wit. They were rather
grateful to him for being so much at odds with the Jansenists.
And he, for his part, felt himself deeply in debt to such good
teachers. Despite everything that separated him from them, despite his aversion to the politics and doctrines of their order, even
despite the selfish strategy of his protestations on certain occasions, he kept a genuinely warm memory of Fathers Tournemine
and Porée and an affectionate regard for the way the Jesuits
instructed young people in their *collèges.* He was well aware that
he owed to them his sense of good taste. He owed them his precision and finesse, his prejudices and his limitations. So strong was
the Jesuit hold on him he could never entirely liberate himself.

Young Arouet's godfather, the abbé de Châteauneuf, introduced him into society. He had presented him to the aging Ninon
de Lenclos,[11] who, charmed by his vivacity, willed him, he tells
us, two thousand *écus* (crowns) to buy books. He introduced him
into the *société du Temple,* that center of freethinking society of
the day where he became acquainted with such epicureans as
Chaulieu, Courtin, the abbé Servien, and M. de Sully—a company
designed to whet two appetites naturally implanted in this youthful bourgeois: the appetite for pleasure and the appetite for wit.
They provoked the first difficulties with father Arouet who appre-

ciated wit and pleasure but within limits, that is, without compromising what was really solid and substantial. And for him the substantial was an appointment to the judiciary, *une charge de robe*. François-Marie would have none of it. He lacked all seriousness of purpose, taking pleasure only in his follies. He was out late, squandering money when he had it and going into debt to get more of it. He wrote verses and refused to do anything else. He was composing a tragedy and submitting an ode for a competition sponsored by the French Academy. His father approved of his versifying, but only as a social grace; not as a career.

He decided to give the young scamp a change of scene. The marquis de Châteauneuf, who had been named royal representative to the United Provinces of the Netherlands (September 1713), included young Arouet among his pages. At The Hague there lived a refugee, one Mme Dunoyer, an adventuress who fancied herself a writer and who was the mother of a pert and pretty daughter, Olympe Dunoyer (known to her friends as "Pimpette"). Abruptly forsaken by Jean Cavalier, a former leader of the Protestant Camisards[12] whom she was supposed to have married, Pimpette had been married to a certain comte de Winterfeld. She turned the head of the nineteen-year-old page. But this young rascal was not the serious suitor Mme Dunoyer desired for her daughter. He was penniless. She lodged complaints at the embassy. The two lovers were separated. Arouet wrote to "his dear heart" colorful letters filled with love and rebellion very much in the sentimental language of the Dorantes and Chérubins[13] on the stage.[a] Pimpette was quite willing to be abducted. He sent her some men's clothing. Whereupon, the ambassador sent his page back to Paris (December 1713). But the rash and angry youth did not give up yet. He tried to interest Father Tournemine and the Bishop of Evreux in the good Catholic effort to bring a young Huguenot back to France. In the end, Pimpette stayed in Holland and consoled herself, we are told, with Guyot de Murville. Arouet remained neither faithful to nor bitter towards his "dear heart."

Arouet senior, however, after having sought a *lettre de cachet*[14] to get his rogue of a son locked up, and after having contemplated

[a] V. XXXIII, pp. 9–21. [Moland ed.] (Besterman, 7–23) (R.P.)

the possibility of packing him off to the West Indies, relented to the point of installing him as a clerk in the office of Master Alain, a lawyer at the Châtelet, "near the steps of the Place Maubert." There he found a comrade equally disgusted with the legal profession, equally enamored of pleasure and poetry. They became friends for life. This was the good-natured Thieriot, egotistical, lazy, devoted to his pleasures and idleness even to the point of treason and dishonesty. He sponged on Voltaire, who never wearied of helping and forgiving him.

Another misfortune: the Academy did not bestow its crown on Arouet's ode on the Vow of Louis XIII. La Motte's[15] influence awarded the prize to the old abbé du Jarry. Arouet's blood boiled at this denial of justice. A satire was unleashed against the illustrious M. de La Motte, causing a scandal and rekindling the father's anger against this impulsive youth, who did nothing but make a fool of himself. Luckily, M. de Caumartin took him away to Saint-Ange until the storm should subside. In the charming country of the Loing, in the company of an intelligent man whose mind encompassed the entire seventeenth century—both its important affairs and its anecdotal gossip—Arouet, for the first time in his life, acquired some serious ideas. Simultaneously, there were planted the seeds of the *Henriade* and *Le Siècle de Louis XIV* ("The Age of Louis XIV").

The Grand Monarch died (1715), and, in the joy of deliverance and that of an assured peace, the pleasure-seeking era of the Regency[16] burst forth. There was a revolt against the dreary bigotry and oppressive despotism of the last reign—an uninhibited display of cynicism, skepticism, and debauch, a passion for gambling, love, and money; and a bold effervescence of wit, laughter, and satire. But there was also unbridled greed and feverish speculation. One needed money for one's pleasures. There was not a single notable who failed to traffic or gamble with one thing or another. It was in this atmosphere that Voltaire moved on his return from Saint-Ange. He frequented the most unrestrained freethinkers, those with whom a display of wit excused all and redeemed all—first at the Temple, the residence of the Grand Prior of Vendôme, then at Sceaux with the duchesse du Maine.

At the Temple he met Chaulieu, the abbé de Bussy, the

Chevalier d'Aydie, the bailiff de Froulay, the Chevalier de Bouillon, Presiding Judge (*président*) Hénault; at Sceaux, the Cardinal de Polignac, M. de Malezieu, and Mlle Delaunay. M. de Sully took him to the Sully estate where he met the duc de La Vallière and Mme de Gondrin, the future comtesse de Toulouse. He slipped like an eel into all the places where vanity and pleasure were prized: at Maisons, the home of the Presiding Judge whose son was his dear friend; at Vaux, the home of the renowned Marshal Villars[17] and his beautiful wife; in Paris, at Châtillon, the residence of Hoguère, the banker, where he met the poets Danchet and Crébillon and the adventurer Goertz, the muddle-headed minister of Charles XII of Sweden. We find him at Richelieu in Poitou, keeping company with the young exiled duke; at La Source near Orléans, the home of Bolingbroke;[18] at Ussé in Touraine, frequented by the licentious poet Grécourt; at La Rivière-Bourdet in Normandy and the Rue de Beaune in Paris in the home of *la présidente de Bernières*. The good marquise de Mimeure was one of his friends. It was at her mansion he engaged in his first intellectual duel with that salty Burgundian, Piron.[19] The mature, red-headed Mme de Rupelmonde took him to Holland. He spent eleven days at The Hague with the poet Jean-Baptiste Rousseau, whom he had regarded until then as his master. They parted deadly enemies.

He cut a swath at the Opéra, at the Comédie, in actresses' loges. He was unsuccessful with Mlle Duclos but won the fair Suzanne de Livry, only to be cut in on by his dear friend Génonville—for whom he felt no rancor. He was on the best of terms with the celebrated actress Mlle Adrienne Lecouvreur.

He emerged from the Bastille, where the Regent had had him imprisoned, only to gain a foothold in the Palais Royal, the Regent's own household. He was welcomed by Dubois[20] and became a friend of the roué Canillac. He formed a friendship with Mme du Deffand[21] and with the Chevalier des Alleures, and he dined with the prince de Conti.[22]

Of frail health, often ill, and always certain he was sicker than he actually was, he would drink the milk of a she-ass and swipe pills from Mme de Rupelmonde. He went to drink the waters of Forges where he found Mme de Prie, mistress to M. le duc (de Bourbon), a prince of the royal blood and prime minister after the death of the duc d'Orléans. She invited him to her place at Bélébat and to Fontainebleau, the royal residence. He gained access to the court. The young queen Maria Leszczynska took a liking to this amusing and flattering poet. She called him *mon pauvre Voltaire* ("my poor Voltaire") in a tone of complete familiarity. After 1718 he dropped the common name of Arouet and from then on was Monsieur *de Voltaire*.

And so at the age of twenty, the son of the "payer of spices," the law clerk of Master Alain, acquired status in the most brilliant society. At thirty he had forced open the gateway to the court. He payed for it with his wit, his improvisations, tales, epigrams, satires, and poetic epistles, a currency that by no means impoverished him. Without fearing impropriety, he did not strive for it. The licentious writings of Grécourt and Caylus, the public farces in which La Vallière and Maurepas found delight, make one appreciate Voltaire's sense of propriety, the effervescence of his wit and gaiety, and the impertinence of his fancy. There was reason to be intoxicated, and he was. He believed in the social privilege of wit. "Are all of us here princes or poets?" he asked the prince de Conti. Surely this utterance reveals the audacity of the adventurer who knows that, in the easy-going world of people in search of amusement, one is classified according to his pretentions. But we can also detect a full-blown naïveté taking seriously its lordly rank in the empire of the intellect. Yet, in the dizziness of his success, he did not completely lose his head. The various women between Pimpette and *la belle Emilie* did not trouble him deeply. More sensitive than passionate, his heart had need of friendship more than love. He felt strong and lively attachments for young men like Maisons and La Faluère de Genonville. He had solid and enduring friendships, as with d'Argental, and he was capable of admirable, indefatigable fidelities, as with Thieriot.

Above all, amid all the victories of vanity and pleasure, his very bourgeois good sense never lost sight of "the solid and substantial," regardless of what father Arouet might think. He first assured himself a literary reputation, but Voltaire desired to be more than a dinner conversationalist and a witty entertainer into the wee hours. He had an ambition to become immortal and, while living like Chaulieu[23] or La Fare,[24] he dreamed of making his mark beside Racine[25] and Boileau,[3] whose works he knew by heart. From 1715 he was working on an *Œdipe* ("Oedipus"), priding himself on improving "the rough sketch" by Sophocles. And, what was even more audacious at that time, he expected to consign Corneille's version to oblivion. Prepared perhaps by one of his Jesuit teachers, prodded in any case by some observations of Fénelon and the abbé Dubos, he purposed to bring off on his first attempt a dramatic revolution. He wrote an *Œdipe* devoid of love or gallantry. But the actors would not allow a newcomer to lay down the law to them. Consequently, in order to get his play performed, Voltaire had to resign himself to letting the grave-mannered Philoctetes sigh for the elderly Jocasta. Nevertheless, his adroit and brilliant tragedy, first presented on November 18, 1718, caused its young author to be regarded as the equal of Campistron and Crébillon and a worthy successor to Corneille and Racine.

Although France was not lacking in tragedies, she could not claim to have a good epic. Ronsard[26] and Chapelain[27] had confirmed the prevailing opinion that the French did not have *la tête épique* ("a head for the epic"). What a unique thing it would be to give the lie to this judgment! Contrary to Boileau's advice, Voltaire settled upon a subject both modern and national. Guided by the abbé Dubos or beguiled by M. de Caumartin, he chose Henry IV, the only French king who was truly popular and whose legend had begun to excite interest in the wake of the disastrous oppression of the latest reign. Its subject was the very crisis from which present-day France had emerged: dynasty, political order, social life and civilization—a grand and moving theme, patriotic and philosophical, with revolutions, battles, exploits, love, and, to excite the free spirit, rich opportunities to speak one's piece to kings, Church, and monks. His enforced leisure in the Bastille prompted him to set to work. Thereafter he paraded his first draft from salon to salon, from château to château, gathering compliments and corrections, arousing on behalf of his enterprise a curiosity that guaranteed its success in advance of its publication. He would have liked to dedicate to Louis XV the work that honored Henry IV, but his philosophical dedication seemed impertinent. He was even refused an official privilege for printing it. Accordingly, he arranged for a clandestine edition in

Rouen, and the poem *La Ligue* ["The League"—the first title of the *Henriade*] penetrated Paris illegally in the baggage carts of Mme de Bernières (1723). Despite the critics, France saluted her epic poet. Voltaire had achieved glory.

But "the solid and substantial" also included money. He was too thoroughly bourgeois; he had understood only too well the lesson of the Regency and John Law's famous System[28] to be unaware of its importance. Arouet senior died January 1, 1722. He could not know how much his son had basically the same ideas as himself. He would have perhaps reached a reconciliation with him had he learned of the measures his son took to ensure that his poetic vocation did not reduce him to starvation. Voltaire had taken cognizance of the relations between writers and their publishers. He was resolved not to be the poor devil dependent on the miserly wages of booksellers, exploited by them and looked down on by respectable people. He had learned that in order to associate with the Sullys and the Richelieus one must not be a merchant of verses and prose, earning a livelihood from this trade. Rather, if one were to hold his own in society, especially if he were not very "noble," it was indispensable to be very rich. Voltaire set about to achieve that objective.

As a younger man he had borrowed from usurers. At twenty he had put his affairs in order and already, no doubt, had a preference for being a lender rather than a borrower. He was fashionable and fastidious, but he knew how to count. He gambled for effect, but if he accused himself of "losing his bonnet at biribi" [a game of chance], you may be sure he never risked his shirt. He publicized his losses to win public admiration. He was always sober, never compromising his health or his purse in his follies. But economy is good for saving what you have. Young Arouet's first problem was to acquire the coveted wherewithal.

He had pensions from the court—the usual road for a man of letters: 1200 francs from the duc d'Orléans in 1718, 2000 francs from the king in 1722, 1500 francs from the queen in 1725. He received an inheritance from his father, a 4250-pound income—a tidy sum for a poet but insufficient to live in *le grand monde,* in high society. Voltaire speculated. The financiers he frequented gave him a taste for and an understanding of banking and commercial operations, the courage to take calculated risks, and an unruffled conscience in taking huge profits. He invested in the Indies Company, putting almost all his capital in it by 1722. With président de Bernières he negotiated a *caisse de juifrerie,* meaning, no doubt, a commercial enterprise.[a] He amassed a fortune in military supplies, thanks to the Paris brothers [financiers]. He created a society to exploit the lottery of the comptroller general Desforts in which the tickets were payable in annuities and the prizes payable in cash He received a handsome share in the proceeds of the combination. He would buy and sell stocks, sometimes tripling his investments.[b] He put funds into *la grosse aventure* of trade between Cadiz and America. He speculated in the grains of Barbary. He dealt in pictures and prints and began to lend money to financially embarrassed noblemen, taking lifetime annuities in return. On going back to London in July 1726, he had in his pocket a banknote of some eight to nine thousand pounds on the Jew Medina.[c] His was not a poet's purse. Medina's bankruptcy caused him only momentary concern. Economically, he had already acquired a strong back and sturdy limbs. Dumoulin's failure in 1735 was to cost him twenty to twenty-five thousand francs; Michel's, in 1740, thirty to forty thousand. But he would be able to withstand these large losses. Jore attributes to him an income of 28,000 pounds in 1736, of which his creditors seized 18,500.[d]

All this prosperity was not without bitterness—loss of friends, betrayals by mistresses, whistles and catcalls from theatre audiences, wranglings with the wits, lawsuits, etc. One of the constant characteristics of Voltaire's life was its everlasting noisiness, its unending stridency. He was boastful and raucous, screaming to the high heavens whatever good or evil befell him. He was one of those noisy, agitated people whom the indifferent are always happy to see overtaken by some misfortune. Ever on the public stage, ever on the public's lips, nothing that happened to him passed unnoticed or unpublicized. These reverberations, altogether too frequent, robbed him of the world's respect while extending his fame and notoriety far and wide. But until 1725, the

[a] V. XXXIII, p. 62 (Besterman, 102) (R.P.)
[b] *Ibid.,* p. 196. (Besterman, 355) (R.P.)
[c] Hettier, *Une lettre de Voltaire,* Mém. de l'acad. de Caen, 1905. (Besterman, 294) (R.P.)
[d] *Voltairiana,* p. 89.

displeasures he had experienced were not such as to make him form an aversion for the society in which he lived. Certain verses were the cause of his being exiled to Tulle in 1716, but the good Regent, no sooner having signed the order, authorized him to replace Tulle with Sully—a few months vacation on the banks of the Loire in a friend's château! For the *J'ai vu* ("I Have Witnessed") which he had not written and for the *Puero Regnante* ("The Boy on the Throne") which was indeed his, he spent eleven months in the Bastille (May 1717 to April 1718), a by no means disagreeable state prison; in fact, it was rather an honor for an obscure youth and one which enhanced his importance.

More wounding to his vanity were Voltaire's quarrels with the actor Poisson, who threatened to beat him up, and with the stool-pigeon officer Beauregard, who did have him beaten on the Sèvres bridge. Voltaire brandished his sword and pistols for a moment and then brought suit against Beauregard. The public formed the impression that this poet was not a man who would fight a duel. Besides, the character of his adversaries was rather degrading. A respectable man did not have run-ins with an actor or an informer.

In February 1726 a rather sad specimen of a *grand seigneur*, the Chevalier de Rohan, with whom Voltaire had had an exchange of words at the Comédie Française, sent for him to come to the château gate of the duc de Sully, with whom Voltaire was dining. Lackeys set upon him with sticks and clubs while the Chevalier, from inside his carriage, "supervised the workers." Great was Voltaire's rage, greater still when he saw that his good friends, the dukes and marquis, found the incident amusing: a Rohan was beating up a poet, a matter of no consequence. This act of brutality shattered the illusion in which Voltaire had been living. To save his "honor," that is to say, his wordly position, he wanted a duel. He wanted it seriously for several months. But he did not fight. The Chevalier de Rohan disappeared. His family and the court kept him under cover. And just to ensure his safety, they lodged his victim in the Bastille with much courtesy and consideration (April 17, 1726). Voltaire left the Bastille a month later only on his promise to cross over into England (May 1726).

This time Voltaire had had definite experience with the social order, with its inequality and despotism. And the ministry of Monsieur le Duc was well advised to send him into a land of political and individual freedom lest he not reflect sufficiently on the matter while still in Paris. This date, 1726, was decisive in Voltaire's life. Therefore, we would do well to pause and consider: what was he like at that time? what sort of conscience, what philosophy was he about to take to London?

Voltaire was a complex character, not only from the natural variety of his inclinations, but also from the influence of the confused times in which he lived and by virtue of the various social circles he had known and frequented. He was not malicious but rather good-natured and humane, capable of generous impulses, hating injustice. But he was also feverish with self-love, avid to enjoy all pleasures, especially avid to feel, to be, and to act. He was fond of sumptuous living. He was loud, impressionable, irascible, resentful, enthusiastic, restless, curious, insolent, sly, mischievous; a spoiled child. Life wove its tapestry over this natural background. By the time he was thirty, Voltaire had the bourgeois ambition to attain nobility, the bourgeois love of and pride in money, property, and good connections. His morality was that of the big operator, disdaining the small daily wage earner and respecting big business and its speculative ventures. His manner of doing business everywhere was such as to make him regard even his benefactions as so many favors to be repaid in services. He had a taste for comfortable living, fine furniture, jewelry, the luxury of the nouveau-riche. To his scorn for little people and for Jews —the prejudice of all classes—he added the prejudices of a gentleman, a contempt for people who live by their writings. But Voltaire lacked the mainspring of honor. It was not for honor, but for the world at large, that he wanted to duel. It would be possible for him personally to have lived without revenge. To unsheath the sword was a gesture unfamiliar to his bourgeois arm, a gesture whose elegance was unappreciated by his philosophic mind.

He was not carefree about money. He lived ostentatiously for reasons of vanity and he lived economically by reason of heredity. He was never to understand in the least the noble art of letting oneself be taken. Affecting the airs of a *grand seigneur,* he would nevertheless haggle and quibble like a typical bourgeois. As a man of letters he was as peevish and prickly as Molière's Vadius and Trissotin.[29] He would rather pour out insults with a pen than shed blood with a sword, and because of his corrosive humor, he was just like the poor devils of the press he so thoroughly despised. He was like the modern journalist whose indiscretion permits itself unlimited license over the life, dignity, honor, and reputation of another person. In short, his conscience was not molded on any single, definite type. No class recognized in him its hereditary mental or moral outlook. He combined features of them all, and for that reason they all refused to hold him in esteem.

What is worse, he was not content to fuse into his conscience all the consciences of his time. He had to reform or criticize them. He was a freethinker and a philosopher. And nothing rendered his morality more suspect to his contemporaries than three or four liberal or generous ideas which were not yet assimilated into the common ethical code of well-bred people. A courtier, and as such sycophantic and dull, on his knees before the king and the ministers, before the ministers' mistresses, and later on the mistresses of the king, he did only what everyone else was doing. They were contemptuous of him in the first place because he usurped the baser instincts of the nobility, and they were contemptuous of him thereafter because he refused to exploit his strategy merely for personal gain. He wanted to advance at the same time the cause of *la philosophie*,[a] which was judged entirely out of place. He could not rid himself either of his obsequious manner and courtier's soul or of his philosopher's soul, and while he assumed postures indecent for a thinking man, the truths he unleashed were, for a man of the court, ineptitudes and impertinences.

But just what was this *philosophie* in 1726? Let us visualize clearly the thoughts and ideas likely to occur to this clever and irreverent youth, ideas that were gaining currency in the society and environment of the times. M. Brunetière[30] has aptly defined the prevailing intellectual climate, bridled in the seventeenth century by the king's police and by the Church: "For the twenty ways there were to prove the immortality of the soul or the divine right of kings, not one was permitted that would deny them."[b] Yet, by virtue of having reasoned about admissible subjects,

[a] Plan for dedicating the *Henriade* to Louis XV (V. VIII, p. 2, 3).
[b] *Etudes critiques*, IV, 134.

the seventeenth century bequeathed to its successor a taste for reasoning, a general freedom of the mind that was eager to examine everything and was little disposed to satisfy itself with traditional and authoritarian solutions. Houdar de La Motte,[15] Lesage,[31] Marivaux,[32] Mme de Lambert,[33] Mlle Delaunay[34]—all describe for us this intellectual type, which bows only to society's conventions and to considerations of worldly prudence.

The Regency did not create free thinking, *libertinage*. It only added security to its public display. The entire doctrine had already been expressed by Saint-Evremond:[35] Deprive reason of the knowledge of God and of immortality (represented with an ironic respect as "matters of faith"); love tolerance; detest persecution and civil war out of skepticism, urbanity, and humanity; govern one's life according to nature through reason, that is, reject Christianity as anti-natural; rehabilitate the body and its needs; maintain a sense of proportion in the pursuit of pleasure, out of wisdom so as not to harm oneself, and out of benevolence so as not to infringe upon the rights of others—that is the distilled essence of the three volumes in-quarto which Desmaizeaux published in Amsterdam in 1705. Parisian society tailored its practice to these principles. Even apart from the announced doctrine of disbelief, it was a general tendency to separate life from any ultra-terrestrial purposes or sanctions and to become occupied only with the quest for happiness here on earth.

At the end of the seventeenth century, French deism was beginning to appear in a number of books printed in Holland, in the curious *Histoire des Sévarambes* of Denis Vairasse (1677) and in the daring *Voyage au Canada* of La Hontan (1703).[a] John Locke[36] and English deism were starting to infiltrate France. Two men in particular converted free thinking into a philosophy. Fontenelle[37] popularized the Cartesian method, divesting it of the metaphysics into which Spinoza[38] and Malebranche[39] had plunged. He repeated, in clear, concise formulations, that reason consists in doubting, in seeing before believing, and he declared that neither man's needs nor his desires are arguments for truth. Fontenelle took the trouble to demonstrate that the oracles of the ancients

[a] Completed and reinforced in 1704 by the *Dialogue avec un sauvage de l'Amérique*.

were not demon-inspired utterances, and his explanation of pagan supernaturalism as priestly humbug and human gullibility carried over into the dogma of Christian supernaturalism. He taught people the new astronomy of Copernicus,[40] Galileo,[41] and Descartes.[42] He planted in their thinking, quietly and discreetly, the notion of mechanical law in lieu of Providence, and for the ancient heavens whose highest realm is the immutable abode of eternal divinity, he substituted the prodigious spectacle of infinite space peopled with countless worlds, scarcely compatible with the accounts of Holy Scripture. Fontenelle was effecting a change in the outlook of cultivated minds. Rather than oratorical and poetic, he was making men's minds scientific, thereby posing a threat to religion which, in order to subsist, requires that education emphasize the faculties of imagination and feeling.

Richer still was that other fount of free thought, Pierre Bayle,[43] with his *Nouvelles de la République des Lettres* ("News from the Republic of Letters"), his *Pensées sur la Comète* ("Miscellaneous Thoughts on the Comet"), and the *Dictionnaire Critique* ("The Critical Dictionary"), four folios of which there were eleven successive editions in forty years (1697–1740). Bayle waged a war on sorcerers which, in turn, threatened man's belief in miracles; nature's laws prevailed over both sorcerers and miracles. Bayle liberated morality from religion, demanded rights for the conscience in error, rejected constraint or authority in matters of belief, and rejected even the rule of universal consent. Serenely and without fanfare, he practiced a total independence of mind, setting the example for that free criticism which recognizes no domain as off-limits and which subjects to rational examination any and all mysteries, including those of religion and royalty. He was the first to accustom people to attacks on Church dogma that used weapons other than common sense and logic. He put at the disposal of philosophical reasoning the immense arsenal of Protestant theology, spelling out all the philological and historical difficulties that shocked Roman theology. He made it evident that the study of religion furnished ways and means of overthrowing religion itself.

Bayle was listened to. He delighted La Fontaine. That salty bourgeois, Mathieu Marais, in the closed confines of his *Journal*, declared himself "Bayliste." Bayle even conquered women. Mme de Mérignac relished him as "a sublime spirit, lofty, lively, strong, and of a most Pyrrhonic philosophy." Reason was even venturing forth onto political and social terrain. Very prudently and adroitly, yet with great clarity, La Bruyère[44] translated such sentiments (already current among the bourgeoisie) as contempt for courtiers and a hatred for financiers. From his depiction of "characters" La Bruyère moved into the area of social criticism, attacking certain abuses which he called "usages": the privileges of birth, the purchase of titles of nobility, the fiscal system, the judicial establishment, and ecclesiastical wealth. The disaster of the closing years of the reign of Louis XIV prompted individuals to scrutinize affairs of state. Boisguillebert [an economist] and Vauban,[45] moved by the misery of the common people, proposed tax reforms, and Archbishop Fénelon[46] went so far as to denounce despotism and the folly of war. Protestants, after the revocation (1685) of the Edict of Nantes, were questioning royalty itself. Bayle denied that there could possibly be a good despot. Jurieu[47] advocated the people's right against the right of the ruler, and in the name of the social compact he dispensed from the oath of loyalty those subjects who were oppressed by their princes.

Following the death of Louis XIV things began to stir. The nobility and the *parlement*[48] reasserted themselves, and this effort by privileged groups to contest cabinet ministers and state officials for a voice in the government had the effect of a liberal movement. They were especially resentful of a despotism which had for so long subjugated one and all only to end in complete ruin. Bold lampoons invoked the ancient constitution of the kingdom, demanding that the royal power be limited by parliamentary control or made to acquiesce to the sovereignty of the States General. Everywhere—with the abbé de Saint-Pierre,[49] the marquis de Lassay, Massillon,[50] and Montesquieu[51]—there was manifest the same desire for a more moderate kind of monarchy, humane, beneficent, and pacifist. There was even a society founded in 1725 for the study of political questions. To the *Club de l'Entresol* (the entresol being the mezzanine level occupied by the abbé Alary in the residence of Presiding Judge Hénault, Place Vendôme) came the marquis d'Argenson and *président* de Montesquieu. These meetings of men dedicated to the public weal were to become suspect in the government's eyes, and Cardinal Fleury[52] in 1731 advised them to be "circumspect." They read the handwriting on the wall and discontinued their meetings.

The entire spirit of the early eighteenth century was reflected in that bold and light-hearted little book by Montesquieu—*Les Lettres Persanes* ("The Persian Letters"). Charming, sensuous, and bantering, serious and supercilious, it released all the pent-up yearnings for liberty in literature, religion, morality, and politics. The public applauded, without serious reflections, all revolts against the authority of the king and the Church. It mattered little that Jansenism was intolerant or that *Parlement* had the most insufferable ego. They represented opposition to spiritual and temporal despotism. This attitude was enough to earn them an immense popularity.

Such was the air that Voltaire breathed with the utmost delight upon leaving school. His classical fondness for the masters of the seventeenth century did not bind him to their timidity of thought. If he had not yet learned to savor Rabelais, too copious and unrestrained for his taste, he was delighted with Montaigne, the bedside book of all freethinkers. But he went beyond the viewpoints of those sixteenth-century *libertins*, as had Bayle, Fontenelle, La Motte, and all cultivated minds. He early forged for himself a philosophy he rarely expressed in his writings between his twentieth and thirtieth birthdays: "The great and only concern one should have is to live happily."[a]

> Quelques femmes toujours badines,
> Quelques amis toujours joyeux,
> Peu de vêpres, point de matines,
> Une fille, en attendant mieux,
> Voilà comme l'on doit sans cesse
> Faire tête au sort irrité,
> Et la véritable sagesse,
> Est de savoir fuir la tristesse
> Dans les bras de la volupté.[b]

> (With a few women ever teasing and bantering,
> A few friends ever joyful,
> Few vespers, no matins,

[a] V. XXXIII, p. 62. (Besterman, 102) (R.P.)
[b] V. X, p. 221—cf. V. XXXIII, p. 35. (Cf. Besterman, 4) (R.P.)

One damsel, while hoping for better,
That is how one must ever meet head on
The contrary whims of fate,
And true wisdom
Is to know how to avoid sadness
In the arms of exquisite pleasure.)

Add, in his case, good food, opera, and time for study.[a] There was room for the heart in this plan for epicurean living. In becoming philosophical the world becomes sensitive. Voltaire began to delight in the charm of the emotions and the beauty with which they embellish life. He was already experiencing what he would express in 1729, recalling his dear friend Génonville, six years deceased.

Malheureux, dont le coeur ne sait pas comme on aime,
Et qui n'ont pas connu la douceur de pleurer.[b]

(Unfortunate are those whose heart knows not love
And who have not known the sweetness of tears.)

The moral was the art of exploiting for one's happiness all the resources of nature:

Le plaisir est l'objet, le devoir, et le but
De tous les êtres raisonnables.[c]

(Pleasure is the object, the duty, and the goal
Of every rational being.)

Christian morality was swept aside with Christian dogma. God Himself is no more than a hypothesis, but if He exists, He is a reasonable and indulgent God, *un Dieu des bonnes gens* ("a God of good folks") Who blesses those who follow their instincts.

It would be interesting to know whether Voltairian disbelief became from that time on aggressive and didactic. Just what were the exact contents of that famous letter to Julie "marked for consignment to the place of blackest impiety" which caused a devout Rousseau [the poet] to tremble in 1722. Must one, as is usually done, identify it with the *Epître à Uranie* which circulated ten

[a] V. XXXIII, p. 87. (Besterman, 146) (R.P.)
[b] V. X, p. 266 (1729).
[c] V. X, p. 231.

years later and was published in 1738? The latter is a rigorous argumentation against revealed religion. The author concludes with these words to God: "Je ne suis pas chrétien, mais c'est pour t'aimer mieux." ("I am not a Christian, but it is to love Thee better.")

Yet it is not certain that he wrote in this vein in 1722. He was already thinking along such lines, however.

> Nos prêtres ne sont pas ce qu'un vain peuple pense;
> Notre crédulité fait toute leur science. . . .[a]
> Allez, s'il est un Dieu, sa tranquille puissance
> Ne s'abaissera point à troubler nos amours.
> Vos baisers pourraient-ils déplaire à sa clémence?
> La loi de la nature est sa première loi.[b]

> (Our priests are not what a vain people think;
> Our gullibility accounts for all their science. . . .
> Come now, if a God there be, His tranquil might
> Will not stoop to troubling our love affairs.
> Could your kisses displease His clement disposition?
> Nature's law is His first law.)

In April 1726 an anonymous clergyman denounced him to the police and claimed to have lodged a complaint some ten or twelve years earlier, charging Voltaire with "preaching deism openly in the dressing rooms of young noblemen. . . . The Old Testament, according to him, is merely a tissue of tales and fables; the Apostles were harmless idiots, simple-minded and credulous, and the Church Fathers, especially Saint Bernard for whom he has a special dislike, were only toadies and charlatans." The good priest advised them "to lock him up within four walls for the rest of his life."[c]

Having deprived himself of refuge in deity, Voltaire had created a need for a source of strength. His epicureanism accepted the irreparable with resignation and fortitude. Loving money, he attempted to live joyously without it.[d] Ill and having troubles in personal matters, pleading against his brother over the rights of

---

[a] *Œdipe*, Act IV, sc. 1.
[b] V. X, p. 231.
[c] *Arch. de la Bastille,* V. XII, p. 132. (Besterman, 269) (R.P.)
[d] V. XXXIII, p. 138. (Besterman, 220) (R.P.)

paternal succession, he wrote: "Fortune treats me no better than nature. I suffer a great deal in many ways, but I have marshaled all my diminished strength to resist my misfortunes."[a] In political matters he still had no personal grievance against social institutions, but the spirit of the times enveloped him. He was neither respectful nor docile, and received all the more eagerly any suggestions for criticism or revolt that the world at large or the world of literature furnished him. Philoctetes philosophized thus in *Œdipe:*

> Un roi pour ses sujets est un Dieu qu'on révère,
> Pour Hercule et pour moi, c'est un homme ordinaire. . . .
> Un vain peuple en tumulte a demandé ma tête,
> Il souffre, il est injuste, il faut lui pardonner.[b]

> (To his subjects a king is a God they revere,
> To Hercules and myself he is an ordinary man. . . .
> A vain people in tumult have demanded my head.
> They suffer, they are unjust, one must forgive them.)

A "republican" note is struck here and there in his correspondence. "They are going to levy a new tax to have the wherewithal to buy lace and fabrics for the damsel Leszczynska. This is like the marriage of the sun which caused the frogs to mutter."[c] (May 28, 1725).

There is nothing more agreeable than The Hague when the sun deigns to put in an appearance. Here one sees nothing but meadows, canals, and green trees. It is an earthly paradise from The Hague to Amsterdam. I saw *with respect* that city which is the storehouse of the Universe. There were more than a thousand ships in port. Of the five hundred thousand men who dwell in Amsterdam, not a single one is idle or poor, and none is a taskmaster or insolent. We encountered the Pensionnaire [the Dutch chief of state] out walking, unaccompanied by lackeys and in the midst of the populace. *You do not see anyone here who has to pay court or who stands in line to watch some prince go by.* The people are acquainted only with work and modesty. At The Hague there is more splendor and fashionable society because of the many ambassadors present. I spend my time there between work and pleasure,

[a] V. XXXIII, p. 126. (Besterman, 207) (R.P.)
[b] *Œdipe,* II, 4; and III, 2.
[c] V. XXXIII, p. 147. (Besterman, 225) (R.P.)

and thus I live in both the Dutch and French manner. We have here a perfectly dreadful *opéra,* but on the other hand, I see Calvinist preachers, Armenians, Socinians, rabbis, Anabaptists, all of whom are great orators and in truth they are all in the right.[a] (7 October 1722).

Does not this letter from Holland already suggest the *Lettres Anglaises* ("The English Letters")?

The *Henriade* revealed to the public Voltaire's earliest philosophy. One should read the poem *La Ligue* (1723), full of audacious verses, maxims, passionate tirades against the intolerant Church, against wars and religious persecutions, against useless or conspiratorial monks, against evil kings and "proud conquerors."

> Héros aux yeux du peuple, aux yeux de Dieu tyrans.
> Fléaux du monde entier que leur fureur embrase.[b]
>
> (Heroes in the eyes of the people; in the eyes of God, tyrants.
> Scourges of the entire world, which their fury sets ablaze.)

His analysis of fanaticism absolved Jacques Clément [Dominican assassin of Henry III in 1589] of personal responsibility for his act and leveled the charge of regicide against religion itself. There were barbs against venality in legal and military appointments. Under pressure from public opinion and the influence of Montesquieu's *Lettres Persanes,* Voltaire revealed himself a partisan of *Parlement.*[c] According to a contemporary critic, there emanated from this neoclassical epic, its theatrical regularity enlivened by wit, sauciness, and sensuality, "dangerous impressions, especially at a time when the freedom to sit in judgment has perhaps gone too far already."[d]

English thinkers consequently recognized as one of their own the poet of the *Henriade.* Before Voltaire had crossed the Channel, Pope declared to Bolingbroke (April 9, 1724) his sympathy for just such a mind:

It seems to me that his judgment of mankind, and his observations of human actions in a lofty and philosophical view, is one of the principal

[a] V. XXXIII, p. 74. (Besterman, 126) (R.P.)
[b] V. VIII, p. 174 and 193.
[c] V. VIII, p. 123.
[d] *Réflexions critiques sur un poème intitulé "La Ligue"* (attributed to Bonneval, 1724, p. 8.

characteristics of the writer, who however is not less a poet for being a man of sense, as Seneca and his nephew were. Do not smile when I add that I esteem him for that honest-principled spirit of true religion which shines through the whole, and from whence, unknown as I am to M. de Voltaire, I conclude him at once a free-thinker and a lover of quiet; no bigot, but yet no heretic; one who honours authority and national sanctions without prejudice to truth or charity; one who has studied controversy less than reason, and the Fathers less than mankind; in a word, one worthy from his rational temper of that share of friendship and intimacy with which you honour him.[a]

We cannot, therefore, repeat John Morley's assertion—"Voltaire left France a poet, he returned to it a sage"—without some reservations. England matured, armed, and excited Voltaire, but she did not create him.

[a] Ballantyne, *Voltaire's Visit to England,* London, 1893, p. 71.

2

Voltaire in England:
The Philosophical Letters[a]

RELEASED FROM the Bastille on May 2, 1726, Voltaire was in
Calais on the 5th. He disembarked at Greenwich "in the midst
of spring,"[b] and that very evening slept in London at the home
of Lord Bolingbroke. Several weeks later he went back secretly
to France, was unsuccessful in finding the Chevalier de Rohan,
and returned to London at the end of July. Discouraged, financially embarrassed by the bankruptcy of the Jew Medina, and ill,
he was aided, he said, by "an English gentleman" (it was actually
the king[c,1]) and by the merchant Falkener, who offered him hospitality at Wandsworth. He considered settling down permanently
in this country "where the arts are honored and rewarded, where
there is differentiation in status but none other among men except
that which results from merit," in this country "where men think
free and noble thoughts."[d] He felt a ferment of "republican"
feelings. He was expansive, intoxicated with English liberty, a

---

[a] Desnoiresterres, *la Jeunesse de Voltaire: Voltaire à Cirey.* Churton Collins,
Bolingbroke, Voltaire in England. Ballantyne, *Voltaire's Visit to England.*
Revue d'Histoire littéraire, 1906 (L. Foulet). *Revue de Paris,* 1904 (G. Lanson).
Jusserand, *English Essays from a French Pen.*
[b] V. XXII, p. 18. [Moland ed.]
[c] Bengesco, IV, 25; and Hettier, *op. cit.*
[d] V. XXXIII, p. 159. (Besterman, 291) (R.P.)

liberty he enjoyed for two and a half years.[a] In February 1729 he recrossed the Channel and, in April, obtained from Maurepas authorization to reappear in Paris.

Voltaire, who had already known several Englishmen in France, reached England fortified with good recommendations. He even had a few from the ministry, which was a bit embarrassed at treating him as a guilty person, and he also had a letter from the English ambassador to Paris, Horace Walpole.[2] The world of the Tories and the Whigs extended him a welcome. He was introduced to Robert Walpole,[3] Lord and Lady Hervey, the Duke of Newcastle, Bubb Dodington (the future Lord Melcombe), and the dowager Duchess of Marlborough. He was cordially received by the Prince and Princess of Wales. When the latter became queen, she accepted the dedication of the *Henriade* upon publication of the London edition in 1728. He held conversations with the most illustrious writers and scholars in England: Edward Young, John Gay, Congreve, Colley Cibber, Berkeley, and Clarke. He visited Pope at Twickenham and spent three months with Swift at the home of Lord Peterborough. If he arrived in time only to witness the funeral of Sir Isaac Newton, he visited Newton's niece and nephew, Mr. and Mrs. Conduit. An absurd story of Voltaire's alleged involvement in espionage and secret intelligence is probably no more than evidence of his lively curiosity and of the precautions he took not to disclose among the Whigs information acquired among the Tories. He wanted to learn English. He resisted the temptation to get along without it. He could speak French with Bolingbroke and other noblemen or else at the Rainbow Tavern in Marylebone with such refugees as Desmaizeaux, Saint-Hyacinthe, and others. But he felt that English was necessary for him in order to understand what was going on around him and because it deserved to be studied as a literary language. In the seventeenth century a Frenchman learned Italian and Spanish; under Louis XV he learned English and German. Voltaire, who wanted the French to learn English and Italian,[b] marked an intermediate stage in our culture.

---

[a] Mr. L. Foulet reduces the duration of his English sojourn to a little less than two years, from mid-August 1726 to early August 1728.
[b] V. XXII, p. 261; Bengesco, II, 5.

After eighteen months his pronounciation was still bad and he had difficulty following a conversation, but he could read and write well. His two essays, *On Epic Poetry* and *On the Civil Wars of France*, as well as his London letters to Thieriot, are in a very good current English idiom. By going every evening to the Drury Lane Theatre, where Chetwood, the prompter, provided him with a copy of the play, he made himself quite fluent in the spoken language. More than thirty years after his return to France he was still able to converse in English.

Not satisfied with what he could see and hear or with the knowledge that his friends and associates could give him, he launched an appeal to the public, soliciting, for the report he intended to write, all kinds of information on England's great men and on new discoveries or enterprises useful to mankind. The publication of his English *Essays*, the launching of the subscription for the *Henriade* (the proceeds of which were partially squandered by the careless Thieriot), bringing out this edition in which Duplessis-Mornay replaced Rosny at the side of Henry IV by way of punishing the duc de Sully for his cowardly neutrality in the Chevalier de Rohan affair—all this kept Voltaire in the public eye. At the same time he was also working on his *Histoire de Charles XII* ("History of Charles XII") and his tragedy *Brutus*. But, more importantly, a psychological transformation was taking place within Voltaire, a transformation that the public was not yet aware of.

There was no indication at first, when he reappeared in Paris in 1729, that this was a different Voltaire. He resumed his easygoing, dazzling way of life; mixing business with pleasures; speculating and negotiating; flattering the comte de Clermont and his secretary Moncrif; cultivating the minister Rouillé; arranging a marriage between the duc de Richelieu and Mlle de Guise, to the great scandal of the proud house of Lorraine; supping and soon lodging with the comtesse de Fontaine-Martel, a philosophically-minded woman who was intensely fond of the theater. He persuaded her to die "according to the rules," that is to say, with the assistance of a priest. (Since the remains of Adrienne Lecouvreur[4] had recently been tossed into potter's field, Voltaire was convinced of the necessity for such ceremonies.)

He mourned in the death of la Lecouvreur the loss of a great artist and friend, one who had, for a moment perhaps, meant something considerably more to him, and in that of Mme de Fontaine-Martel, the loss of a friend devoted to his glory and who could also think the same thoughts as he. The deepest anguish he suffered was the death of young Presiding Judge de Maisons. "The death of M. de Maisons has left me in a state of despair bordering on stupor. I have lost my friend, my support, my father. He died in my arms, not through the ignorance but through the negligence of doctors. As long as I live, I will never be consoled over his loss and the cruel manner in which I lost him."[a]

But with Voltaire, life quickly gained the upper hand. He did not forget Maisons. He enshrined him in *Le Temple du Goût* ("The Temple of Good Taste"). But *Eriphyle*, a tragedy, could not wait. He had to finish and correct it. There was the necessity of helping establish Linant, a promising young poet, and the necessity of extricating printer Jore from an awkward predicament. He could not linger long in "the sweetness of tears." Little by little his English fever broke out in writings that took his public somewhat by surprise. The poet was becoming an historian in *Charles XII*, an historian precise, impartial, just, without flattery or satire, a philosopher without polemic, demonstrating in a lively, colorful account how a great man, avid for war and glory, could bring about the ruin of his kingdom. He was Shakespearean and republican in *Brutus* (performed December 11, 1730) and again in *La Mort de César* ("The Death of Caesar") which he dared not risk on the stage. He was Shakespearean in *Eriphyle*, which was a failure (March 7, 1732); Shakespearean again, but in a gallant and French manner, in that tender and brilliant *Zaïre*, so well suited to please women, a masterpiece in tragedy in Louis XV style, whose performance (August 13, 1732) was a veritable triumph. He was impatient now to take greater risks and present to the French people his reflections on England.

Voltaire knew that anything coming from him was suspect. His indignation over the treatment of Mlle Lecouvreur had almost cost him a run-in with the authorities. He had had to attribute to the late Chaulieu his own *Epître à Uranie*. Even his *Histoire de Charles XII* was denied the privilege of publication.

---

[a] V. XXXII, p. 230. (Besterman, 417) (R.P.)

For, having spoken well of Stanislas, father of the queen of France, he had not dealt tactfully enough with Stanislas' adversary, Augustus II, king of Saxony. The dedicatory preface to the merchant Falkener had created difficulties for *Zaïre*. A general protest had greeted *Le Temple du Goût,* that excellent example of Voltairian criticism, blending classical tradition with worldly taste and personal temperament. Voltaire pulled his punches, but the liberties he did take, and with such moderation, seemed nothing less than scandalous. The writers whom he scratched, screamed. Those he omitted screamed louder. A *grand seigneur* complained about a compliment. It seems his rank did not permit him to receive such in print.

Nevertheless, Voltaire finished his *Lettres* on England, presenting one copy to Thieriot who took charge of having them published in London in both English and French, and another copy to Jore, an adventurous bookseller who accepted the risks of the enterprise. For a moment he had hopes of securing a publication permit or at least a tacit permission. Cardinal Fleury had laughed at the letters on the Quakers which Voltaire read to him (omitting certain portions). A censor, the abbé de Rothelin, saw trouble only for the thirteenth letter on Locke and the soul. But in the end, Voltaire had to abandon any hope of authorization, official or otherwise. He waxed indignant. He wrote, without publishing it, his notable letter to an official of the office of censorship (June 1733), a spirited plea for freedom of the press and of ideas. But simultaneously, since one had to take risks, he doubled his wager, adding to his observations on England his commentary on Pascal.

Meanwhile, people were beginning to talk about this scandalous publication in preparation. Cabinet ministers became uneasy and hostile. Voltaire grew frightened and resisted the pleas of the impatient Thieriot and Jore. Every week that passed detracted from the novelty of his work. Publications on England were now proliferating. Apart from the Dutch journals or the *Lettres* of the Swiss Béat de Muralt, which, by comparing English and French manners and morals, had wounded the national pride of the abbé Desfontaines (1725), and without going back to Boissy whose *Français à Londres* ("Frenchmen in London") had brought to the stage the contrast between the two peoples, provoking a riposte from Marivaux (1727),[a] there was also Father Catrou's *Histoire des Trembleurs* ("History of the Quakers") (early 1733). And the abbé Prévost, who had already used his knowledge of England in his novels, published in June 1733 the first issue of *Pour et Contre* ("The Pro and Con") in which he promised to "include each time some interesting item touching on the genius of the English, the sights of London and other parts of the isle, and on the daily progress they are making in science and literature."

Voltaire could not prevent publication of the English translation which appeared in mid-August 1733, but he still succeeded in holding up the French edition for nearly a year. He was in Burgundy for the marriage of the duc de Richelieu to Mlle de Guise when he received word that a *lettre de cachet*[5] had been issued against him (May 3, 1734). Copies of a pirated edition by Jore had been seized. Voltaire hastily passed over into Lorraine. *Parlement* issued a decree on June 10th to burn the book and arrest the author. Voltaire's friends—Mme de Richelieu, Mme d'Aiguillon, and the marquis de Matignon—tried to appease Chauvelin, the Keeper of the Seal. He was not inflexible, but Cardinal Fleury became angry. This scandal was a threat to his slumbering despotism. Above all, the Solicitor General and the Jansenist *Parlement* were intent on punishing the imprudent and impudent philosopher. Voltaire had to spend an entire year in Champagne. Paris was not reopened to him until March 1735 on his promise of good behavior. For ten years the parliamentary decree remained a constant threat to him.

Persecution merely spurred on the success of the *Lettres Philosophiques*. Five editions were printed in 1734; five more from 1734 to 1739. "Whenever they announce the arrival of some monster," remarked the abbé Molinier, "the public flocks eagerly to see it. The mind, no less than matter, produces monsters. Almost everyone wanted to see these letters."

Voltaire did not give a graphic or pictorial description of the country and its manners, although a remaining fragment of an early sketch shows that he had given some thought to it. The Jore edition contains twenty-five letters. The first ones (I–VII) deal

[a] *L'Ile de la raison*, prologue.

with religion and, at the very outset, with the Quakers (I–IV). He had consulted good sources: Barclay, Croese, Sewel, and the life of William Penn. He had seen Quakers in London. While he described their enthusiasm, their assemblies, and the adventures of their leaders with an amused impertinence that angered them, he gave a sympathetic account of their virtues, their evangelical simplicity, and their critical views of sacraments and dogma that Catholics felt to be directed against the Church. Then, in a broad manner, he made fun of Anglicans and Presbyterians, but in an even broader manner he lampooned the French clergy for its wealth, its worldly morality, etc. He spoke briefly of the Antitrinitarians and maintained silence out of prudence, not ignorance, on the subject of deists, who were so numerous at that time in England. From the spectacle of religious life in England he drew a conclusion—an echo of Bayle and Montesquieu, but still as new as it was shocking in France: "If there were only one religion in England, we should have to fear despotism. If there were two, they would cut each other's throats. But there are thirty of them, and they live in peace and happiness."[a]

Amusing and rather naïve were the rejoinders from French ecclesiastics. The abbé Molinier suspected Voltaire of wanting "to multiply Quakerism" among us. The abbé was slightly wide of the mark. The Jesuits were busy legitimizing the tithe: "M. de Voltaire is unaware that the custom of paying tithes to priests goes back to antiquity, even to the time of Abraham and Melchizedec. A Wit does not understand facts and traditions." In Voltaire's remark about "Churches where certain ecclesiastics are fairly satisfied with 50,000 pounds revenue and where the people are good enough to put up with it," the Jesuit journalist of Trévoux[6] heard "a cry of sedition and banditry." But, fortunately, the journalist added, in France "people know how to live and to respect their superiors." This was to be true for another fifty years.

Three letters (VIII–X) describe England's political régime. More than Rapin Thoyras, Muralt, or Montesquieu, Voltaire idealized English life, political liberty, the constitutional monarchy, equality of taxation, the honorable status of commerce

[a] End of letter VI.

(young lords did not disdain being merchants in the city), and the comfortable lot of the peasant. He exalted the pacific greatness of this nation of businessmen, masters of the sea and bankers to princes, disinterested guardians of Europe's liberty. No mockery in these pages: short, compact, incisive sentences without hesitations or reservations:

A man, because he is a nobleman or because he is a priest, is not exempt here from paying certain taxes. . . . Everyone pays. Each one gives, not according to his rank (which is absurd), but according to his income. . . .

The English nation is the only one on earth that has succeeded in controlling the power of kings by resisting them.

The reproach most often directed against Englishmen is their execution of Charles I, who was treated by his conquerors as he would have treated them had he been successful.[a]

The abbé Prévost preferred to ignore the letters dealing with such delicate subject matter. Others denounced the "horrible consequences" of these maxims fashioned "to arm the king's subjects and foment insurrection." The abbé Molinier scoffed at those great words *freedom* and *slavery:* "Chains are hard to bear, but happily, this is a poetic expression commonly used in love as in politics, and one which should cause no more anxiety in this country than it does to the lovers in Cythera."[7]

Letter XI, on the subject of inoculations against smallpox, introduces us to English philosophy. Inoculation was an act of philosophical freedom. For proof we have the riposte hurled at Voltaire: "The French nature is revolted by the system of inoculation; we submit to the decrees of divine Providence."

Next come the letters on Bacon, Locke, and Newton (XII–XVII)—an enthusiastic endorsement of the experimental method and of its founder Francis Bacon; the demonstration by Locke and Newton of its application to metaphysics as well as physics; a lively critique of scholastic reveries and of the "fictitious tales" of Descartes and Malebranche; an energetic defense of Locke's principle: that God Almighty was able to give matter, which did not of necessity possess it, the power of thought. These letters

[a] V. XXII, pp. 109, 103, 104. Text of 1734.

arrived at the moment when the *tourbillons* ("vortices") of Descartes held sway in the Academy of Sciences and when theologians, long since perturbed by Cartesian metaphysics, discovered in Locke a spirituality that could be enlisted in the cause of religion. Despite Father Buffier's esteem for John Locke, despite Maupertuis' book on Newton, Frenchmen remained attached, partly for reasons of national pride, to their fellow countryman René Descartes.[8] Nevertheless, a general tendency was abroad to regard metaphysics with suspicion and defiance. Physicists and geometricians were daily gaining more credit and influence. People of social prominence and cultivated women were delighted to hear that these philosophies they found so incomprehensible were really only so much sound and fury. The public was ready for Voltaire.

After religion, politics, and philosophy, it was literature's turn. In five letters (XVIII–XXII) Voltaire wrote about tragedy, comedy, and poetry. He presented Shakespeare, Otway, Dryden, Addison, Wycherley, Vanbrugh, Congreve, Rochester, Waller, Butler, Swift, and Pope, characterizing each rapidly and interpolating excerpts from their writings with his own judgments. He noted the lack of good taste, the unevenness, of English poets but also the power of their genius, their "overblown style, too far removed from nature, too closely copied from Hebrew writers." He admired their naturalness, their impetuosity of imagination, and their energy, which was often sublime. He discerned a relationship between their literature and their political régime: liberty had left its imprint on the writings of English poets and was the reason literature was held in such high esteem in this land where "it is common for people to think."[a]

Lastly, Voltaire considered literature from a social point of view (letters XXIII–XXIV) in order to applaud the esteem accorded men of letters, who in England secured appointments and positions of dignity, whereas in France. . . . He compared the organization of the Royal Society of London with that of French academies. But here, in spite of his criticism, he gave France the edge. In this final letter he expressed a point of view dear to the eighteenth century and true at that time. It was the age of

[a] V. XXII, p. 162.

academies. They were truly centers of intellectual and scientific life, serving simultaneously as workshops for research and as institutions of higher learning. Voltaire thought well of them and wanted to make them even more useful, particularly the French Academy.

The actual *Lettres Anglaises* end at this point. The 25th letter of the Jore edition gives us fifty-seven comments on Pascal, which were completed in 1742. These observations find their source in the same inspiration that dictated Voltaire's letter on Locke. The adversary was well chosen. Blaise Pascal,[9] that man "whom little minds hardly dare to examine," was the only apologist for revealed religion who really mattered in French letters and who was respected by the public at large. He was the only one who could prove, not the God common to Christians and deists alike, through a reasoning that was both philosophical and commonplace, but specifically Jesus Christ and Christian mysteries, which were incomprehensible by any single method of argumentation. By virtue of his genius he had made people believe in the success of his "demonstration." By attacking him, no matter what precautions Voltaire might take in the choice of quotations, Voltaire was coming to grips with religion itself. For that reason this 25th letter gravely weakened his case, except in the eyes of the Jesuits who had their own reasons for being indulgent to a censor of Pascal.

The Protestant Bouiller scorned Voltaire's audacity, calling him "a butterfly who would attack the bird of Jupiter." While it would be a mistake to equate Voltaire's common sense with the fervent genius of a Pascal, and while one must recognize in his criticism of the *Pensées* ("Meditations") certain trivialities and errors, one cannot deny that in more than one instance it is Voltaire who is right rather than Pascal. He is right in contesting a number of fanciful or unsubstantial subtleties of Pascalian argumentation. He is right, for whoever is not Catholic or Christian, in his judgment about the nature and destiny of man. He was especially right, within the spirit of his age, for anyone who was not a Jansenist. The eighteenth century Frenchman could not regard life as evil and reason as impotent. Here the Jesuits found Voltaire in the right. At least they conceded he was right *rationally speaking* to say that man can be what he is without "the fall from grace" and that only *faith* can assure us of original sin. Bouiller could defend Pascal only by weakening him and by minimizing the personal nature and qualities of his *Apology*.

The *Lettres Philosophiques* were a great event in the intellectual life of the eighteenth century. It may be said that they contained nothing new, since Frenchmen had already discussed Locke, Newton,[a] the Quakers, the English parliament, Shakespeare, and even inoculation. Nevertheless, it was a very new work and a literary landmark. More than the *Histoire de Charles XII,* it was a revelation of Voltairian prose—limpid, alert, and sharp-edged, an incomparable filter of ideas bubbling over with delightful wit. Nowadays we are tempted to say: "a superficial clarity, pleasantly light and charming." Yet the abbé Prévost found the letters on Locke and Newton too "serious," not sufficiently "brightened up" with "agreeable invention." Voltaire was not the pure artist who writes to satisfy himself. He took the measure of the public that he sought to win over. In these *Lettres* philosophy discarded the attitudes of detachment and the covert malice of Bayle, the disguises affected by Fontenelle and Montesquieu. It took stage center, boldly and simply. It exposed itself without a mask, wielding its lethal weapon, that *ironie perpétuelle,* which would forever exasperate the Solicitor General.

Voltaire exercised his right to think out loud on all subjects previously regarded as taboo in public discussion. The state of drowsy lethargy in which old Cardinal Fleury endeavored to keep men's minds was suddenly shattered by the piercing tones of a trumpet—a clarion call. Those insolent letters announced a completely revolutionary program. It was no longer just this little item or that little item, a partial and sketchy sort of criticism. Voltaire had gathered up everything—political freedom, religious freedom, philosophical freedom, the amelioration of human life, the experimental method, and the social value of the intellect. Even Newton on optics was not something harmless. Not so much in its results as in its method, it seemed to strike a blow for scientific freedom. In linking Newton and Locke to Bacon, Voltaire thrust into view, above the admissible sciences (each one

---

[a] Voltaire studied Newton in the writings of Pemberton and Fontenelle and with Maupertuis. It was Maupertuis who converted him.

regarded from a religious viewpoint as something separate and distinct), the menacing spectacle of a science that was one both in spirit and in method. The cumulative effect of all his remarks on England landed like a huge rock, its impact shaking the very foundations of French society. Remove from his writings the things he criticized—oppressive religious unity, the wealth of the clergy, its political power, royal despotism, and the privileges of the nobility. Visualize what he desired—equality of merchant and nobleman, graduated taxation, the separation of faith and reason, the sovereignty of the experimental method, scientific and literary freedom. What is left of the France of Louis XV? Was there not a sweeping revolution in his program?

The *Lettres Philosophiques* was the first bomb dropped on the Old Régime. That was why it tore the parliamentarians away from their quarrels over the papal bull and unified them in an effort to stifle these letters under the protective covering of the court, the bishops, and the Jesuits. That is why the good Fathers, who did not yet despair of their former pupil—since he disliked Pascal—agreed that the suppression of his book was very wise *(fort sage)*. Jansenists, ultramontanes, and Protestant clergymen perceived for the first time the new face of the *philosophe*.[10] "Just what is a *philosophe?*" said the abbé Molinier. "A kind of monster in society who feels under no obligation towards its manners and morals, its proprieties, its politics, or its religion. One may expect anything from men of their ilk."[a]

[a] The abbé Molinier, p. 81.

3

Voltaire at Cirey :
Physics and Metaphysics[a]

IN SPITE of a permit granted by the police lieutenant, Voltaire's sojourn in Paris was an unhappy one. He resolved to remain at the château de Cirey where he had waited for the storm to blow over: at Cirey-sur-Blaise, described with horror by the poet's young and worldly niece, Mme Denis, as "a lonely place terrifying to humanity, four leagues distant from any habitation, in a country where there is nothing to see but mountains and uncultivated terrain." Actually it is located in a lovely valley, fresh and green, surrounded by two heavily wooded hills; the coal extracted from them nourished several iron works now no longer in operation. The place is charming, but it is indeed isolated, far from the main highways. Via Saint-Dizier it was just a short distance from the border of the duchy of Barrois. At the first warning one could pass from the domains of the king of France

[a] Desnoiresterres, *Voltaire à Cirey*. Longchamp (and Wagnière), *Mémoires sur Voltaire*, 2 vols., 1825. E. Asse, *Lettres de Mme du Châtelet*, 1882; *Lettres de Mme de Graffigny*, etc., 1879. Léouzon Le Duc, *Voltaire et la police*, 1867. *Mém. de la soc. des lettres de Saint-Dizier*, 1892–1894 (abbé Piot), *Cirey-le-Château*). Duc de Broglie, *Frédéric II et Louis XV*, 1885. *Revue d'histoire littéraire*, 1902 (P. Bonnenfon, *Sur Voltaire et J.-B. Rousseau*). Dubois-Reymond, *Voltaire comme homme de science*, trad. *Lépine*, 1869. Saigey, *les Sciences au XVIIIe siècle; la physique de Voltaire*, 1873.

Gabrielle, Emilie de Tonnelier de Breteuil, Marquise du Chatelet,
By Nicolas de Largillière (about 1736)
The Columbus Gallery of Fine Arts

into those of the Duke of Lorraine. Cirey meant rest, study, and security.

There was love also, at least at the outset. The marquise du Châtelet, to whom the property belonged, had, after brief affairs with several lovers, become the poet's mistress at the age of 27 in 1733. After the mysterious episode of the Charonne inn, where they went to enjoy fricassee of chicken, and the equally mysterious foursomes at Voltaire's with the duchesse de Saint-Pierre and M. de Forcalquier, their liaison became a matter of public knowledge, and by reason of its duration, altogether respectable according to the mores of the age.

Imagine a tall, thin woman with sharp facial features and a pointed nose: that is the face of *la belle Emilie,* a face she is pleased with and for which she spares nothing to enhance it: curls, pompons, precious stones and jewelry, all in super-abundance, but since she wants to appear beautiful, though nature decreed otherwise, and since she wants to appear wealthy, despite her limited means, she is obliged, in order to afford the superfluous, to do without necessities such as chemises and other bagatelles.[a]

These are the remarks of a woman, Mme du Deffand. There are two reasons for discounting them: Mme du Châtelet was by no means ugly, and she was even quite attractive. She was certainly flirtatious, fond of adornment, of an impulsive, passionate nature, and boldly, aristocratically immodest even to the point of bathing in front of a *valet de chambre,* whom she did not really regard as a man. And she was rather fond of gambling. She knew Latin, Italian, and English. She was passionately interested in mathematics, physics, and metaphysics. Moreover, she understood them. She read Leibnitz and included Maupertuis and Clairaut among her friends. She was a "thinker." Another good gossip of the day tells us that every year she reexamined and reappraised her principles. She wrote on scientific and philosophical subjects. People regarded her as a pedant, but she was sincerely dedicated to her studies. She preferred the use of her mind to the trivia of society. She was not devout or even a believer. She was not a busybody or a slanderer or in any way malicious. As

[a] Mme du Deffand, *Corresp. complète,* V. II, p. 763.

the mistress of M. de Mopinot, she might have said that, except in bed, she meant to be treated as a man. She had a man's mind, a man's heart—honest, forthright, steady, and capable of strong affections. All in all, she was superior to the women who made fun of her.

And so it was that Voltaire came to live in her château, alongside the tactful marquis. At that time such an arrangement was not considered improper. Voltaire was like a member of the family, advancing funds in their financial difficulties, decorating and remodeling the home in which he built a long room for himself with an attractive "rococo" doorway, a bit too heavily cluttered with all sorts of ornaments, emblems, and mottoes. In this hideaway there was no social chatter, no procession of visitors. They lived *en famille:* Monsieur, Madame, the friend, the son, the tutor Linant (a poor devil whom they did not dismiss because he would not have found employment elsewhere), the tutor's sister, who was no less indolent and incapable than her brother and whom they also retained out of pity, one or two neighbors like good old Mme de Champbonin, nicknamed *Gros Chat* ("Big Puss"), or old cousin Tichateau. That was the usual cast of characters at Cirey.

The ten or twelve years Voltaire spent there were years of great productivity. The lady who was his friend became his protector. And she worked to keep him from the public, from the plaudits of noisy acclaim. She wanted him all to herself, but it was for his benefit that she prevented him from circulating dangerous thoughts he had expressed in writing. She put firmly under lock and key such items as Voltaire's *Métaphysique* and *La Pucelle* ["The Maid"—a verse travesty on Joan of Arc]. She guided him toward less scabrous topics, toward the studies she was fond of. She urged him to work on science, mathematics, and physical experiments. Voltaire gave in. His intellectual curiosity could gallop off joyfully in any direction. But he could not wholly forsake his pleasure and his destiny. He could not give up poetry or history. He was never able to hide his talent under a bushel. Whether in print or manuscript, he simply had to entertain the world or else scandalize it. He had to hear the ever-resounding cry: Voltaire! Poor Emily was at a loss to know what to do.

Voltaire's repose was as restless and excitable as his temperament, a strange mixture of dazzling successes, feverish studies, unrestrained polemics, alarums and excursions, impulses to rush off to the great theaters of Paris, to the court, or to the homes of flattering princes.

He endowed his nieces. He kept writing. He turned out touching and terrifying tragedies: *Alzire, Mahomet, Mérope.* He was rhyming stanzas, odes, and, above all, epistles which the marquis du Châtelet was not always happy to see in circulation, particularly when they celebrated too affectionately *la belle Emilie.* Voltaire was finishing concurrently those follies entitled *Jeanne* and *Les Discours en vers sur l'homme* ("The Discourses in Verse on Man"). Life was good in the paradise of Cirey. Voltaire was optimistic. He produced *Le Mondain* ("The Man of the World").

> Oh! le bon temps que ce siècle de fer
> (Oh, how good this age of iron is!)

this age in which one had champagne and coffee, Germain silverware, Gobelin tapestries, Rameau's music, and the chorus girls of the *Opéra.* Unfortunately, he expressed contempt for Adam (a man uncivilized and unrefined) as well as for that terrestrial paradise which lacked modern comforts. Theologians began to growl, and the poet was off in haste to Holland.

Voltaire experienced a glorious delight in finding himself courted by the crown prince of Prussia, a prince fond of the arts and philosophy and much abused for indulging these affections by his father, the sergeant king. Frederick initiated an active correspondence with Voltaire, making him his teacher of French spelling and poetry, an illustrious, tuition-free teacher who was compensated for his labors with compliments and little gifts. Kaiserling was dispatched as ambassador to Cirey to present to the poet, to the prince's friend, a writing desk and some verses. Theater and a nocturnal display of fireworks honored the envoy and celebrated a new social phenomenon—that of a king's son paying court to a man of wit, *un homme d'esprit.*

With his friend Mme du Châtelet, Voltaire studied physics, purchased laboratory equipment from the abbé Nollet, installed furnaces, observed, and experimented. They sent reports to the Academy of Sciences, which failed to award them any prizes. Whereupon Voltaire threw himself into metaphysics, writing about the subject and arguing about it with the marquise and the prince. He pushed vigorously ahead with his *Siècle de Louis XIV* ("Age of Louis XIV"). And since he doubtless had unexpended energy left to burn, he could not pass up an opportunity for a quarrel or a scandal. There was a lawsuit against Jore, that "rogue," resulting in a two-sided decision which threw the bookseller's case out of court but also damaged the writer's reputation. There were virulent exchanges of defamations in print with old Jean-Baptiste Rousseau and above all, a war on the abbé Desfontaines whom he bombarded with *Le Préservatif* only to be counterattacked with the *Voltairomanie*. All the dirt they kicked up with such obvious relish served only to disgust people of good breeding, and Voltaire lost more from his bad temper than did the "pamphleteer." The valuable service Voltaire had rendered the abbé in extricating him from the Bicêtre hospice, where he was being held on a nasty morals charge,[a] the very real lack of good manners on the part of the befriended party, who forgot much too quickly any sense of gratitude or obligation—all this disappeared in a storm of mutual recriminations, crude and slanderous, which sullied their authors more than their intended victims. The retraction of sorts finally elicited from Desfontaines did not repair the loss of esteem suffered by Voltaire, an esteem less jeopardized by his enemy's insults than by his own scandalous, undignified outbursts, his clamors to the police, to the judiciary, and to the ministers of state, and by the coalition of friends and clients whom he incited to move on his behalf. The situation was not improved by the lamentable Thieriot incident in which his old friend [Thieriot] refused to act, leaving uncertain whether his failure to do so was motivated by considerations of honor or by selfish cowardice. The public at large forgot the original cause of the dispute and, in view of subsequent events, adopted an attitude of contempt for Voltaire.

He had another deep cause for displeasure with the government. It had suppressed a collection of writings in which there appeared a few harmless observations taken from his *Siècle de Louis XIV*. Out of chagrin and convinced that no one could

[a] His dossier is disturbing. *Arch de la Bastille,* XII.

write history in France, he left his work half finished and undertook, in complete privacy and for Emily alone, a study of universal history. Of greater peril was the *Mahomet* ("Mohammed") affair. Greeted in Lille in 1741 with universal acclaim, the play was regarded in Paris the following year as an act of outrageous impiety. He had to withdraw it in order to prevent *Parlement* and its Solicitor General from resurrecting their decree against the *Lettres Anglaises*.

Around 1739 Voltaire felt the urge to travel. A lawsuit of Mme du Châtelet took them both to Valenciennes, to Brussels, and to The Hague. In the latter city he published the splendid refutation of Machiavelli, which the Prussian prince had composed, and then attempted unsuccessfully to suppress it at Frederick's request. Having now become a king, Frederick no longer felt inclined to practice the maxims expressed in his book. Somewhat disenchanted with the philosophy of sovereigns, Voltaire did not, however, resist the friendship of the conqueror of Silesia. He went to see him at Cleves and at Rheinsberg. In 1740 he went as far as Berlin.

He returned there in 1743 through another shift of fortune, entrusted with a mission from the French government. Its purpose was to persuade the king of Prussia (France's old ally, who had cynically dropped her after acquiring Silesia) to take up arms on our behalf. It was no easy task. Voltaire failed, no more and no less than had he been a professional diplomat. But he was smothered with flattery. Simply to have him all to himself, the king of Prussia undertook a bit of deception designed to sow dissension between Voltaire and the French minister. The motive was so flattering that the poet overlooked the unethical royal methods.

Everything was sheer delight for him in the joy of breathing the atmosphere of a court. He was on most familiar terms with the king's sisters. He spent two weeks with the eccentric Wilhelmina, Margravine of Bayreuth, who showed him her little Versailles, her *Hermitage*. He returned dazzled by operas, theatre, and hunting parties. All was enchantment. He flirted with the future queen of Sweden, Princess Ulrica, and proffered her an exquisite madrigal which, from the standpoint of protocol, appeared impertinent.

Souvent un peu de vérité
Se mêle au plus grossier mensonge;
Cette nuit, dans l'erreur d'un songe,
Au rang des rois j'étais monté.
Je vous aimais, princesse, et j'osais vous le dire!
Les dieux à mon réveil ne m'ont pas tout ôté;
Je n'ai perdu que mon empire.[a]

(There is often a bit of truth
Mingled with the most outlandish falsehood;
Last night, in the illusion of a dream,
I had risen to the ranks of kings.
I loved you, princess, and I dared to tell you so!
The gods, on my awakening, did not take everything from me:
I lost only my empire.)

How far away, at that moment, were the château de Cirey and the incomparable marquise!

The poor woman was heavy of heart on seeing with what ease her lover could leave her for a prince or an actress, for Frederick or la Gaussin.[b] But he came back to her, however. He always had an affection for her. Yet he could no longer be happy in their liaison or content to remain at Cirey unless permitted to escape continually. He was weary of the rustic retreat and weary of their intimate conversations. He wanted to enjoy his fame and glory. At the premiere of *Mérope* (February 20, 1743) he had appeared in the loge of Mmes de Boufflers and de Luxembourg and had kissed the latter's hand, to the enthusiastic applause of the audience. Not since the days of *Zaïre* had he known such a triumph. Joys of this sort intoxicated him and made him regard as dull and boring the quietude of that far away valley where love was always beckoning him.

And so we have given the reader a sort of bird's eye view of ten years in the life of Voltaire. If we wish a somewhat closer glimpse, let us follow that "chatter box," Mme de Graffigny, who came from Lorraine to Cirey in 1738. Voltaire, elegantly dressed and powdered, received her with warm embraces and wept on hearing her recount her misfortunes. He showed her his bed-

---

[a] V. X, p. 528 [Moland ed.]
[b] *Arch. de la Bastille*, XII, 24.

room, his paintings, his porcelains, his jewelry, his clocks, his silverware. He had in all things "an extremely discriminating taste." In his study she saw his books, his laboratory equipment. Emily's apartment was also magnificent, making the visitor more sensitive to the "repulsive filthiness" of the rest of the château.

She dined with Voltaire. The poet's *valet de chambre* stood behind his chair. Everything was first handed to him, "like pages of the king's gentlemen." Voltaire took nothing from anyone else's hands. The supper was "correct and elegant," seasoned with "charming talk, enchanting talk" sometimes lasting until midnight. "What didn't they talk about! Poetry, sciences, the arts, everything in a light and bantering fashion." Occasionally, Voltaire would read to the enthusiastic guest his *Siècle de Louis XIV,* his *Mérope,* some of his epistles, his *Discours* on man, his *Pucelle.* They acted out plays in the pretty little theater installed in the attic: "The decorations are colonnades with pots of orange trees between the columns." There was a single loge, which the mistress of the château could reach from her bedroom by means of a hidden staircase. The walls were adorned with bright and lively paintings. Hardly had she arrived when Mme de Graffigny was assigned a part in a play. They performed *L'Enfant Prodigue* ("The Prodigal Son"), and they rehearsed *Zaïre* for a performance the next day. There were moments that were simply feverish. "In twenty-four hours we rehearsed and played thirty-three acts, including tragedies, operas, and comedies." When the theater was idle, there were the marionettes, "the play in which Punchinello's wife thinks she has killed her husband by singing *fagnana, fagnana!*" Or else Voltaire showed pictures with his magic lantern, commenting on each "with remarks that made you die laughing," pictures in which he put friends and enemies together, Richelieu alongside Desfontaines.

In the midst of these pleasures there was frenzied intellectual activity. Ordinarily, Mme du Châtelet spent the night working. She would sleep for two hours. Voltaire would lock himself up all day in his room, sometimes arriving in the middle of the evening meal only to run back, after eating, to sit down again at his writing table. But he had his moments of relaxation, delightful moments. He was "as lovable a child as he was a wise philosopher." But "a furiously self-centered author"; one must not praise anyone else in his presence. He would fly into a rage at the mention of Jean-Baptiste Rousseau.[1] He was a spoiled child and a pouter. He would pout for a glass of Rhine wine, which Mme du Châtelet forbade him to drink because it disagreed with him. He would sulk for a suit of clothes that she did not want him to wear. They would quarrel—in English—over anything at all. Already Voltaire was "the eternal invalid," dosing himself to suit his fancy and drinking coffee. Yet as soon as he was off on some topic, he would forget all his maladies in a sparkling display of malice and gaiety.

But suddenly we find Voltaire and Emily convinced that the visitor has sent to her friends some portions of *Jeanne,* the dangerous *Jeanne.* They become frightened. Terrible scenes ensue, especially for the guest. She leaves the room, crestfallen, in tears, running a temperature, obliged to go to bed. Ah! The indiscretion was not hers after all. They apologize. They flatter her. But the spell is broken. The charm has ended. She escapes from this inferno which she had first mistaken for a paradise.

Of the vast and varied literary output Voltaire composed at Cirey, the writings that give special color to the period are those on metaphysics and science. Under the influence of Mme du Châtelet he wanted "to assess his ideas" on God and the soul, and in 1734 he wrote a *Traité de Métaphysique* ("A Treatise on Metaphysics") which she prevented him from publishing. It would have created an uproar. Emily was a disciple of Leibnitz.[2] Voltaire followed in the footsteps of the "wise" Locke[3] and the English philosophers.

He believed in God. He had proofs that satisfied him, the proof that derives from the orderly system of the universe, the proof that requires a first cause, a prime mover. He was very definitely a *cause-finalier,*[a] a believer in ultimate causation. With a moral proof, with the need for a sanction for good and evil, there was no question in his mind. For Voltaire and his mistress, metaphysics was an introduction to physics. God was the first law, the first truth of physics. God was a necessary hypothesis. "In the opinion that there is a God one finds certain difficulties,

[a] V. XXII, p. 200.

but in the contrary opinion there are absurdities."[a] And thus proceeding from "doubt to doubt" one comes "to regard the proposition that *there is a God* as the most plausible thing man can conceive."[b] This God will never make martyrs or executioners. He resides in the mind like the notion of the atom. He is not a mystical reality.

Attached to this God are the necessary laws of the universe. Moreover, we know nothing about His nature or attributes. All arguments about Providence and God's justice are just so much idle talk. To Jansenist pessimism Voltaire had only recently objected that man is not so wretched as Pascal made him out to be. And now to Leibnitzian optimism he replies:

How do you know that things cannot be better? The world is whatever it is capable of being. Life is neither very good nor very evil. It is tolerable since, generally speaking, people find it so. What we call "evil" are the natural effects of general laws. Death is of exactly the same order as birth, and the latter implies the former. We must accept life, nature, and her conditions, utilizing them as best we can.

This is already the philosophy of *Candide* but with a less sarcastic tone, with a more smiling indulgence for the world's mediocrity. At this time Voltaire is less hostile to Leibnitz than to Pascal, and he peppers the still effervescent Jansenism with his *Mondain*.

On the subject of the soul, Voltaire's attitude is clear: "I do not claim to have demonstrable proofs against the spirituality and immortality of the soul, but all probabilities are against it."[c] He uses Locke's proposition that God was able to give matter the property of thought—a contradictory proposition for a Cartesian who defines matter as extension in space. Not so for Voltaire, for he begins by denying that extension is the essence of matter. Those incomprehensible words *mind* and *matter* are for him only general terms under which we classify two kinds of properties relating to a single substance. But why make God intervene? Why not admit, with Collins,[4] that thought can be produced

[a] V. XXII, p. 201.
[b] V. XXII, p. 202.
[c] V. XXII, p. 215.

naturally, "by a special arrangement and organization of matter?"[a] The fact is that if the substance which possesses material properties can, through modification, produce thought without any special gift from God, then this God himself would disappear. The organizing intelligence would merge with the organized universe and pantheism would emerge from deism. But Voltaire was fearful of Spinoza.

Immortality, rationally unintelligible, was regarded by Voltaire as a hypothesis useless to society. On the question of free will he was greatly perplexed. He did not yet profess the rigorous determinism he would espouse thirty years later, conceding then that his ideas had changed.[b] He admitted the existence of free will, using as proof the fact one feels he has the capacity to make choices. Freedom of the will, for Voltaire as for Shaftesbury,[5] was the reflective will that rules the senses, resists passions, and follows reason. The will is "limited, variable, and, in a word, of no great consequence since man himself is not very consequential."[c] It is "the health of one's soul,"[d] often impaired, never perfect. But do not motives control our will? Precisely. And the arguments which induced Collins to establish a moral determinism were for Voltaire, as for Chubb, evidence of one's personal liberty. "I obey necessarily, but willingly, this command of my reason."[e] Which is to say that freedom of the will is only a conscious adherence to clearly conceived motives, a substitution of intellectual determinism for the kind that is emotional or instinctive.

Nevertheless, we can choose only what we do choose. And Voltaire concludes by limiting personal freedom, in accordance with Locke's definition, "to the ability to do what we want to do."[f] I desire to walk because I can visualize the pleasure or utility of walking. I am free to do so provided I am not crippled or imprisoned. When one reaches this position, "free will" has become little more than a word. We are very close to denying

[a] First reply to Clarke, p. 113.
[b] V. XXVI, p. 57.
[c] V. XXII, p. 414.
[d] V. XXII, p. 218.
[e] V. XXII, p. 414.
[f] V. IX, p. 388; V. XXII, p. 416.

it completely. In 1748, after explaining the doctrines of Clarke, Voltaire added: "We must admit that terrifying objections may be raised against the idea of freedom—we must acknowledge that these objections are answerable only with a vague sort of eloquence."[a] Actually, Voltaire had changed his views less than he believed. He had, above all, dared to become consistent with himself.

In the end he had to face up to the problem of ethics and morality, but Voltaire did not elaborate a metaphysics on morals. He sketched an experimental and positive kind of morality. There was no absolute good or evil, no innate moral ideas. Virtue consists in (1) obedience to laws; (2) the conformity of our actions to the general good; (3) the conformity of our actions to certain natural feelings which all men experience from the social framework and the general conditions of existence.[b] Among mankind's natural feelings the virtuous ones are those which, according to Shaftesbury, contribute to the good of society. But how can virtue be defined as "obedience to laws"? If that were true, the Solicitor General was virtuous in burning the *Lettres Anglaises*. The magistrate who applies the laws is more virtuous than the writer who, in spite of the laws, prints thoughts contrary to those laws. Voltaire agreed that obedience to laws is the mortar of the social edifice; hence, obedience is a useful idea, virtuous in and of itself. He agreed that, in the opinion of his fellow man, the citizen who lives in accordance with the laws of the land is regarded as virtuous. But that fact neither prevents nor forbids attempts to bring imperfect laws more into line with the natural feelings of humanity and justice and into conformity with the common good of the body politic.

Even more emphatically than Shaftesbury, Voltaire rejected religious sanctions, judging them implausible and, above all, useless. Did fear of the world to come ever restrain a conqueror? We must be content with human and social sanctions: fear of punishment and a respect for public opinion which holds the power of approval or disapproval. Let us also take into account the fact that the well-bred person has a natural inclination for

[a] V. XXII, p. 416.
[b] V. XXII, pp. 224–226.

virtue, that is, that in the normal development of a healthy
individual, social sentiments play a very strong role. And let us
also count upon education to cultivate and fortify these feelings.
Sanctions, then, are incomplete, uncertain, and fragile. But so
is man incomplete, uncertain, and fragile. He can only build and
develop from what he is.

In his *Métaphysique de Newton* he was to add an examination
of the fundamental hypotheses of science.[a] At times expository,
at other times interpreting Newton and Clarke, combating Descartes and Malebranche and especially Leibnitz (of whom he
wished to disabuse Emily), filled with Bayle, Locke, Collins, and
Chubb, freely eclectic in following the English thinkers, he
admits atomism, the immutability of species within a limited
evolution beginning with the principle of an infinitely varied
initial arrangement of matter.

What is most interesting to us in Voltaire's metaphysics is his
method, which he borrowed from the English deists. Here are
its essential principles:

(1) Separation and Independence of Reason and Faith

"My sole task is to think in human terms. Theologians make
divine decisions. That is something altogether different. Reason
and faith are contrary by nature."[b] Collins had said: "Reason
does not prove either the immateriality or immortality of the
soul: as a philosopher I doubt; as a Christian I believe."[c] This
attitude, more politic than rational, must not be judged in the
abstract. It was relative to the circumstances of the age. It was a
modus vivendi, a concordat, if you like, that freethinkers offered
the still powerful churches. By making reason and faith move on
different planes, they were trying, without limiting or contesting
religious authority, to assure the human spirit unlimited freedom
for research.

[a] V. XXII, pp. 427–438.
[b] V. XVII, p. 149.
[c] *Essai sur la nature et la destination de l'âme humaine,* p. 16.

(2) *Extension of the Experimental Method to Metaphysics*

"I appeal to your conscience," said Voltaire to Leibnitz, "on the subject of monads;[6] do you not sense to what extent such a system is purely imaginary?"[a]

"Let us first analyze things precisely and thereafter we will try to see, with a great deal of caution, whether or not they can be reduced to a few principles."[b]

"I can do no more than follow the path of analysis which is the walking-stick nature gave to the blind; I examine everything, piece by piece, and I see whether I can then make some judgment on the whole.[c] Whenever we cannot avail ourselves of the mathematician's compass or the physicist's torch, it is certain that we cannot advance a single step."[d]

"If we wish to know what Newton thought about the soul and its manner of functioning, and which of all these notions he embraced, I will reply that he subscribed to none. What then did he know about this subject, he who had reduced the infinite to mathematical terms and who had discovered the laws of gravitation? He knew how to doubt."[e]

Voltaire did not reject metaphysics. He consented to speculate about God, the soul, and human freedom, for "I was young then," he was to write in 1771. But he regarded metaphysics as reasoning about things of which one had no knowledge. Accordingly, it was necessary to be very cautious, gather facts, and make a few inferences, a few simple, clear, and uncomplicated hypotheses. Above all, one must not spend too much time at it. He brought metaphysics into the realm of the layman. He separated it from theology, keeping only a minimum which he saw no advantage in eliminating; namely, the concept or the word *God*. He made metaphysics an extension of science. He asked the sciences for all the answers they could furnish to metaphysical

[a] V. XXII, p. 434.
[b] V. XXII, p. 203.
[c] V. XXII, p. 209.
[d] V. XXII, p. 204.
[e] V. XXII, p. 427.

questions, and he assigned to science many of the problems philosophers had always considered their own private domain. He envisaged new sciences to clarify doubts that philosophical systems vainly thought to resolve: psycho-physiology, child psychology, animal psychology. And if he is often flippant, it is because he did not anticipate that these sciences would offer him good collections of controlled data and because he drew hasty conclusions based on a few dubious or incomplete observations.

With Voltaire, science moved into first place, the position occupied until then by metaphysics. Thus he contributed to the general movement which, since the beginning of the century, had drawn men's minds toward scientific studies. Literature, like metaphysics, was yielding ground to the sciences. The education of the socially prominent was becoming scientific. Fontenelle had induced women to read about astronomy. Montesquieu was lecturing at the Academy of Bordeaux on the adrenal glands and explaining the cause of the echo. For several years since 1735 the abbé Nollet had been conducting a course in Newtonian physics, performing curious experiments that drew a large audience, including women. Shortly thereafter the king's apothecary, Rouelle, was to offer a course in chemistry in the Royal Zoological Gardens. Tax collector Dupin de Francueil brought to it a spectator named Jean-Jacques Rousseau.

Churchmen at this date did not fear experimental science. It gave less cause for alarm than metaphysics. The abbé Pluche[a] and the Jesuits favored these precise and useful studies so long as the practitioners refrained from formulating any general views. As for youths "destined to fill all the positions of Church and State," Pluche desired that the two-year course in philosophy be devoted primarily "to geometry and mathematics" and to the natural sciences. He wanted, for the completion of their studies, at least in the large cities, a *droguier* [a collection of drugs and chemicals], a botanical garden containing the common plants, and a "systematic course in experimental physics."

In this movement, which culminated in the *Histoire Naturelle* ("Natural History") by Buffon,[7] Voltaire and his mistress played their part with their instruments and their furnaces. There is no

[a] *Le spectacle de la nature*, V. IV, p. 470.

point in dwelling on their experimental efforts. The *Eléments de la Philosophie de Newton* were, for their day, a good popularization in which Voltaire sought to establish an agreeable style of writing for the public presentation of scientific truths. He had found Fontenelle too ornate and wanted only order and clarity. "You will find that my explanations are quite clear," he wrote to M. Pitot of the Academy of Sciences. "I am like those little brooks which are clear and transparent because they are not very deep. I have tried to present ideas in the same manner as they entered my head. I have gone to a lot of trouble to spare the same for our French readers."[a]

He composed a *Mémoire sur la nature du feu* ("Memoir on the Nature of Fire"), a *Dissertation sur les forces motrices* ("Dissertation on Motive Forces"), another *Sur les changements arrivés dans notre globe et sur les pétrifactions qu'on on prétend en être les témoignages* ("Concerning Changes That Have Occurred on Our Planet and Petrified Objects Which Are Claimed to Be Evidence Thereof"), also an account *Sur un Maure blanc amené d'Afrique à Paris en 1744* ("Concerning a White Moor Brought from Africa to Paris in 1744"). All this has no present value and in fact had very little to begin with. We must note, however, that Voltaire failed to win the Academy of Sciences award on the nature of fire because his report contained nothing but observations, experiments, and calculations. The Academy wanted explanations in terms of the Cartesian system. Voltaire, on the other hand, had a fairly accurate notion of the experimental method and its requirements.

He had it, but he continually fell short of its realization, for he had neither the patience nor the leisure time to prolong or extend his research as much as was needed. He also fell short because, and most importantly, if he discarded systems, he did not discard his passions, and he resisted truths that he disliked. He was unsympathetic to the study of fossils for fear of finding confirmation of the Biblical account of the Flood. And it was for just that reason the same study intrigued Burnet and Woodward and Scheuchzer and the good abbé Pluche. They were as unscientific in gathering facts as Voltaire was in disputing them.

[a] V. XXXIV, p. 280. (Besterman, 1281) (R.P.)

With a little more scientific detachment Voltaire would not have brushed aside certain incontrovertible evidence with the sorry joke he made and for which he has often been reproached: that fossils of fish found in the Alps were simply refuse dropped by travelers, and that fossil sea shells had merely fallen from the hats of pilgrims.[a] He would have examined more closely the inescapable implications of these indications of earlier conditions of the world and, by delving more deeply, would have understood what Buffon clearly demonstrated, namely, that this new science, far from proving the hypothesis of a universal flood, definitely liberated the human mind from just such a belief. Voltaire did not have sufficient confidence in truth itself. In a broad manner he had defined rather well the scientific method, but he could not impose on himself the necessary intellectual discipline to practice it from day to day.

In the history of science, as in that of metaphysics, Voltaire is unimportant. He was strictly an amateur. But even this fact is significant, that a man of letters, a poet, should give so much attention in his life and in his thinking to these specialized studies. Nor were they useless to him. Condorcet[7] held that they "enlarged the scope of his poetic ideas" and "enriched his verses with new imagery." I think the poetic gain was a meager one. But the sciences did furnish Voltaire with the concepts of the universe and of life itself on which he erected a metaphysics that served his purpose and that dominated his practical politics and morality. Having rejected the theological structure of man's relation to the universe, he turned to the natural sciences for the model of a method for studying mankind and for clarifications on the cosmic enterprise which would reveal the position, the power, and the destiny of man. His general knowledge of the over-all nature of things served to formulate his idea of the potential degree of perfectibility and happiness which mankind could hope to achieve, collectively and individually. If wisdom consists in conforming to universal order, then science alone, which reveals this order, leads man to wisdom. Principles of good conduct presuppose good physics. "It is useful," said Condorcet discreetly, "to disseminate in men's minds accurate ideas about

[a] V. XXIII, p. 222.

matters that seem to belong only to the sciences, whether it is a question of important general facts on the nature of the world or of everyday facts visible to all. Absolute ignorance is always accompanied by errors, and errors in physics often serve as a prop for prejudices of a more dangerous sort."[a]

With Voltaire, then, began the domination of the sciences even in the thinking of those who were not scholars or scientists.

[a] V. I, p. 214.

4

Voltaire the Courtier (1744–1753):
Versailles–Berlin[a]

WITH SELFLESS devotion, Mme du Châtelet set about the task of getting her friend readmitted to the court. The year 1743 had rid Voltaire of an enemy with whom there could be no more pretenses of reconciliation, old Cardinal Fleury. But he still had adversaries in Bishop Boyer and the minister of state, M. de Maurepas. Close friends of the king, the duc de Richelieu and the duc de La Vallière, were working on his behalf. And so were the king's mistresses, Mme de Châteauroux and, after her, the very attractive Mme d'Etioles, soon to become the marquise de Pompadour.[1] He had known her as a child and was one of her courtiers. In fact, he may have been one of her first confidants. We see him now at the court of Versailles, promenading among the gardens, seated "in one of the king's own sedan chairs, borne by four Swiss porters"[b]—then as a guest at Etioles (June and July 1745)—then as a purveyor of diplomatic notes, of royal entertainment, and of verses for official occasions. As part of the festivities marking the marriage of the dauphin (February 23,

[a] Desnoiresterres, *Voltaire à la cour; Voltaire et Frédéric; Mémoires de Voltaire*. Collini, *Mon séjour auprès de Voltaire*, 1807. *Lettres de M. de Marville*, V. II. *Zeitschrift für franz. Sprache und Litt.*, V. XXVII (Haupt) et V. XXVIII (Mangold). Mangold, *Voltaires Rechtstreif.*, Berlin, 1905.
[b] *Journal du commissaire de police Narbonne*, p. 610.

1745), Voltaire presented a comedy-ballet, *La Princesse de Navarre*. He composed his *Poème de Fontenoy* and, as "a good citizen," he took a poetic interest in "the happiness" of Mme de Pompadour.

At the same period he wrote a long, vapid letter to Father de La Tour to appease the Jesuits. He flattered the Italian cardinals and Pope Benedict XIV, who smilingly accepted the dedication of *Mahomet ou le Fanatisme* ("Mohammed or Fanaticism") August 17, 1745. He wanted to tranquilize all the anxieties his name aroused. He received his salary: a 2000-pound pension (April 1, 1745); then the promise, followed by the issuance, of the official title "Gentleman of the Chamber" in 1746; and shortly thereafter a seat in the French Academy, where he was received on the 8th of May, 1746. Why then, in the midst of these triumphs, did he insist on dispatching police and archers in pursuit of a few libelous verses by the poet Roy, who was in a jealous rage over his old enemy's election to the Academy instead of himself? It is claimed that Voltaire personally led the police into the Rue Saint-Jacques to conduct searches in certain suspicious lodgings. The upshot of a long lawsuit against Travenol (a violinist at the Opéra in whose place they had found some satirical brochures) was the publication of the *Voltairiana,* or in other words, the greatest collection of defamations ever leveled against Voltaire.

Meanwhile, he was losing his foothold at the court. The king, a proud and timid soul, was too indifferent to literature to appreciate Voltaire and too much the gentleman to care to associate with him. Mme de Pompadour was friendly but not disposed to take sides in the matter. She openly favored one of the poet's rivals, the old tragedian Crébillon, and was sensitive and suspicious herself, her ear always cocked to catch any allusions to her bourgeois origins. The duc d'Ayen was unhappy over Voltaire's interference in the management of the Théâtre des Petits-Cabinets. There was general ill will on the part of the courtiers, jealous of this low-born intruder who, with his wit and cleverness, had come to challenge them on their home ground. They were inclined to see impudence and impertinence in every trifle he turned out. There were just too many reefs and shoals for Voltaire to navigate. He would notice things that a good courtier must overlook. He would announce in English to Mme du

Châtelet, who lost 80,000 francs one night gambling at the queen's table, that people around her were cheating. This remark was understood and created a scandal, and Voltaire had to go into hiding at Anet. He came back, but his fall from favor was prolonged and depressing. He wisely "converted to profit" the king's earlier bounties, divesting himself of his position as a "Gentleman of the Chamber" for some 60,000 pounds.

He fled with Mme du Châtelet from the great stage of Versailles to the small princely courts at Lunéville and Commercy, to good King Stanislas, to Sceaux and Anet with the duchesse du Mainè,[2] paying his way with comedies and tragedies and with entertaining philosophical tales. *Memnon* (1747), which later became *Zadig,* was probably born at Anet. In spite of his short stories, in spite of his tragedies *Sémiramis* and *Oreste,* the five or six years Voltaire spent as a courtier were the most sterile and wasted years of his life. The death of Mme du Châtelet (September 10, 1749), caused by a pregnancy from intimacy with a young officer, Saint-Lambert, marked a turning point in Voltaire's life, giving it a new direction. He wept in grief over the poor faithless woman whom he loved with such staunch affection. He went to collect his furnishings at Cirey and settled in Paris on the Rue Traversière-Saint-Honoré where his niece, Mme Denis, kept house for him. In his quarters on the third floor he installed a theater in which he performed his *Rome sauvée* ("Rome Saved"). He played the role of Cicero with bombast; at his side, little Lekain, a young actor whom he had just discovered, was acquiring stage experience. Some six or eight months later Voltaire left for Berlin.

Mme de Pompadour had become increasingly aloof. He had been denied entrée to the king's presence and refused admission to either the Academy of Sciences or the Academy of Belles-Lettres, to which he had aspired. He was too outspoken in defense of minister Machault and the minister's *impôt du vingtième,* a 5 percent income tax from which the clergy were seeking exemption. He soon compromised himself by supporting ministerial policies. Meanwhile, Frederick was tempting him with brilliant and substantial offers and protesting his eternal friendship for Voltaire, the poet. Emily was no longer there. Still smarting from his treatment at court and consumed with a desire to show the king of France how a man of intelligence could be honored and rewarded in a foreign land, he set out by way of Cleves and Wesel, through "the vast, bleak, and detestable terrain of Westphalia," that "godforsaken country" to be recalled in the opening lines of *Candide*. He arrived in Potsdam July 21, 1750.

He departed from Potsdam on the 26th of March 1753, angry and embittered. His correspondence reflects all the stages of his feelings:[a] at first dazzling enchantments and heady sensations—the grenadiers, the opera, the suppers, the honors, the pension—everything was pure delight. To be loved and flattered by a conqueror: what a triumph! A bit of anxiety troubled him as he moved into the regular routine at Potsdam, but the king of Prussia was still . . . "the finest of men." But by fall he was growing disenchanted and by Christmas he was longing for the Seine and his home in Paris. Already the magic spell was broken. There were quarrels and reconciliations, periods of serenity followed by bitter disputes, until the final and irrevocable disillusionment: "I am going to make for my instruction a little dictionary used by kings. 'My friend' means 'my slave.' " (December 18, 1752).

The details of this tragicomedy are given in his correspondence and in the writings of Desnoiresterres. There was a clash of personalities between king and poet. Both great men were hypersensitive, incapable of receiving the sarcasm they enjoyed using at the expense of others. The king was not too sure of himself—a despot, harsh, scornful, inconsiderate of the pride and dignity of others, intensifying his Prussian militarism with French persiflage, wounding with his wit those whom his power had crushed. Brutally and ungenerously, he hurt and humiliated those he called his friends. Voltaire was vain, demanding, fretful, and jealous—jealous of Baculard d'Arnaud who became his victim, jealous of Maupertuis[3] whom he tried but failed to destroy—always harassed and always harassing. The king's entourage, at first deferential to the poet, kept watching for opportunities to sow dissension. They would retail to the one the remarks of the other, not without injecting additional venom. Then there was

[a] V. XXXVII, pp. 147, 157, 171, 191, 217, 218, 543, etc. [Moland ed.] (Besterman, 3604, 3619, 3685, 3728, 4486, etc.) (R.P.)

that diabolical temperament of Voltaire's, constantly exploding. If Voltaire was pillaged and insulted by La Beaumelle, who decided to publish an edition of the *Siècle de Louis XIV* for the express purpose of defaming its author, and if we cannot feel unsympathetic to Voltaire for failing to take a philosophical view of this affront, yet he was not always so clearly in the right. A dubious attempt at speculation, ending in a raucous lawsuit with the Jew Hirschel, greatly displeased Frederick—even more so the polemic against Maupertuis and the *Diatribe du docteur Akakia,* which the king burned after having had a good laugh over it. Voltaire and Maupertuis were just two Prussian "functionaries," the one a chamberlain, the other the president of the Academy. The king, who would condone anything in private, wanted propriety in public. He insisted that his functionaries should not compromise themselves in shady dealings and that they should respect, outwardly at least, each other's dignity of position. He was not paying a good price for an Academy president to have him devaluated by public ridicule.

At last, on January 1, 1753, Voltaire handed back to Frederick his "key, his order, and his pension," which he now called his "cap and bells" and "ornaments ill-becoming a philosopher."[a] They were returned to him and he was not granted permission to leave until March 26th. After a stay in Leipzig, where he had business with booksellers, and at Gotha and Cassel, where the duchess and landgrave compensated in part for the king's disfavor, he reached Frankfort. There, from June 1st to July 7th, he was held prisoner by "M. le baron de Freytag," a military councillor in residence to his Prussian Majesty, who was under orders to seize the traveler's key of office, his Prussian Cross of Merit, and above all, that copy of *Œuvres de Poésie* ("Poetic Works") in which there was material to provoke all the courts of Europe against its royal author Frederick. Voltaire screamed to high heaven, exaggerated fantastically every incident, any bit of mistreatment he and his niece experienced. And yet, at the heart of this ridiculous episode, if one considers only the official correspondence of baron Freytag, this much deserves thoughtful consideration: a Prussian citizen was arbitrarily detaining a

---

[a] V. XXXVII, pp. 554, 562. (Besterman, 4507, 4520, 4553) (R.P.)

Frenchman and a French woman for a period of five weeks, arresting Voltaire in public, keeping him under military guard in a free city of the Empire, seizing and searching all his luggage, and confiscating all their money which, as of August, had not yet been returned and may never have been. One must admit that for Voltaire this was no laughing matter.

On leaving Frankfort he was in embarrassing circumstances. He stopped at various places: Schwetzingen, at the home of the Elector Palatine who had a charming little theater; Strasbourg, where he finished for the Duchess of Saxe-Gotha his factual, rapid survey of the *Annales de l'Empire* and where he protested before two notaries the fraudulent publication of the first two volumes of his *Histoire Universelle;* Colmar, where he contemplated settling down; Senones, in Lorraine, but in Empire territory, where he closeted himself for six weeks to work on his *Histoire Universelle,* utilizing the knowledge of Dom Calmet and the library of the Benedictine abbey; Plombières, where his niece and his two "angels," the d'Argentals, came to keep him company. He was upset and feeling wretched. Paris was off limits and France itself uncertain. Germany was odious; Switzerland attracted him by its reputation for freedom. Earlier, in Berlin, he had sounded out gentlemen from Berne who proved reluctant to extend a welcome to such a guest. Finally, after a stop at Lyons where the theater public and the Academy, in session, gave him an enthusiastic reception, but where Cardinal Tencin refused to invite him to dinner and passed the word that he was unwelcome in that locality, Voltaire crossed over into Geneva the evening of December 12, 1754, dined with Dr. Tronchin, and took lodgings in the château de Prangins which was made available to him.

Voltaire's years of apprenticeship were over. It was high time; he was going on sixty. Berlin had been his last training school. There he had learned the delight of being his own master and master in his own household. The lesson had been the more effective for being so harsh. Nevertheless, Voltaire had wasted less time with the king of Prussia than with the king of France. The only freedom he had missed was that of his feelings and emotions. As for his freedom to think, he was by no means a slave in "the palace of Alcina." Voltaire had worked. He had finished his *Siècle de Louis XIV,* which was published in Berlin by Henning, printer to the king, in 1751. And what excitement he had known! What new intellectual horizons had opened up during the two-and-a-half year contact with a king who carried Bayle in his traveling bag and who had no fear of ideas! Those delightful suppers of which he could only speak with enthusiasm twenty-five years later, those carefree suppers that lasted so late into the night that the servants, standing along the gleaming woodwork, thought their legs would drop off from fatigue—those *soirées* had been like a second England, even headier and more intoxicating. Between the king and a host of venturesome spirits who asked only to rend the veil from every temple—the eccentric marquis d'Argens; that fool La Mettrie,[4] the atheist physician; the profound and mordant Maupertuis; the jolly major Chasot; the serious and precise Darget, reader and secretary to Frederick; the amiable and adroit Algarotti, the women's expert on Newton; the honest Lord Marshal Keith and his brother; the fat Lord Tyrconnel, envoy of France, a sharp-tongued epicurean; and that amusing scamp Pöllnitz, the only German in the assemblage, who had traveled the world over (and was familiar with its religions), and who knew all the juicy gossip of Europe—in this atmosphere Voltaire opened into full bloom. He left Berlin trained and equipped for the Ferney campaign, an expert in arguments that would undermine the Church and a master tactician for conquering the public.

For Frederick he had written his tale of *Micromégas,* perfecting the form of his philosophical short stories. He had composed his first dialogue in the manner of Lucian. He had launched the buffoonery of *Akakia.* He had brought from Berlin (along with his cross and key, with the *Œuvres de Poésie,* and a large residue of spite and resentment) three redoubtable weapons: *le conte* (the short story); *le dialogue;* and *la facétie* (the broad jest). For the last twenty years of his life he was to make continual use of them, exploding social institutions and oppressive beliefs, religious or otherwise.

5

Voltaire's Tastes: Poetry and Tragedy[a, b]

UNTIL THE publication of *Le Siècle de Louis XIV* (1751), Voltaire was regarded by the public primarily as a poet. Therein lay his uncontested renown. his *gloire*. His scientific and philosophical writings were looked upon as entertaining diversions, almost impertinences or, at any rate, as the whims of an intellectual who nursed a desire for universality. But scarcely anyone denied his superb good taste or the genius of his verses and tragedies. These gifts earned for him the respectful friendship of the critic Vauvenargues[1] whose personal bitterness and physical suffering were assuaged somewhat by the chance to provoke this sharp analytical mind into developing its literary judgments.

Nowadays, when we no longer dream of investing it with

[a] Vernier, *Voltaire grammairien.* Alexis François, *la Grammaire du purisme et l'Académie au XVIIIe siècle.* Deschanel, *le Théâtre de Voltaire,* 1896. H. Lion, *les Tragédies de Voltaire,* 1896. J.-J. Olivier, *Voltaire et les comédiens interprètes de son théâtre,* 1900. Jusserand, *Shakespeare en France,* 1898. Lounsbury, *Voltaire and Shakespeare,* 1902. *Zeitschrift für franz. Spr. und Litt.,* V. XXIII (Koehler, *Sur les unités*). Lessing, *Dramaturgie.* La Harpe, *Cours de littérature.* Joannides, *Répertoire de la Comédie française.*

[b] In the *Œuvres complètes,* Moland ed.: Vols. II–VI (theater), VIII (*Henriade*), IX–X (poems, satires, epistles, odes, various works in verse). *Zaïre,* ed. by M. Fontaine, 1889. *Sémiramis,* ed. by J.-J. Olivier, 1946. Attention is called to the fact that the text of *La Pucelle,* established by Beuchot and retained by Moland, is particularly unreliable. Cf. L. Jordan, *Archiv für das Studium der Neuren Sprachen,* 1912 (R.P.)

authority and regard it simply as history, eighteenth-century French taste is quite attractive to contemplate, and Voltaire was one of its most perfect examples. "A classical taste," we call it. Yet how far it had already come from the classicism of Racine and Boileau! The Quarrel of the Ancients and the Moderns[2] had put an end to the worship of antiquity and to the austere disciplines of great classical art. In their *collèges* the Jesuits were fashioning refined taste, a delicate, timid kind of taste, less marked by simple grandeur than by the light, graceful, witty touch. During the final sad years of Louis XIV's reign, Versailles surrendered its protection and domination of letters to the latest literary coterie, to the newest salons, and to the small princely courts. There was less concern for pure beauty or cold majesty and more attention to charm, elegance, and piquant delight—a refinement of language that was relaxed and exquisite, neither mannered nor untidy. There was still the desire for nobility of style, but for an amiable sort of nobility. Literature became an adornment of life, one of life's pleasures contributing to happiness—the goal of human endeavor. Pleasure was the supreme law and, by the same token, a justification of both the traditional and the new.

For the models of antiquity national models, our [French] masterpieces of the seventeenth century, were substituted. Respect for them demanded that they be imitated. Through education, academic and otherwise, classical rules and definitions of the different literary genres entered the minds of the new generations and commanded respect in the name of *bienséances* (proprieties) and *convenances* (decorum). Guided by the Dictionary of the Academy and by works of great writers, Racine in particular, they realized the ideal of linguistic purity. Any thought or idea intending to make its appearance before the "three thousand connoisseurs" of the Parisian public had to clothe itself in the restrained vocabulary and the accepted imagery authorized by the literary masters. Good taste was part of good tone. People found pleasure in these slavish practices, which distinguished a man of the world from *le peuple,* the common herd, or a refined Frenchman from a barbarous Englishman or crude German. Yet, at the same time, conformity to these practices minimized inequalities of social status by establishing an equality of culture, a fraternity of the cultivated. Good taste became a Freemasonry of the intellect.

No one believed more deeply in good taste than Voltaire. And no one was more conscious of it or more thoroughly imbued with it than he. None was more lively than Voltaire in his pleasures nor more delicate in his displeasures. And no one was more aware of its limitations. Throughout the reign of Louis XV, from Marivaux and Vadé, La Chaussée and Rousseau, down to the very eve of Mirabeau[3] and Chateaubriand,[4] Voltaire maintained the easy nobility of style and limpid elegance whose secret he had learned from Hamilton[5] and La Fare.[6] Never affected, trivial, flamboyant, or ponderous, whenever he expressed pleasantries, atmospheric color, or emotions, everything was clear, of a piece, and light in style. He exercised taste even in his insults and his abusive trash. He would inhibit himself and stifle his emotions in deference to his principles. His natural vigor would increase in inverse ratio to the dignity of the literary form and consequently in direct ratio to the freedom of the genres. In all the great forms of literature there were too many rules, too many imperious models and fixed tones of style. Accordingly, he refracted the light of others more than he generated any light of his own.

He judged French writers with the same disciplined restraint he imposed on his own natural vivacity. He spared neither Crébillon nor Jean-Baptiste Rousseau, nor Marivaux, nor Montesquieu, nor Jean-Jacques Rousseau. He disapproved of the *comédie larmoyante*—the sentimental comedy, the *drame*[7] and the *Opéra-Comique*. Time and again he called his century "the dregs of all time." The great Corneille was often guilty of not writing French and he lacked good taste. There was much to criticize in La Fontaine.[19] Hence his admirations were pitifully circumscribed to a short period of time and to a handful of works of *le grand siècle*, the age of Louis XIV. A few of Boileau's epistles, a few of Racine's tragedies: these, in short, were the flawless "diamonds" affording the connoisseur unadulterated pleasure. These were the eternal masterpieces in which genius had attained correctness—treasures of perfect art and beautiful language.

This sense of good taste, in Voltaire as in other Frenchmen of his time, claimed for itself a superiority it took for granted, an attitude that was close to impertinence. It claimed a universal empire. It identified itself with universal reason. Voltaire made lofty, dogmatic judgments about ancient and foreign writers. He felt he had improved on the writers of antiquity and had "perfected" them, and he was volunteering for the task of civilizing foreigners. Voltaire's curiosity was insatiable. Everything amused him—the Bible and Shakespeare, Saadi and the Chinese. He noted the different tastes of peoples, but he was not tempted to conclude therefrom any relativity of tastes. Rare indeed were the civilizations or eras in which anyone understood the meaning of imitating beautiful nature, *la belle nature*. A few thousand Frenchmen knew it. They guaranteed the indisputable glory and, in this respect, the unquestioned superiority of our nation. Voltaire was chauvinistic in one thing only—taste. But on that subject he was categorical. Apart from the sublime good taste of our own masterpieces, there was probably some evidence of genius to be found elsewhere, but it was an uncouth and barbarous genius. Shakespeare had "some great and terrifying moments" but "ideas that were bizarre and gigantesque," "not the least trace of good taste" nor "the least awareness of rules." The Bible was the product of a coarse and ignorant people. He would judge *Hamlet* or the Biblical prophets exactly as he would excerpts of Chinese literature given him by Father du Halde. He found delight in looking at unusual samplings of the human spirit. They interested him and he made fun of them. He would find traces of reason and poetry that enchanted him and then absurdities and crudities that disgusted him. He liked to introduce new beauties to his public. But he would first clean them up, polish them, adjust them to good taste and reason, and then rejoice over having made these beauties presentable, decorous, colorless, and bloodless.

He had, moreover, his own fine, subtle personality, perceptible to the man of letters who can distinguish tastes and styles by quarter tones. He had a weakness for the voluptuous graces and the elegant buffoonery of Ariosto. He allowed a little Italianism to brighten up the bareness of French rationality. He also had a weakness for Swift's caustic humor. Into his light and sparkling French wine he infused a bit of pungent gin. He admired the harmonious paintings of Raphael, but he purchased Titians and Téniers. He was sensitive to the powerful style of English poets, "imitators of Hebrew poets," and to the bold imagery of the orientals. He would have liked to give a bit more color and warmth to the polite refinement of our own poetry. Even Racine sometimes seemed a bit pallid to him. If to us Voltaire appears timid and restrained, those of his contemporaries whom he displeased reproached him for excessive color and boldness of style. He frightened them. He took too many risks.

From the seventeenth-century masters and his Jesuit instructors Voltaire retained the notion that poetry has a beauty and dignity superior to prose. He would not for a moment suspect that twenty lines of his *Jeannot et Colin* or his *Pot Pourri* ("Miscellanies") were worth more in the artistic scale than an entire canto of his *Henriade.* He would not for a moment be tempted by the paradox of Houdar de La Motte [who theorized that poetry is independent of conventional forms and need not be expressed in verse], an idea that attracted such minds as Marivaux, Montesquieu, and Buffon because the paradox was true for them and their time [but not for their contemporary, Voltaire, who remained wedded to seventeenth-century literary doctrines]. Voltaire would never want odes in prose or tragedies in prose. He was always the most ardent advocate of verse. More than La Fare and La Chaussée, he was to continue the classical modes of writing.

And yet he could conceive no other role for poetry than did his adversary, La Motte. It was conventional language and form. It had no other purpose or content than prose. It was a decorative and agreeable manner of speaking. It incorporated figures of speech too audacious for prose and regular cadences, which prose was free of. Each poetic genre had its scale of styles and metrical forms. The very difficulties resulting from these numerous rules were responsible, in large measure, for the beauty of one's verses provided, of course, that the difficulties were elegantly resolved. The higher the genre in the poetic hierarchy, the less freedom there was. Voltaire disappeared in his odes. Inferior to Jean-Baptiste Rousseau in rhetoric, equal to La Motte in dispassionate clarity, he discoursed on *Fanatisme* ("Fanaticism") or *Ingratitude* or the *Félicité des Temps* ("The Felicity of the Age"), using the literary devices of hyperbole, metonymy, prosopopoeia, and allegory. He regarded himself as a lyric poet for having written some rhymed stanzas to "the Gentlemen of the Academy who went below the equator and up to the Arctic Circle to measure degrees of latitude." The poet Malherbe[8] was the pure model to emulate —the poet who concealed true lyricism from Voltaire and from all other French poets for some two hundred years.

His epic poem, the *Henriade*, was thought to be of greater value than his odes. Today we consider it no more than a pale pastel, half-faded and blurred, but we can still understand the enthusiasm it generated. After *Clovis* and *La Pucelle* ("The Maid"), it was a jewel. Its brilliant oratorical qualities; its effortless versification, deemed forceful as well as correct; its skillful handling of the classical rules; its allegories, historical *tableaux,* pathetic scenes in noble, graceful style; all the pomp and splendor of an epic, attenuated, lightened, and continually humanized by some lively, unconventional detail—in a word, this highest lesson in classic art, rendered in a pretty Louis XV style, still grandly theatrical but on the lighter, brighter side—all this should suffice to explain for us the popularity this epic poem enjoyed for fully a hundred years.

Although the rules for the great types of literature hampered Voltaire, often to the point of neutralizing him, he could still leave his hallmark, especially in the *Henriade*, with ingenious little details in construction, flashes of sparkling wit or sensuous imagery, a special kind of bold and provocative philosophizing. As he descended the ladder of the literary hierarchy, his personality became more visible. His philosophic poems on *L'Homme* ("Man"), on *La Loi Naturelle* ("Natural Law"), and *Le Désastre de Lisbonne* ("The Lisbon Disaster"), in which we still find him stilted and involved, either writing in a coldly rational manner or else applying a bit of glossy veneer to give an outward charm, these poems were for Condorcet, whose judgments reflected contemporary opinion, among "the finest monuments of French poetry." He found in them "a variety of moods and a kind of lyrical abandon, a touching emotion, an enthusiasm ever noble, ever true" which gave them "a charm for which Voltaire alone knew the secret."[a] We can appreciate better the popularity of his *Epîtres* ("Epistles"), which were a kind of didactic poetry, freer in style; a less inhibited, more lively poetry, seasoned with badi-

[a] V. I, p. 216.

nage and satire, less ponderous than Boileau's epistles and more philosophical than those of La Fontaine.

When we get down to his *genres badins*, his light verse—comical, mischievous, and puckish—we are truly in the presence of a poet. His public enjoyed these bagatelles all the more for regarding them as inconsequential. But for us today they have considerable artistic merit. *La Pucelle* still has some of the dignity and artifice of a great literary form. The heroic comedy had its rules. In this work Voltaire did a lightweight travesty on Ariosto just as he had done on Virgil and Tasso in the *Henriade*. Today we are merely bored by this "infamous" *Pucelle*. It has lost its bite as well as its charm. Its numerous details and exquisite couplets do not conceal the cold sterility of this attempt at saucy satire, laboriously lengthened into twenty-one cantos. But that was not the opinion of Voltaire's contemporaries. That gay parody touching on everything, that irrepressible verve parading its bawdy buffoonery, was clothed, so they thought, in raiment of flawless form—an embodiment of the impeccable precision and academic elegance marking a literary masterpiece. By comparison with *Philotanus* or *Le Balai* ("The Broom") it ranked very high. Worldly sophisticates, women, and even princesses took an uninhibited delight in reading it.

In all the lesser, free-form genres (he scarcely attempted any others, and I know of only two sonnets by Voltaire), in satires, short stories, stanzas, madrigals, epigrams, in everything we call light verse—the lofty style and coldness of classical regularity disappeared. But the man of good taste remained. Careful and discriminating in his choice of language, he avoided in his vitriolic abuse, even in his most scurrilous subject matter, any slipshod writing or repulsive language. Inferior to La Fontaine in the short story, where his character delineations are much weaker; outstanding in the writing of satire in which, after d'Aubigné,[9] Régnier,[10] and Boileau,[11] he was a true innovator by virtue of his amusing and devilish humor, equally free from ponderous moralizing or literal realism; delightful in his stanzas and epigrams, Voltaire was a poet after the fashion of Marot,[12] Voiture,[13] the La Fontaine of the *poésies diverses*, Chaulieu, and Hamilton. He had a uniquely personal charm in his facility, malice, fantasy, and mirth. His was a poetry compounded of light and airy graces—nothing vague, nothing dazzling.

It was not that he lacked feelings or moods. These could be irascible, affectionate, tender, and sad. But he culled them, sifted them, and filtered them through his mind. The spontaneous reaction of common sense, which resolves happiness into pleasures, rejected those painful emotions which, when explored in depth, have opened up the sources of present-day lyricism. Art and poetry for Voltaire were created to delight the soul, not to sadden it. He incorporated in his verses only those feelings one may savor with pleasure. Nothing poisonous was admissible. A note of regret over a love that is lost or the brevity of life, a touch of hedonistic pleasure or epicurean melancholy, a burst of wrath or hatred, always ending in amused mockery, a glimpse of nature—graceful and ornamental—like a beautiful setting for society's elegance:

> Beaux jardins de Villars, ombrages toujours frais;
> (Beautiful gardens of Villars, ever cool and shady.)

—that was enough to produce the poetry Voltaire dreamed of. Action was the serious side of life; poetry was meant to adorn and enhance it.

Today we judge a poet by his imagery and prosody. The loftier and nobler the literary genre, the colder and more commonplace was Voltaire's imagery. It thawed out in the lesser genres. It was never very rare or very new. Rather it was his treatment, his development, his special twist, the comic way he used it, that endowed it with artistic value. His versification fulfilled the eighteenth-century notion of poetic beauty. Weak or facile rhymes, pauses seldom varied, the short, breathless phrase—we today find this art flaccid and monotonous. But in those days, verses without breaks and without jolts or shocks, with regular cadences changing only the position of the mute "e," with their smooth, silent gliding of light, clear syllables—such verses were savored for a fluidity and harmonious softness regarded, until the time of Delille and Chénier, as the very essence of metrical perfection. Voltaire declaimed his loftier verses with deliberate bombast, carefully scanning every line, marking the rhythm with studied precision. Read his pretty stanzas addressed to Mme du Châtelet or his *Adieux à la vie* ("Farewell to Life"), his translations of Shakespeare, Addison, and Dryden in the eighteenth letter of his *Lettres Philosophiques,* or his *Poème sur le Désastre de Lisbonne,* and you will see that Voltaire's verses reflect the same melodious ideal as those of Lamartine who, moreover, was influenced by Voltaire. Lamartine[14] played the same musical instrument but with a different touch and power. He had other songs to make it sing.

The type of poetry to which Voltaire brought the most passion, and in which he pleased his contemporaries most, was tragedy. He was madly in love with the theater, as was his public. There was an almost childlike naïveté in those refined sophisticates who took such fresh pleasure in causing or watching the movements of those human marionettes known as Gaussin, Dumesnil, Clairon, or Lekain. We wonder today at the ease with which they could be satisfied, at the few demands placed on their imaginations. For us Voltaire's plays scarcely exist any longer. It is hardly necessary to repeat our objections—their timidity, incoherence, artificiality, and the false or feeble note they strike. This has been said often enough. But in their day they were new and powerful. Let us try to view them in the light that illumined them when they enchanted Frederick the Great and Vauvenargues, Mme de Pompadour, and Marie-Antoinette.

Racine had infused into the compact plot and psychological analysis of French tragedy elements of passion and poetry that Corneille was more and more neglecting. He had rediscovered them in the Greeks. Racine left a theater public avid for the occurrence on stage of some unforeseen turn of events and equally fond of analyzing the heart's desires. But it was a public obsessed with a craving for poetic pathos which it did not fully comprehend, and which could be gratified by strange oddities and expressed in whimsical aversions. During the final years of Louis XIV, an awakening of sensibilities—a taste for love and voluptuous delights —attenuated in all literature the severity of classic art. Then, and particularly during the unrestrained era of the Regency, opera opened up the public eye to the charms of *décor,* stage sets, and scenery. The *palais à volonté* ("palace at will"), the barest suggestion of a set as used by the Comédie Française, began to appear inadequate. The performance of Racine's *Athalie* in 1718 inaugurated a new era, one in which the purely literary impression sought visual reinforcement, increasing the illusion of reality with bonafide *mise-en-scène*, direction, staging, sets, and the use of extras.

Meanwhile, the longing for Racinian emotions was having its effect. In the work of his successors, in the gentle melancholy of the pale Campistron, in the tender melodramas of La Grange-Chancel, in the violent bombast and complicated plots of Crébillon,[15] the theretofore tightly knit form of rational tragedy was unraveling a bit, and the public was acquiring a taste for improbable situations, for unnatural passions, for *coups de théâtre* (electrifying surprises); for *incognitos* (confused or concealed identities), providing theatrical suspense and anxious expectations, to be followed by terrifying or heart-rending recognitions and revelations.

Then came little Arouet who, alongside the outmoded *Œdipe* ("Oedipus") of Corneille and the coarse, unpolished one of Sophocles, had placed an *Œdipe* of glossy newness and gleaming freshness, a pert and ingenious *Œdipe* in which the improbability and horror of the theme were made to conform to literary and social proprieties and were brightened up with philosophical witticisms. Did they not even say that this bold youth intended, in his theatrical début, to fulfill a Platonic yearning of Fénelon's, namely, to divest Cornelian and Racinian tragedy of their love themes, pretending that there was no room in "Oedipus" for lovers' sighs or gallantry? Voltaire had yielded to popular taste only after the actors refused to play a loveless tragedy. His brilliant initial triumph augured well for the future. Everyone was watching to see if he could repeat himself, but they were disappointed. Hisses and catcalls for *Artémire* and *Mariamne* told the story.

While La Motte was elaborating his paradoxes in countless prefaces and discourses, in his plays he gracefully renounced them all, offering the spectacle, so typically French, of bold theoretical criticism followed in practice by dutiful adherence to established routines. However, a few timid novelties enlivened his *Romulus* and his *Macchabées*, rather pallid opera scenarios, and his tender *Inès*, which kept his audience in tears in 1723. Throughout all this, Voltaire remained enmeshed in tradition.

But on his return from London, what fireworks! What a jostling there was of old habits and prejudices! He defended the use of verse and perhaps saved it from La Motte's attempt to drive it out of the theater and even out of the ode. But in *Brutus,* the republican tirades, the stage setting for the house of the consuls with the Capitol in the background, the senators in red togas standing in a semicircle around the altar of Mars—all this on a stage which, until then, had known only *l'habit à la romaine,* Roman garb imitated from the bas-reliefs of Trajan's Column— the ghost in *Eriphyle* inspired by *Hamlet,* the first phantom ever offered to the *Messieurs du Parterre* ("the gentlemen in the pit") since the foundation of the Comédie Française—and jealous Orosmane killing the tender Zaïre, a graceful transposition of *Othello,* this was Shakespeare *en biscuit* ("in capsule form"). And then those heroic names of Lusignan, Châtillon, and Montmo- rency—a brilliant evocation of chivalry in the land of the sultans —brought French history to the stage as English history had been in *Henry V* and *Richard III.* In his unsuccessful *Adélaïde* he again used those popular names from French history: Duguesclin, Vendôme, and Coucy. And he pulled off a few daring surprises: a prince of the blood with his arm in a sling; the brusque roar of a cannon replacing the polished phrases of a messenger of bad tidings. Again there was republican vitality in *La Mort de César* ("The Death of Caesar") and Shakespearean inspiration in pre- senting Mark Antony haranguing the populace, a populace that spoke, applauded, or protested; lictors bearing the body of Caesar beneath his blood-stained robe; Mark Antony descending from the tribunal to kneel beside the body. Who in the 1730's played with greater freshness and originality on the minds and emotions of French society?

In addition, Voltaire denationalized his public, arousing its curiosity about other peoples and other lands. He entertained it with a procession of heroes and heroines of every nation and every era: Spaniards and Americans in *Alzire;* Moroccans in *Zulime;* Arabs in *Mahomet;* Romans in *Rome sauvée;* Chinese in *L'Orphelin de la Chine;* Sicilian Normans in *Tancrède.* His tragedies were a tour of the world and a lesson in universal history.

And what exciting combinations of intentions and inventions! There was philosophy and Christianity in *Alzire*; philosophy, irreligion, and English pathos in *Mahomet;* Greek tragedy in

Mérope and *Oreste*, in which the plot was purged of love and the pathos accompanied by occasional shafts of free thought; magnificent and effective stage sets in *Sémiramis,* in which a phantom comes out of a tomb—an Aeschylean specter, not a Shakespearean one. For Voltaire had had enough of Shakespeare now that La Place had translated him and the French public seemed to be taking to him. Father Brumoy, in his *Théâtre des Grecs* ("The Greek Theatre"), furnished him with new material. From that time on Voltaire reversed the language and emphases of his judgments on Shakespeare. Formerly he had been saying: "No taste, but what genius in that English barbarian!" Now he was saying: "A few felicitous ideas, a number of effective passages, but what crudity! a drunken savage!" And then there was the triple duel with Crébillon to whom he gave lessons in tragic simplicity, Greek pathos, and Roman history.

Finally, after all kinds of triumphs and failures, the creative period of Voltairian tragedy came to a close with two new and unusual works: *L'Orphelin de la Chine* ("The Chinese Orphan") and *Tancrède.* In the former we see Mlle Clairon in "Chinese dress" consisting of "a double skirt of white cloth, a corset with green embroidery and a network of gold tassels," with "a robe or polonaise of gauze, flame-colored and lined with blue taffeta," "without hoopskirts or sleeves and with bare arms," practicing gestures, "foreign, so to speak, often putting one or both hands on her hips, and sometimes a clenched fist to her forehead." Coupled with this touching Idamé we see the fierce conqueror [Genghis Khan] who, little by little, succumbs to her feminine charms of reason and virtue. In this role we see the actor Lekain in a striped gold and crimson tunic, his hefty butcher's arms emerging from wide, short sleeves; on his back a lion skin and a quiver full of arrows; a Turkish saber at his side; and an immense bow in his hand. On his head he wears a huge helmet made from a lion's head adorned with eleven large plumes and a red aigrette. This "authenticity" of costume perfectly matched Voltaire's verses. He had portrayed a father and mother sacrificing their son to save the heir to the throne—the tragic conflict between monarchical loyalty and natural affections—the philosophical contrast of a humane, peace-loving, civilized China and a coarse, uncouth Tartar, a warrior and a nomad. It was a chapter from Voltaire's world history, from his *Essai sur les Moeurs*, transposed into a melodramatic setting.

With *Tancrède* (a subject he borrowed from Mme de Fontaine, who had taken it from Ariosto), he brought to the French stage a taste for things "troubadour," that period which preceded the romantic Middle Ages. Set among the Normans of Sicily, it was the story of a girl falsely accused, who finds a champion in an unknown knight. Voltaire seasoned his touching scenario with the misunderstandings of jealousy and all the familiar ingredients of the *drame* and classical tragedy. On a stage only recently cleared of spectators, knights of the Middle Ages strode back and forth, buckled in the armor of sixteenth-century tourneys. The stage, bedecked with shields, sashes, and coats of arms, displayed pavilions and an arena erected for the combat in which a somber Tancrède saves the life and honor of the long-suffering Aménaïde. In the scene in which the actress Clairon "traverses the stage, leaning from exhaustion on the executioners around her, her knees collapsing, her arms dangling as if lifeless," suddenly recovering her strength to utter a plaintive cry at the sight of Tancrède —in this scene Voltaire created something artistically new.

Corneille and Racine had written tragedies for the mind. They had put into their verses, into the characters' speeches, all that they cared to communicate to their audience. Apart from the effects he produced with his brilliant style of writing, Voltaire had additional things to say to his audience, things to be communicated by the actors' gestures, by the "props" and symbols of sets and costumes. His tragedies were imperfect until performed. The actress Champmeslé had simply interpreted Racine's lines, but Clairon added her stage business to Voltaire's verses, and it was this collaboration that created Idamé or Aménaïde. It was for this reason that Voltaire kept driving his actors, prompting and coaching them, even physically shaking some of them to get a certain effect, a certain intonation, transition, or interpretation that he, Voltaire, wanted. He tried to transfer to the players a bit of his own *diable au corps*, his own diabolical verve and energy.

All his plays were heralded by much fanfare and public controversy. Before a production, Voltaire would drop confidential remarks to friends and newspapers. After its performance he would fire away with prefaces, dedications, discourses, and letters.

Always there was gossip, and sometimes scandal—and of such prolonged duration that it was impossible to ignore. Even the slightest innovation acquired, from its advance publicity and subsequent commentaries, an importance out of all proportion to its actual effect on stage. But then the public was grateful to Voltaire for having exercised such restraint while attempting something bold and new. If a few critics condemned his "excesses," for the most part they applauded him for keeping his imitations of Shakespeare and the English theater within the bounds and dictates of French taste—good taste, that is—and for not permitting emotional outbursts to reach the point of savage grief or violence where one's feelings ceased to be pleasurable. For Voltaire the theater was to remain a delightful game, a festivity for sophisticates. The velvet glove of his "Racinian" verse and style, tailored to his public's taste, cushioned any violent shocks with a soft, smooth, and harmonious elegance. In feverishly overblown couplets, in dialogue of carefully controlled sensationalism, in convulsions that observed all the delicate proprieties, our great-grandparents enjoyed the illusion of having reached, for a moment, the terrifying brink of tragic horror.

The tragedies that he conceived with such enthusiasm—correcting and rewriting untiringly, always anxious and hopeful of improving them, calmly discussing them with himself and his friends, and which, after so many revisions, still kept an air of facile improvisation—were simply clever reworkings of all the best known and most reliable dramatic clichés from Greece, England, and France. Here are some of the familiar features: sons, fathers, and mothers killing, or about to kill, their fathers, mothers, or sons; fraternal enmities; homicidal jealousies; unnatural passions and crimes against nature; disguised identities fraught with peril; human life overpowered by crushing fatalities. Voltaire freshened up the theatrical assortment of situations, characters, and passions by his novel stagings, his historical evocations, his sketches of remote times and places and historical personalities. He introduced a few psychological novelties—an English type of feminine fragility almost[a] unknown before Voltaire —the weak and charming creature who lives only for love, less

---

[a] This "almost" is for La Fosse; La Valerie in his *Manlius*.

moral or cerebral than the Junies and Aricies of Racine and less strong-willed than his Hermiones and Roxanes. And then, with his curious trio of charaters in *Mahomet*, Voltaire was the first ever to attempt in our theater a rational analysis of religious phenomena. He depicted Mohammed, the creator of a religion, as a tragic Tartuffe[16]—a man of genius, unscrupulous as to the means of attaining his ends, a man who dominates the superstitious masses through deceit and imposture and who contrives a miracle in the final scenes. Beside the prophet are the two persons he manipulates, two idealistic young people who are fascinated by him and responsive to all his suggestions: a young nun, credulous and fearful, and a young man, Séide, not unlike Jacques Clément [the Dominican assassin of Henry III]. Séide, a somber, tormented disciple of Mahomet, is driven by a mad compulsion for murder and martyrdom to the point of committing parricide.

Voltaire's novelties were never entirely new, nor was his use of tradition simply traditional. He produced various combinations from Sophocles, Corneille, Racine, Quinault, Shakespeare, and even Metastasio, seasoning them with sensibility and Voltairian philosophy. There was always something unexpected to titillate his public and always something old and reliable to avoid disappointing traditional tastes. By 1760 Voltaire had fulfilled his dramatic intentions. Others went further and faster than he. Without changing his ideas, he rearranged them. His earlier experiments now acted as a restraining influence. Diderot and *le drame*, Shakespeare and English violence were threatening the national edifice of classical art. But, most importantly, during his last years at Ferney Voltaire had too many other things on his mind. He was imbued with a zeal for social action and philosophical propaganda. Theatrical pleasures had to take second place.

Nevertheless, there still trooped forth an amusing procession of tragedies, often more amusing for the reader than for the audience. There were the anti-Christian tableaux of *Olympie*—and a curious attempt at historical tragedy in the *Triumvirat* (in which, unfortunately, Voltaire's notion of good taste banned from his verses the color and excitement he placed in his notes)—a bourgeois pastorale, *Les Scythes* ("The Scythians") in which the patriarch of Ferney donned a shepherd's costume for his tragic role. There were obvious contemporary themes in *Les Guèbres* ("The

Guebrians"—Persian Parsees) as well as in *Les Lois de Minos* ("The Laws of Minos") with their pleas for religious tolerance and their attacks on the priesthood. In all of this there was more intellectualism than art. We are therefore correct in calling these plays *brûlots éteints* ("extinguished firebrands").

But after 1760 and his retirement to Ferney, his plays were still performed. They revived his masterpieces of thirty years before, plays that continued to prove effective. Their bold innovations were developed still further, independently of the author, by the treatment they underwent with the new changes and progress in stage techniques. Act II of *Mérope*, for example, was presented in 1763 in a setting by Brunetti—"a wooded grove outside the city, consecrated as a royal burial ground. It is filled with a number of ancient tombs and different forms, cypress trees, obelisks, pyramids, everything that characterized the pious veneration of the ancients for their dead. Among these tombs can be seen that of Cresphonte, adorned with everything precious that Mérope could provide." The audience was gripped with emotion, both historical and lyrical, at the sight of this stage spectacle conveying a poetic feeling for the past as well as for death. How far people had come from *Andromaque* where Hector's tomb is nowhere but in Racine's verses, visible only to the imagination!

During the Revolutionary era and the Empire there was to be a neoclassical reaction in tragedy against Voltaire and the *drame*, but a reaction that retained many elements of Voltaire's tragedies. Ironically, it was Voltaire who, thinking to consolidate classical tragedy, had actually condemned it. He had accustomed the public to melodramatic and romantic effects which he had masked behind his brilliant and bloodless Alexandrine verses. He made the classical unity of place impossible to maintain. The great moments in his theater—Mérope raising an axe to slay her son; Séide stabbing Zopire near the altar where the old man is praying and then the old man dragging himself, bleeding, across the stage; Ninias emerging with bloody hands from the tomb of Ninus, where he has just killed his mother—all these scenes are pure pathos, almost devoid of psychological interest, and of a very theatrical pathos, incapable of being produced without the resources of the stage and scenic effects. They required, in short, a visual experience to achieve their full effect. Du Belloy, Lemierre, and Ducis added only a few innovations to what Voltaire had already done. They continued the action from the point where Voltaire had stopped or was no longer present, but they moved in the direction Voltaire had indicated. Voltaire is the great representative name marking the transition from classical tragedy to romantic drama, from Racine's *Athalie* (1691) to Hugo's *Hernani*[17] (1830). His importance and influence are immediately evident the moment we consider the records of the Comédie Française. In 1763 Corneille was performed 16 times at the Comédie, Racine 17 times, and Voltaire 48 times; in 1775 it was Corneille 10 times, Racine 17 times, and Voltaire 54. In 1789 it was Corneille 18 times, Racine 28, and Voltaire 42. The 18 performances of Du Belloy, the most frequently played of the younger dramatists after 1765, coupled with the 22 performances of Chénier's *Charles IX*—a Chénier[18] just arrived on the scene— all these together scarcely counterbalanced the popularity of Voltaire.

In 1805 Voltaire had only 28 performances against 57 for Corneille and 59 for Racine, but Crébillon, Ducis, Lefranc de Pompignan, Longepierre, and Poinsinet de Sivry reached a combined total of just 9 performances. Voltaire alone had managed to hold the theater public between the classicism of Louis XIV and that of the Napoleonic Empire. It was the year of *Les Templiers* ("The Templars"), which was given 33 times. Finally, in 1828, Corneille fell to 5 and Racine to 26. Voltaire remained at 28. If Ducis alone of all the eighteenth-century dramatists held a respectable place alongside him with ten performances in 1828, nine of those ten were Ducis' translations of *Hamlet* and *Othello*. Clearly, the public was more interested in Shakespeare than in Ducis.

As for Voltaire's comedies, they scarcely deserve mention. His only success was in *le comique larmoyant,* the tearful, sentimental comedy, which was alien to his natural inclinations and notions of good taste. *L'Enfant Prodigue* ("The Prodigal Son") and *Nanine* marked for him the limits of his willingness to mix the literary genres. These two comedies enjoyed a long popularity. During the First Empire they were still being performed and esteemed for their tepid philosophy of prudence and discretion.

It is rather surprising that this great master of mockery and sarcasm, whether in his tragedies or his comedies, was successful only in touching people's sensibilities. His true genius was constrained and inhibited, as we have indicated, by the traditions and masterpieces of classical comedy. In a few *divertissements de société* (light society skits) he did attempt a more whimsical, action-packed comedy in the English manner, but his great powers of comic invention were never freely and completely released except in the characters and dialogues of his buffooneries (*facéties*) and his celebrated philosophical tales.

6

Voltaire the Historian[a]

THE GREAT results of Voltaire's studies in history appeared during the years 1751 to 1756, a culmination of twenty years' work and research. We must pause at this point to examine his historical writings, for at Ferney, during the last two decades of his life, Voltaire will be engaged chiefly in polemics or historical criticism. He will hardly have time to be an historian.

The seventeenth century had had some fine scholars of history, erudite men who published collections of texts and critical dissertations. But except for Bossuet,[1] it did not produce a single great historian, one concerned both with accuracy of fact and literary excellence. Tillemont, Cordemoy, and Fleury had produced a number of solid, conscientious works, which, however, lacked distinction. *Les beaux esprits,* the literary wits, gave their

[a] *Histoire de Charles XII,* 1731. *Siècle de Louis XIV,* 1751. *Annales de l'Empire,* 1753. *Essai sur l'histoire générale et sur les moeurs et l'esprit des nations* (various chapters, *Mercure,* 1745–46, 1750–51; *Abrégé de l'histoire Universelle,* unauthorized ed., 2 vols., 1753; V. III, authentic, 1754), complete authorized ed., 1756. *Histoire de Russie,* 1759, 63. *Précis du siècle de Louis XV,* 1768 (incomplete, 1755 et 1763). *Histoire du Parlement de Paris,* 1769. A. Geffroy, *le Charles XII de Voltaire et le Charles XII de l'histoire* (*Revue des Deux Mondes,* 15 Nov. 1869). E. Bourgeois, *Introduction* to the Hachette ed. of *Siècle de Louis XIV.* R. Mahrenholtz, *Voltaire als Historiker* (*Archiv de Herrig,* V. LXII). Minslow, *Pierre le Grand dans la littérature étrangère,* 1872 (cf. Bengesco, I, 398–403). Langlois, *Manuel de Bibliographie historique,* pp. 317–318.

readers lots of eloquence, many pompous speeches, elegant portraits, and a number of reflections both subtle and profound.
They neglected just one thing: the essential. French history,
above all, was the hapless prey of servile rhetoricians. The fear
of the Bastille and a hope for government pensions had a dismal
effect on the historian's taste for truth and objectivity. An independent soul, like Mézeray, would plunge himself, with little
reliable information, into malicious and venemous satire. This
was called "liberty." Vertot and Saint-Réal were merging history
with the novel, with pure fiction. The demarcation line was so
ill-defined that Father Lelong inscribed, side by side with the
scholars Duchesne and Labbe and among contemporary French
historians, the name of Courtilz de Sandras, the creator of the
Mémoires de d'Artagnan.

They knew that the public wanted, first and foremost, to be
entertained. According to Mézeray, historical accuracy would be
of no profit to him, save with a handful of people, and would
perhaps do him a disservice with the others. In any event, it
would scarcely win him compliments commensurate with the
extra amount of work entailed. Accordingly, he spared himself
the trouble. Father de Villiers wrote in 1699:

We have seen a man entrusted with the task of writing a history of
France, who, after having composed and written everything about this
nation of first importance, inquired as to who that person Duchesne
might be. He had not even heard of this author, nor of any of the
authors whose works Duchesne had collected and utilized. Imagine
where he found his historical information, not knowing that one should
read the only authors who provide it.[a]

By the end of the seventeenth century and the beginning of the
eighteenth, would-be historians began to acquire more accurate
ideas of what the study involved. They stopped adhering to the
hoary admonitions of Cicero and Lucan on the duties of an
historian. Bayle,[b] Father Daniel, Fénelon, and Lenglet-Dufresnoy[c]
perceived and gave the public some notion of the indispensable
requirements for historical research. French society as a whole,

---

[a] P. de Villiers, *Entretiens sur les contes de fées,* 1699, p. 60.
[b] Bayle, *Dict. crit.;* articles on *Concini, Abimélech, Elisabeth,* etc.
[c] *Méthode pour étudier l'histoire,* 1713 and 1729.

previously out of touch with scholars and men of letters, was beginning to make contact with them through the Academy of Inscriptions, the literary salons, and the coffee houses.

However, as so often happens, practice was slow to catch up with theory. Rapin de Thoyras wrote, with critical alacrity, a history of England based on source materials. It received favorable comment. But a huge, resounding success greeted the work of Rollin, an outspoken, uncritical compiler of ancient history. Those who formulated theories were the first to avoid their application. Lenglet-Dufresnoy expressed some of the most childish beliefs and ludicrous certitudes. Father Daniel—who wrote a beautiful Preface—when shown "eleven or twelve hundred volumes of original documents and manuscripts at the King's Library" spent "*an hour* glancing at them and said that he was quite satisfied. That was all the use he made of this immense collection." Later he confided to Father Tournemine "that all those documents were just so much useless paper, of no value to him in writing his history."[a]

Literary and social proprieties, like so many swaddling clothes, enveloped historical writing along with every other form of literature. Hénault discreetly objected to Voltaire's candid opinion of a certain prince: "It's all right for fireside talk, but one doesn't put that sort of thing into writing."[b] And always the powers temporal and spiritual were hovering over the historian. Even Hénault, to avoid being harassed, was obliged to "suppress more than three quarters" of his book, "that is to say, the most interesting parts."[c] In order to strike a compromise between his conscience and his desire to be let alone, he tactfully limited his condemnation of the Saint Barthlomew's Day Massacre[2] to a quotation from Archbishop Péréfixe.

Voltaire arrived on the scene, then, at a time when they were just beginning to place a premium on truth, critical judgment, and personal independence in the writing of history; but it was still a time when these virtues were rarely exemplified. There was originality just in striving for them, and one could already

---

[a] Lenglet-Dufresnoy, *Méthode*, IV, 47, *Supplément*, 2nd part, p. 159.

[b] Lion, *Le Président Hénault*, p. 68.

[c] *Ibid.*, p. 269.

look forward to being paid by the public for one's troubles.

L'Histoire de Charles XII ("The History of Charles XII") marked Voltaire's début as an historian (1731). He chose modern history [the recent meteoric career of the Swedish king Charles XII (1682–1718)], a subject crammed with adventure and unusual personalities. He had reread Quintus-Curtius[a] but rejected the classical fondness for long, contrived speeches and portraits, preferring to quote or analyze authentic remarks, comments, and letters. Depicting men and events by means of significant and small details and carefully documented circumstances, sifting and evaluating anecdotes, pruning them of crude or vulgar details, Voltaire wrote a fast-moving, historical account, lively, never ponderous, marked by a sensitive, elegant touch, and as eminently readable and interesting as a novel. Everyone was immediately aware of its qualities, while the critics denounced it as being only a novel.[b] Today we know it was something far better. Admirably well-informed for his time, having consulted all available documents and witnesses, Voltaire strived to get at the truth with complete impartiality. If he did draw a moral, a philosophical lesson, from the life of Charles XII, condemning in a king his fondness for war, conquests, and martial glory—it was a lesson that spelled itself out naturally from the given facts. Voltaire had no need to invent or falsify to discover the moral. The partial corrections of La Motraye, Nordberg, or the former grenadier Popinet,[c] clearly reinforced rather than weakened the impression of general solidity in this historical work. Only nineteenth-century historians, for whom the Swedish archives were opened, brought to Voltaire's account any significant corrections or additions. By its light and exquisite form, this good historical writing blended well with the subtle shadings of the palette that produced the contemporary masterpieces of *Zaïre* and *Manon Lescaut*.

Le Siècle de Louis XIV ("The Age of Louis XIV") is a work of greater weight and scope. Conceived as early as 1732, and perhaps in 1729; begun in 1734; well along by 1738, then dis-

[a] V. XXXIII, p. 193 [Moland ed.]. (Besterman, 350) (R.P.)
[b] *Voltairomanie*, p. 6. "A poem in prose," said the abbé de Parthenay (*Histoire de la Pologne sous Auguste II*, préface).
[c] *Mercure*, Jan. 1746.

continued because of government hostility; resumed in 1750; completed and published in Berlin in 1751; retouched in 1756; and brought to its definitive state in 1768; *Le Siècle de Louis XIV* is a great historical work, one that still has considerable significance in our own day since its views and interpretations continue to be discussed and debated by present-day historians.

A French Protestant, intelligent but an adventurer, a man with few scruples but with a thirst for money and publicity—Angliviel de La Beaumelle seized upon the work in 1753 and had it reprinted with comments of his own, occasionally judicious and useful but, for the most part, satirical and insulting. Voltaire, outraged at being robbed and defamed at the same time, launched a riposte with his *Supplément au Siècle de Louis XIV*. It was the beginning of his feuds with La Beaumelle in which, as always, he overstepped the bounds of moderation and made his public forget that the first wrongs had been committed by his adversary.

La Beaumelle, who had intelligence and knowledge, had made only slight modifications in the *Siècle de Louis XIV*. Hénault had not been able to do more. The work was a solid one. No one in the eighteenth century was capable of challenging it. Voltaire had spent his youth among the survivors of the great reign, at the Temple, at Saint-Ange, at Sully, Sceaux, Vaux-Villiers, and La Source. In England he had seen some of the leading figures of the War of the Spanish Succession: Lord Peterborough, Lord Methuen, the Duke of Marlborough's widow, not to mention Bolingbroke. With all his collected anecdotes and confidential information, he might very well have chosen to write some interesting "Memoirs of Others" on Louis XIV. Instead, he preferred to write history.

Methodically, he resumed his inquiries and interrogations, following every lead, knocking on every door, going from the duchesse de Saint-Pierre, Torcy's sister, to Cardinal Fleury. He read everything that had been published by way of histories and memoirs—200 volumes, he tells us. He ferreted out the unpublished. He had the memoirs of Torcy,[3] Dangeau,[4] and Villars[5]— the papers of Louvois,[6] Colbert,[7] and Desmarets.[8] He even had access to the state archives, and in the Louvre collection found some curious documents on the question of the Spanish succession. After publication of the first edition, he remained alert for

everything and anything that appeared. He made his own corrections and emendations and even profited from the critics when
he found their criticisms valid, no matter how hard those critics
sought to wound him.

Voltaire created a work of the first rank, as solid and accurate
as it was possible to be in the period when he was writing. If his
method does not meet all the exacting demands of research today,
it marked a genuine advance over that of his predecessors. It is
very close to the method of Sainte-Beuve[9] in his *Port-Royal* and
Causeries du Lundi—an indefatigable and limitless curiosity
with a literary finesse applied to the discernment of historical
truths. Nothing was more false in its over-all judgment than the
criticism of Presiding Judge Hénault. Voltaire, he said, saw only
the surface of things. Voltaire lacked the serious tone of history.
Voltaire defamed his own country. He had an aversion for the
great men of France.[a]

Voltaire illuminated most intelligently the great problems of
his subject matter: the Spanish succession, the revocation of the
Edict of Nantes, the characters and roles of the great actors—
Colbert, Mme de Maintenon,[10] and the king of France. He studied
them seriously. We must not let Voltaire's epigrammatic style
conceal from us the serious moderation of his judgments and
analyses. With the exception of his views on religion, Voltaire,
for once in his life, sinned on the side of optimism rather than
satire and cynicism. If he did not regard Turenne's conversion
as a disinterested decision, was it out of personal animus or was
it not the truth? Indulgent to the king's mistresses and favorites,
Voltaire awarded the king, all things considered, somewhat the
lion's share of credit for the splendors of his reign. He was the
first to see Mme de Maintenon as she really was and to indicate
the true importance of Colbert, who was in disfavor with his
contemporaries. He was sufficiently moderate and objective about
the revocation of the Edict of Nantes[11] to displease the Protestants; although pointing out on the one hand the injustice,
cruelty, and disastrous consequences of this intolerable measure,
he also condemned the Cévennes revolt in the name of public order
and out of disgust with the *illuminés* [Protestant fanatics].

---

[a] Lion, *Le Président Hénault*, p. 67ff.

Broadly speaking, his entire book is but a glorification of the French mind, of seventeenth-century French civilization, and of the king who was its splendid embodiment. The philosopher, who hated war, was hard put to it not to be dazzled at times by the military grandeur and the conquests of a refined and civilized France.

Since the time of Gibbon, not a single critic has failed to condemn the plan of the book, which fragments the subject matter and destroys its continuity. The reader encounters the battle of Malplaquet (1709) and the last somber days of the aged monarch before he is treated to the sumptuous royal entertainment of happier days such as *Les Plaisirs de l'île enchantée* ("The Pleasures of the Enchanted Isle"). He follows the events of the war in Holland before learning about Colbert's tariffs, and he sees the Pope allied with the Protestant princes before having heard of *la régale* [the right assumed by the king to seize the revenues of a bishopric during its vacancy]. But this parceling out of his material corresponded to the analytical nature of Voltaire's mind and to the organizational intention of his ideas.

While public opinion in 1730 was unfriendly to Louis XIV, against whom there had accumulated all the rancors of those who were out of power and all the antipathies of philosophers who were revolted by his despotism, Voltaire, the man of intelligence and a poet above all, saw in his long reign the prodigious development of the human mind with its masterpieces of arts and letters. France failed, to be sure, in her effort to achieve a universal monarchy, but she established over all of Europe the predominance of her language, her refinement, her culture, and her great writers. Whence the enthusiasm that produced Voltaire's original plan for the *Siècle de Louis XIV,* altogether French and classical. There was also a deeper implication—an *arrière-pensée:* what a contrast between the court in which appeared simultaneously a Condé, a Colbert, and a Racine[a] and the present court, in which there was no Condé or Colbert and from which Voltaire was also absent! The government of Louis XV was expected to learn a lesson from the history of its predecessor.

The work unfolded on successive theatrical levels. After the

[a] V. XXXII, p. 493.

grandiose proscenium depicting victories and conquests, there appeared the person of the king, the life and manners of the court, the refinement of the nobility, and the inner workings of the government, its useful institutions, and its ecclesiastical affairs. Finally, like a magnificent stage backdrop, there was the marvelous décor of arts, letters, and science, representing the outstanding achievement and superiority of seventeenth-century French civilization. The *Siècle* was planned and arranged as an apotheosis of the human spirit.

Between 1738 and 1742 the arrangement was modified. Ecclesiastical affairs interrupted its progress. These were relegated to the last pages. They constituted the obverse side of the coin, the sad side of the otherwise resplendent reign. Religious quarrels and persecutions, superstition and fanaticism—that was "the history of fools." The seventeenth century, unsurpassable in poetry and the arts, left room for improvement—a task to be performed by philosophy in the age of Louis XV and Frederick the Great. This explains the sarcastic tone in his treatment of religious affairs, and it also explains the final chapter on Chinese ceremonies, no longer surprising when one considers it as a symbol of reason driving out fanaticism.

All the facts of the seventeenth century were gathered under two headings: a glorification of human intelligence and a derisive contempt for human stupidity. These ideas presupposed a larger, less partial, more historical concept—that of producing the history of an age and not merely the history of a king.[a] This idea had been barely perceived in theory by Fénelon and totally neglected in practice by all the historians, by Bossuet as well as by Daniel. Voltaire is the first historian of civilization. And civilization was not a fortuitous or secondary consideration with him. It was linked to the deepest feelings within his nature, to his *philosophie du bonheur,* his philosophy of happiness.

. . . Of those who have commanded battalions and squadrons, only the names remain. The human race has nothing to show for a hundred battles that have been waged. But the great men I speak to you about have prepared pure and lasting *pleasures* for men yet to be born. A

[a] V. XIV, p. 155; V. XV, 105; V. XXXIII, pp. 483, 492, 506; V. XXXV, p. 414, etc. (Besterman, 819, 840, 864, 2089, etc.) (R.P.)

canal lock uniting two seas, a painting by Poussin, a beautiful tragedy, a newly discovered truth—these are things a thousand times more precious than all the annals of the court or all the accounts of military campaigns. You know that, with me, great men come first and heroes last.

I call great men all those who have excelled in creating what is useful or agreeable. The plunderers of the provinces are merely heroes.[a]

Accordingly, it was the development of civilization and the dissemination of reason—but of a reason applied to one's wellbeing—that Voltaire wanted to describe and illustrate. And in so doing, he believed he was rendering a service and creating a work worthy of a good French citizen and a citizen of the world. But it was impossible to portray the progress of mankind without giving his own views on its motivating force—another design interlocked with his other purposes—another series of relationships to be singled out and scrutinized.

For fifteen hundred years the Providential concept of history had dominated men's minds. It had found its most brilliant and eloquent expression in Bossuet's *Discours sur l'histoire universelle* ("Discourse on Universal History"). Voltaire eliminated divine guidance from the study of history. Events were the necessary results of universal laws. Unforeseen shocks and coincidences (we call them chance) determine peoples' destinies. A glass of water spilled on a gown—and Marlborough falls from favor and peace is restored between England and France. A village priest and a councillor are walking one day toward the town of Denain —and Marshal Villars has discovered the road to victory. Fortunate successes provide certain countries at certain times with powerful motivating forces that contribute enormously to the advancement of civilization: those forces are the country's great men. And when a great man is lucky enough to influence sovereign authority, his actions—his efficiency and output, if I may put it thus—are simply immense. This supreme good fortune has happened just four times in the western world since the beginning of recorded history: (1) the Hellenic age of Philip and Alexander; (2) the age of Caesar and Augustus; (3) the age of the Medicis and the Italian Renaissance; and (4) the age of Louis XIV. Thus, in Voltaire's mind, the compelling forces of great

[a] V. XXXIII, p. 506. (Besterman, 864) (R.P.)

moments in history were the happy combination of great men and sheer luck—*le hasard*. They constituted the motivating power that Bossuet had ascribed to Providence.

The tone and spirit of Voltaire's *Siècle de Louis XIV* derive from this multiplicity of viewpoints, which, through the varied shades of light shed on the events of the time, gave a joyous expression to the ever keen and alert intelligence of the eighteenth century. We must also take into account the writer's art of achieving his ends in producing this historical exposition. As always, Voltaire wanted to be clear, concise, and elegantly casual. He simplified his material, disentangled complexities, and lightened the subject for his reader's enjoyment. He wanted his account to be as interesting as a stage play, as a tragedy. He succeeded in that respect with regard to the history of wars and treaties, in which chronology tied the events cohesively together. We follow the Sun King from his dazzling sunrise to the blood-red rays of his melancholy sunset. We are prepared for the stage entrance of Louis XIV by an introduction rigorously assessing the reign of Louis XIII and Cardinal Richelieu. Then the young king appears, to put the country back on its feet in a few short years and bring it to a position of preeminence among all the states of Europe. Next we see everything directed toward the invasion of Holland. There is a brisk movement in which Louis XIV reaches the gates of Utrecht. This is the moment of a dramatic *péripétie*—a sudden reversal of fortune. Four cavalrymen enter Muyden, the location of the locks, and in short order they have departed. They had almost achieved, and then unwittingly ruined, Louis' grand design for universal domination. This one small incident sets off a chain reaction of dire events. At Nimwegen, Louis is stopped; and at Ryswick, his royal grandeur is dealt a crushing setback. The Peace of Utrecht comes as a welcome relief to the reader only because he was expecting to see France herself collapse in total defeat.

There are no portraits. Life is mobile, never standing still. Louis' features are on every page of the book, variously sketched —a man of many moods and facets.[a] There are no long speeches, but there are many reflections, the mark of the philosopher. His

[a] V. XV, p. 123.

mind reacted to his subject matter with all kinds of comments, criticisms, and pithy observations.[a] It would be wrong to imagine that this unending and scintillating display of wit and comment consisted only in reviling the clergy and slandering those in high places. Of course the major premises and prejudices of Voltairian philosophy are everywhere in evidence: impiety, love of peace, tolerance, a taste for luxury, bourgeois pride, the concept of the public good, cosmopolitanism, and a passion for literature. But in addition, what a variety of ideas! There are quick estimates of individual and collective motives, doubts about perfect altruism or unmitigated evil, lucid analyses of factors leading to success or failure, remarks about the use of the rifle and bayonet in the wars of Louis XIV, etc. It is a constant exercise in reasoning by a rational mind that needed to see clearly in all matters. Every fact presented is accompanied by an explanatory note that also classifies it.

Augustin Thierry[12] condemned this method,[b] but it delighted the eighteenth-century European reader who sought, above all else, an understanding of events. It is not that Voltaire lacked color or was incapable of giving visual qualities to his writing. He had a fondness for the specific detail, the precise statistic, the isolated fact that suggests the picture as a whole. Marshal Créqui at Trier, in front of his garrison that had revolted and wanted to capitulate, flees "into a church." Marshal Marsin, at the siege of Turin, holding a council of war, "takes from his pocket" the letter from the king. Lavallière [the king's erstwhile favorite] exchanges her life at court—he does not say "for life in a convent" but—for "the hair shirt, bare feet, fasting, the choir at night, and singing in Latin." Here is his description of a courtier to the king:

In those days they wore a cassock over a doublet decorated with ribbons, and over the cassock they put on a cross-belt from which hung a sword. They wore a sort of lace collar and a hat adorned with two rows of plumes.[c]

[a] Note, in what has been called *le Sottisier* (V. XXXII), how much Voltaire was fascinated by documents and source materials. (*Voltaire's Notebooks,* Besterman ed., 952) (R.P.)

[b] *Lettre V. sur l'Hist. de France.*

[c] Chapt. XXV.

Voltaire sensed the theatrical pomp of Louis' reign in its many fêtes, tournaments, the Royal Household, and the journey to Flanders. He portrayed it according to the tastes of his own age, in the manner of Coypel [court painter to Louis XV] and not Van der Meulen [court painter to Louis XIV]. However, it is true he refused to give it much visual color. He knew and reported that Colbert had "thick eyebrows that joined, a rude, common face, and a glacial countenance," but Colbert *cared very little* as to "the way in which he wore his collar" and "the bourgeois manner that the king said he kept at court." The nobility in Voltaire's history are denied such details. Any vulgarities or unseemly matters are swept aside or veiled by the decorous tone of aristocracy.

More especially, Voltaire did not want anything picturesque that was unrelated to an idea. A visual image was for him a means of explaining something. He spoke to the reader's imagination only when necessary to provoke thought. The little details, the piquant anecdotes, anything concrete merely served as a symbol. Through sensation he moved toward an idea, and he sought to give his reader only certain, carefully chosen sensations (free from any vulgarity) which would easily lead the reader to an awareness of certain informative and instructive relationships. The clear, refined color of the *Siècle de Louis XIV* was entirely intellectual.

Apart from Voltaire's malevolent enemies, whom nothing could disarm, there was unanimity of opinion on this work which corresponded so perfectly to the mental outlook of the age. Mme de Graffigny, Frederick, and the marquis d'Argenson were enthusiastic admirers, and Lord Chesterfield expressed the public attitude when he said: "It is the history of the human mind written by a man of genius for men of intelligence."[a]

A similar—and even stronger—impression was produced by Voltaire's *Essai sur les moeurs et l'esprit des nations* ("Essay on the Manners and Spirit of Nations"). In 1740, when he had given up trying to finish his *Siècle de Louis XIV* in France, Voltaire set about the task of writing an abridgment of world history for

[a] Desnoiresterres, V. IV, p. 211.

Mme du Châtelet. She had acquired a distaste for the study of the past because of the childishness and the verbosity of the authors, and the lack of any philosophical spirit in their writings.[a] There was no shortage of *Annales mundi,* of *Historiae ab origine mundi* or *ab ortu imperiorum,* or of *Histoires du monde* or *Histoires universelles,* in Latin or French, long works in big folio volumes or compact studies in duodecimo—dry, factual erudition or histories elegantly inaccurate. And not one of them went beyond political and military facts.

The only work of superior literary value was that of Bossuet. But Bossuet's history was so wedded to Catholic dogma that it lost its authenticity and usefulness for independent thinkers. Voltaire did not want to redo Bossuet. Ancient history scarcely interested him. But he proposed to do a continuation, less mediocre than the writings of La Barre, who was unknown, or Massuet, and by continuing Bossuet to destroy and replace his philosophy of history. Voltaire began with Charlemagne [where Bossuet had left off] and brought his history down to the time of Louis XIV.

He threw himself into his work with customary fervor. The monthly *Mercure* published in 1745–1746 some fragments of this new "history of the human spirit" and, in 1750–1751, the "history of the Crusades." In 1753 Jean Neaulme printed at The Hague the *Abrégé de l'Histoire universelle depuis Charlemagne jusqu'à Charles-Quint* ("A Summary of Universal History from Charlemagne to Charles V"): two volumes whose appearance the author protested in letters, newspapers, and before two notaries. He himself published the third volume to establish the authentic tone and spirit of his work. In 1756 he gave a complete text to the Cramer brothers, publishers in Geneva, under the title: *Essai sur l'histoire générale et sur les moeurs et l'esprit des nations depuis Charlemagne jusqu'à nos jours.* He welded to this general history his *Siècle de Louis XIV* and some chapters on Louis XV. The definitive text appeared in 1769 under the simplified title: *Essai sur les moeurs et l'esprit des nations.* ("Essay on the Manners and Spirit of Nations"). His general history—excluding the

[a] V. XXIV, pp. 41, 543.

material on Louis XIV and Louis XV—was expanded from 144 to 197 chapters. At the same time the work received an appropriate introduction: *La Philosophie de l'histoire par feu M. l'abbé Bazin* ("The Philosophy of History by the Late Abbé Bazin"), printed in 1765. It was a rapid survey of the origins of civilization and the great peoples of antiquity, leading the reader to Charlemagne and the Middle Ages. Thus Voltaire embraced human development as a whole.

It is evident that such a work, dealing with eight-and-a-half centuries of history, was not based on original source materials. Rather, it was a compilation. We would like to know what tools Voltaire made use of. Failing a complete study of the matter which would give us reliable information, I have made a few samplings. His two chapters on Mohammed he took almost entirely from Gagnier and De Sale—two good authorities. On China he consulted Du Halde. For church history and the history of the Crusades his guide was the excellent Fleury. For the history of England and Joan of Arc, the dependable Rapin de Thoyras. These are good guarantees of reliability. It is true that for Henry IV he scarcely went beyond Mézeray. Sometimes, however, he appears to have gone back to documents referred to by his authors to collect some significant and characteristic detail. He was also fond of curious, little-known papers and documents.

All in all, Voltaire seems to have done an excellent work of popularization. Daunou and the authors of *L'Art de vérifier les dates* ("The Art of Verifying Dates"), and the English historian Robertson praised his historical accuracy. Nonnotte wrote two volumes on the *Erreurs de Voltaire: erreurs historiques, erreurs dogmatiques.* Voltaire wrote him an inept reply. He would have done better to let his *Essai* speak for him. For Nonnotte did not weaken or invalidate Voltaire's work. To be sure, he made some corrections of details. Errors and oversights were inevitable in a work of such magnitude, especially in view of the fast and sometimes dizzy pace at which Voltaire wrote. But very frequently it is Nonnotte who is mistaken, who quibbles and alters the texts. Was Voltaire wrong to find the legend of Florinda and Roderick "very suspect"? Nonnotte denounced as lies certain well-established facts—facts that put the Church or the monarchy in a bad light. He accepted as historical truth anything that religious hatred imputed to Protestants and heretics. He continually labeled as "historical errors" whatever contradicted his dogma and the passions that went with his dogma. He was erudite but not in the least critical. Voltaire was much closer than he to genuine history.

The philosophy in the *Essai sur les Moeurs* consisted basically of three ideas, two of which we have already noted in *Le Siècle de Louis XIV*. In the first place, there was the intention to write the history of the human spirit, of civilization, and not merely a history of kings. Secondly, it was Voltaire's idea to recount the changes and revolutions in commerce, social customs, and the arts—not simply wars and treaties. His third purpose was to write a history of the world, and not just of Europe. Chevreau and Puffendorf had previously given attention to Africa, America, India, and China in their universal histories, but with them it was only a kind of statement of material fact. They wrote about every country they saw on a world map. Voltaire was motivated by a philosophical concern. Reducing history to western civilization and its Graeco-Judaeo origins was a mutilation of history. In the remote past, in the mists of pre-history—before Romans, Greeks, Jews, or even Egyptians—one could already discern the civilizations of Chaldeans, Chinese, and Hindus. The world had a history, indeed many histories, long before the one presented in Holy Scripture. What a joy for Voltaire to kill two birds with one stone—to discover truth and deal a blow to religion at the same time! Since the time of the Renaissance and the great maritime discoveries, neither historian nor statesman could limit his purview to Europe. All nations were interdependent, linked to one another by trade and commerce.[a] Drinking coffee from Arabia in a cup from China, Voltaire saw his historical horizon expand.

These three concepts formed the framework and controlled the development of his *Essai sur les Moeurs*. Voltaire started and ended with the Orient. He devoted 90 of his 197 chapters to tableaux of the manners, institutions, arts, and spirit of different

[a] V. XI, p. 158; V. XXIV, p. 28.

peoples and different eras. Even in those chapters dominated by accounts of wars and political history, Voltaire still chose the most significant facts about the status of civilization.

I would like to discover what human society was like, how people lived in the intimacy of the family, and what arts were cultivated, rather than repeat the story of so many misfortunes and military combats—the dreary subject matter of history and the common currency of human perversity.[a]

He was interested in the way people dressed in the Middle Ages—how they provided light and heat—how they worked—the price of meat and bread—when they invented eye glasses—windmills—pottery—fireplaces—how their houses were covered.[b] He visualized the Norman pirate ships, the supplies of "beer, sea biscuit, cheese, and smoked meat" with which they set out on their voyages.[c] Only precise facts give a clear understanding. Voltaire set down his selected, pertinent details and his unusual anecdotes. In Voltaire's work we have come a long way from those historians who made no distinction between the Francs of Clovis [sixth century A.D.] and Frenchmen of the court of Louis XIV. He grasped the differences between earlier and contemporary civilizations, and he grasped them with more excitement than serenity. He made fun of or waxed indignant over those countless centuries that failed to resemble his own.

The cosmopolitan outlook, kept in the background in his *Siècle de Louis XIV,* now came to the fore. There was no "chosen people," no superior race. Each society in its turn had contributed to human development. The author proposed "to render justice to all nations." Excluding the Providential point of view and all doctrines of finalism, he offered a rational concept of history. Humanity has produced itself, haphazardly, slowly, under the pressure of instincts, needs, and circumstances which, piece by piece, have formed human laws, manners and morals, industry and the sciences, and here and there scattered a bit of comfort, justice, and liberty among the many miseries and brutalities of

[a] V. XII, p. 53. Cf. V. XXXIX, p. 207. (Cf. Besterman, 6560) (R.P.)
[b] V. XI, p. 275; V. XII, p. 55.
[c] V. XI, p. 305.

life. The role of the great man—so conspicuous in his *Louis XIV* —is overshadowed now by the role of chance and the unconscious movements and changes among the masses which, alone, bring about progress. The individual has become much more a result than a cause.[a]

And yet Voltairian history was profoundly idealistic. Aware that understanding and feeling are the motivating forces of moral determinism, he tried to give his readers an image of the past that would make them the working agents for his ideal. This ideal could be defined as a rational conception of human relationships. Experience has revealed that there are certain general conditions that make for human happiness or unhappiness. The most obvious of those causing unhappiness—conditions for which man, not nature, is responsible—are war and fanaticism. Millions of men have died since the dawn of history because of the ambitions of kings and the absurdity of dogmas. The remedy is to disabuse mankind. Less easily dazzled, less credulous and gullible, that is, more rational and sensible, the human race will be more reluctant to consent to its miseries.

But, Oh, how slow is the progress of reason! The historian's blood begins to boil when he contemplates the tissue of horrors and stupidities that constitute history. He is seized with impatience. He is furious with society's dupes and victims for cherishing or adoring their tyrants. His anger is exacerbated when he considers the historians who preceded him. From the days of the earliest crude chroniclers of the Carolingian kings down to the tactful Jesuit and the polite academician, there they all are, or almost all—childish, untruthful, servile, grovelling on their knees in the face of force—glorifying deception, banditry, and injustice, and incapable of viewing manfully their kings and priests. All, or almost all, had applied themselves to perpetuating the errors that have held mankind in thrall. With his eyes on their recorded accounts, Voltaire repeated the narrative with passionate irony, conspicuously displaying all the facts that shed light on "the excesses of absurd insolence in those who governed and the excessive stupidity of those who let themselves be so

[a] V. XII, p. 66.

governed." By his underscoring and emphasizing with sarcasm all the "crimes" of kings and clergy, he hoped the public might finally become enlightened and exercise its will.

Voltaire's *Essai* was, accordingly, a work of ardent humanitarian proselytizing. It was not that he had no intention of being fair, even to kings and popes.[a] Everything was not bleak and savage even in the darkest ages. "It is very maladroit to slander the Inquisition." The monks cleared the forest and undertook studies and research. Their cloisters became "a safe refuge from tyranny" in a period of general barbarism. Voltaire knew how to side with the Templars against Philip the Fair. He joined the clerical battle and the royal struggle for empire as the thread of continuity ensuring a haven of safety for civilization during the confused Middle Ages. He saw in the papacy a moral force holding in leash the passions of violence and military brutality.

Still, we cannot deny that his humanitarian impatience and explosive temperament very often made him falsify and misinterpret history. Even from his own point of view, he should have been a little less harsh on that poor humanity which, deprived of divine assistance, somehow managed, with so much pain and suffering, to raise itself above the animal level and to achieve a degree of rational existence. Every shred of morality, justice, and liberty was a victory for the human spirit. For that reason, the least bit of progress should have been regarded by Voltaire as a pearl of great price. And however desirous he was of inciting the living to shake themselves free of age-old shackles, he ought not to have heaped so much abuse on the dead, on those who showed more virtue in their barbarous times whenever they observed a few ethical principles than we show today in the development of such principles.

He was much too inclined to project into the past the ideas of the present. He did not recognize that the Church—in Voltaire's day a force for reaction and oppression—was, for a time, a force for progress and liberation. He "rehabilitated" the persecuting Roman emperors as defenders of the laity and secular society. He disguised the mystical Julian as a rational philosopher. He invented a flattering picture of Moslems, Chinese, Hindus,

[a] V. XI, pp. 309, 343; V. XII, pp. 66, 353.

and all civilizations that were not Christian. Yet we must not push this kind of criticism too far. The Romantic or religious historians of the nineteenth century have given us an idealized picture of the Middle Ages, one that is false. In its reality there was some justification for Voltaire. Achille Luchaire's unbiased and arresting description proves it. But above all, we must understand that if Voltaire was too severe in judging the Middle Ages, it was less from religious antipathy than from rationalism. His religious hostility rejoiced in ideas imposed on him by his rationalism. It was the enlightenment of his age and not mere anti-Christian prejudice that decried fanaticism, brutality, ignorance, and irrational fervors. Neither the abbé de Saint-Pierre[a] nor Presiding Judge Hénault[b] dared to excuse the Crusades. Some think it was the eighteenth-century philosophers who disparaged the Crusades. But would they include the abbé Fleury? No one more clearly condemned the Crusades than he.[c] The opinion of the Middle Ages held by this rational Christian scarcely differs from Voltaire's. Enlightened minds that had received a classical education, whether pious or impious, could not look with indulgence on those "crude, uncouth" centuries.

In the eighteenth century the psychological sciences were such that it was impossible to speak of religious phenomena, miracles, Joan of Arc, or Saint Francis of Assisi, as even a nonbelieving historian can speak of them today. There was no middle ground between absolute faith and absolute disbelief. One had to choose between the supernatural or downright fraud. Montesquieu, who was quite critical of Voltaire's history, could not think otherwise of Joan of Arc than did Voltaire.[d] In the eighteenth century the supposition of pious fraud and deception was actually the most rational point of view. Voltaire was in complete accord with the spirit of his age. That accounted for the success of his *Essai*, which, from 1753 to the Kehl edition [1784], was reprinted at least sixteen times. The abbé Audra made an expurgated abridgment of it for *collège* use, in which he retained "the principles of reason

[a] Goumy, *l'abbé de Saint-Pierre,* p. 200.
[b] Hénault, 1768 ed., pp. 976–979.
[c] *Disc. sur l'hist. ecclés.,* 269, and the entire 6th *Discours.* Cf. also the 3rd *Discours* concerning the Middle Ages.
[d] *Pensées,* II, pp. 59, 253.

and humanity." Until the Catholic and Romantic reaction of the nineteenth century, it was Voltaire who furnished cultivated minds with their concept of the march of civilization.

It is superfluous to say that Voltaire's method no longer suffices. But it marked a stage in the transition from traditionalist history to scientific history. Voltaire did not seek a meaning of history outside of history. Historical certainty was not measured for him by the harmonious agreement of facts with certain dogmatic tenets. It depended solely on the quality of the materials used by the historian. His principle frees us from having to respect his errors, and we are not bound by his conclusions except to the extent that we find documents corroborating them. People no longer argue about *Le Discours sur l'histoire universelle*. They argue about Voltaire. They refute him. The fact is that his history admits of the same criteria as our own. Herder[13] and Michelet,[14] Thierry and Guizot[15] only replaced him by continuing him.

If Thierry had been fair, he would have noticed that most of his criticisms of the histories of France did not apply to Voltaire—that we do not find in the *Essai* those simple-minded legends, that sustained atmosphere of false coloration, or that "abstract type of dignity and heroism" of which he complained so much. And he would have noticed that if Voltaire did not communicate the feelings and sensations inherent in his material, the reader at least acquires an idea of the differences in eras of history and the multiplicity of races, peoples, and institutions. After Bossuet, history as we know it had to be created. After Voltaire, it needed only to be perfected. That is what has allowed Hettner[16] to write that "the whole modern conception of history emerges from Voltaire's *Essai sur les moeurs*."

7

Voltaire at *Les Délices* and Ferney[a]

Philosophers need to have two or three holes in the ground to escape from the dogs who chase them.

Tavernier . . . when asked by Louis XIV why he had chosen a property in Switzerland, replied, as you know: "Sire, I was rather glad to have something I could call my own.[b]"

THESE REMARKS of Voltaire expressed his feelings when he escaped from Berlin, sentiments not unlike those of Scarmentado[c] [Voltaire's creation, forerunner of the sorely-tried Candide]. He

---

[a] Longchamp et Wagnière, *Mémoires sur Voltaire et ses ouvrages*, 1825, 2 vols. Desnoiresterres, V. V–VIII. Perezy et Maugras, *Voltaire aux Délices et à Ferney*, 1885. Maugras, *Voltaire et Jean-Jacques Rousseau*, 1886. L. Foisset, *Voltaire et le président de Brosses*, 1858. H. Tronchin, *le conseiller François Tronchin et ses amis*, 1895. E. Asse, *Lettres de Mesdames de Graffigny, d'Epinay, Suard*, etc. (on their visit with Voltaire), 1878. *Zeitschrift für franz. Spr. und Litt.* (Stengel, *Lettres de Voltaire et de Mme de Gallatin au landgrave de Hesse-Cassel*), 1887, V. VII. *Revue de Paris*, 1905 (H. Jullemier). (Voltaire, *Commentaire historique*, 1776.) (*Correspondance avec les Tronchin*, Delattre ed., 1950. *Boswell on the Grand Tour, Germany and Switzerland*, Frederick A. Pottle ed., s.d.) (R.P.)

[b] V. XXXIX, p. 198. (Besterman, 6519) (R.P.)

[c] Compare the name "Scarmentado" in the tale probably written in 1753.

crossed over into Switzerland, where he rented a house at Monrion situated midway down the mountain slope between Lausanne and the lake, a winter residence sheltered from the north winds. For his summers he acquired, at Saint-Jean near Geneva, an estate costing 87,000 pounds which he christened *Les Délices* ("The Delights"). At a glance he could take in the sweeping vista of "Geneva, its lake, the Rhone, another river (the Arve), extensive countryside, and the Alps."[a] Later on (since Monrion lacked a garden and sufficient cooking facilities) he leased for nine years in Lausanne a large and comfortable dwelling whose façade had fifteen windows affording a magnificent view of the lake, Geneva, and the Savoyard Alps.

His soul was filled with a delightful sense of tranquillity and well being. He gazed with enchantment on the elegant and grandiose setting of the lake surrounded by mountains. He was so affected by the beauty of Alpine landscape that he was moved to express his feelings in poetry, recalling the heroic memories of Switzerland's struggle for freedom. Voltaire was lifted to heights of lyricism.

But he did not linger long in those lofty heights. The call to action again took hold of him as soon as he felt he was safe from harassment. He began to build, plant, and work at his gardening at *Les Délices*. He attempted to have his six mares bred to an over-aged Danish stallion—a fruitless enterprise, alas! He entertained at dinner the most distinguished people in the country. He played host to all notable travelers passing by way of Lausanne and Geneva, such people as Palissot [the writer], Lekain [the actor], the Mesdames d'Epinay and du Bocage, the English philosopher Gibbon, and the Italian Jesuit Bettinelli. He made frantic efforts to disclaim his authorship of *La Pucelle* [an irreverent treatment of Joan of Arc]. He revised his *Histoire Universelle*. He wrote a Chinese tragedy. He argued against Providence and Leibnitz over the earthquake at Lisbon. He expressed anguish at the outbreak of the Seven Years' War in 1756. He patched things up with Frederick, King of Prussia, while still nursing a grudge against him. He tried to intervene to reestablish peace. He wrote to English friends on behalf of the luckless Admiral

[a] (Besterman, 5640) (R.P.)

Byng.[1] He enlisted in the cause of the *Encyclopédie* and argued
with Gresset [a French poet] and Haller [a Swiss physiologist].
He went to visit the Elector Palatine and mourned the death of
the Margravine of Bayreuth. He prevailed on D'Alembert[2] to
write his article "Geneva" for the *Encyclopédie*, and in that article to praise rational Christianity, the pure deism of the modern
Calvinists. And furthermore, he persuaded D'Alembert to refuse
the Genevan pastors the satisfaction of a retraction their piety or
politics demanded.

The trouble stirred up by the article on Geneva gave him cause
for reflection. Little by little, he was coming to realize the incom-
patibility of his temperament and point of view with the spirit of
Calvinist Geneva. The "Magnificent Council" [the city's ruling
body] forbade its citizens and townspeople to take part in or to
witness a tragedy performed at Voltaire's residence, and they
invited Voltaire to abstain from erecting a theater on territory
belonging to the Christian Republic. They would permit him
to engage in "histrionics" only at his place in Lausanne or at
Monrepos, the estate of the marquis de Gentil [outside the jurisdiction of Geneva]. But at Lausanne there were other nettles of
Calvinist zeal to sting and scratch the philosopher.

And so he returned to French territory. In the vicinity of Gex,
a half-hour from Geneva, he bought the estate of Fernex (he was
to spell it Ferney, the way it was pronounced), and he leased the
county of Tournay from *Président* de Brosses for life tenure. This
time Voltaire was well situated with maximum security. Like a
fox with the hounds in pursuit, he had, as he said, his front paws
in Lausanne and Geneva and his rear ones planted in Ferney and
Tournay. He was to build his stage and tread the boards at
Ferney, especially at Tournay in his *entresol*, thus enabling him
to thumb his nose at the "Magnificent Council," the Consistory,
and all those Protestant preachers. And if thunderclouds gathered
over Paris or Versailles, a short ride in his carriage would bring
him over the Swiss border, where he could snap his fingers at the
French ministry, the *Parlement*, and the Church. For a moment
in 1765, after the death of the Chevalier de la Barre [a victim of
religious fanaticism] a frightened Voltaire was to toy with the
idea of founding a colony of philosophers, "a truth factory" with
its own printing press in the vicinity of Cleves on Prussian soil.

From 1760 on, he stayed generally at Ferney where he lived like a prince. His fortune was immense and continually increasing. He had funds in business enterprises and banking houses[a] in Cadiz, Leipzig, and Amsterdam. But his available capital he invested chiefly in life annuities and at high interest rates, which were willingly granted him because of his age and "cadaverous face."[b] Among his debtors were French noblemen, German princes, marshal Richelieu, the Elector Palatine, and the Duke of Wurtemberg—slow payers all, who eventually settled up without Voltaire's losing any more than he did with Jews and bankers, and who liquidated the interest on their overdue obligations by doing him favors and giving him protection when demanded. Voltaire's notary told Collé in 1768 that his client had 80,000 pounds of revenue from life annuities, 40,000 pounds from real estate, and 60,000 pounds from securities. In 1776 an authentic record reports 177,000 pounds of income from annuities in addition to 235,000 anticipated revenues.

His upkeep and expenses at Ferney were enormous. The château he built was not large, but it was elegant. Day-to-day maintenance was costly enough, but when he entertained, when he gave theatrical performances, there were usually in addition to the regular personnel sixty to eighty invited guests. In 1768, after carrying out a thorough reorganization of his household, Voltaire set up a budget for Ferney of 40,000 pounds per annum, including the maintenance of twelve horses and a staff numbering sixty.

The usual guests at Ferney included his niece, the plump Mme Denis,[c] who spent her time quarreling and then patching things up with her uncle;[d] his faithful secretary Wagnière, who replaced Collini; and, in 1763, the copyist Simon Bigex and Father Adam, a Jesuit whom Voltaire had taken in and who became his partner at chess. Between 1760 and 1763 he added to his ménage Corneille's great-grandniece, the dark-complexioned Marie, unattractive but with beautiful big dark eyes. He raised the girl and settled a dowry on her. Later he took in Mlle de Varicourt,

[a] V. XXXVIII, p. 189. (Besterman, 5071) (R.P.)

[b] Collini, *Mémoires.*

[c] *Lettres de Mme de Graffigny,* etc., p. 263.

[d] V. XXXVIII, pp. 186–187. (Besterman, 5067) (R.P.)

"beautiful and good," to whom he gave no dowry since the man she married, the marquis de Villette, was very wealthy and did not want any money.

There was always some visitor living at Ferney for weeks or months on end—a never-ending procession that included his other niece, Mme de Fontaine; the marquis de Florian, whom she remarried; and the handsome "Florianet." And there was cousin Daumart, one of the king's musketeers, or else the supple Ximinès, or little La Harpe and his wife, or poor Durcy de Morsan, following his personal misfortunes, and the duc de Villars, a great tragedian. Then there was always a swarm of Genevans on hand, constantly going and coming from the city to Ferney, more like members of the family than visiting friends. There were all the Tronchins [lawyers and doctors with whom Voltaire established close relations], the Rilliet household, the two Cramers, Mme Gallatin, and Huber, the witty designer of silhouettes who often infuriated the patriarch of Ferney. Nor let us forget *Monsieur le Fornicateur Covelle.*

And what a stream of visitors from every state and every nation! Voltaire became a European curiosity, one of the "musts" for every tourist. Ferney was the Mecca for freethinkers and sensitive souls. One after the other they filed by: D'Alembert,[2] Turgot, the abbé Morellet, the musician and *valet de chambre* of King Laborde, the Chevalier de Boufflers, Chabanon, Grétry [the composer], the Englishmen Sherlock and Moore, the Prince of Brunswick, the Landgrave of Hesse, Mme Suard, the marquis de Villette—and so many others one could hardly count them all. It was a declaration of principles and a personal affront when the Count of Falkenstein, the future Joseph II, did not deign to detour for a stop-over at Ferney.

Several visitors have left us their impressions. They show us the tall, bony old man with alert and sparkling eyes, wrapped either in his Persian robe or, on important occasions, dressed in noble bronze-colored attire with a large wig and lace sleeves extending to his finger tips—neat, erect, lean, lively, and sober. He would take only a few cups of coffee with cream. And as he believed he was always on the verge of dying, he was forever consuming drugs and medicines. He would work part of the day in bed where he also received visitors. He was very much the *seigneur de village*, the village lord, jealous of his rights and honors, a proprietor and landowner with every fiber of his being. He was proud of his buildings, his plantations, his flocks, his church, and passionately concerned with finding markets for his manufactured products: watches and silk stockings. He behaved with royal graciousness towards friends and vassals who celebrated his birthdays with triumphal arches, fireworks, and unctuous verses of praise and flattery. He was always mad about theater, poetry, and wit—a delightful conversationalist of bewitching charm and gaiety. But he was capricious, whimsical, irritable, and despotic. He was generous to those who flattered him, stingy and quibbling with whoever rubbed him the wrong way. He would haggle over the sale of a hunting knife or go to court against *Président* de Brosses over a few cords of wood that he was furious to have to pay for in the end. He was a meddler and intriguer in the city affairs of Geneva. He took delight in ridiculing everybody. Always bitten and always biting, he was pursued by a pack of enemies that he increased without cause: Fréron, La Beaumelle, Chaumeix, the Pompignans, Nonnotte, Patouillet, Larcher, and Cogé. He was never in repose, always insistent upon having the last bark or the last bite. He was the diabolical tormentor of the unhappy Jean-Jacques Rousseau,[3] whom he would be ready to accept as a member of his household. At every chance he would claw and scratch the great Montesquieu, whom he had defended during his lifetime. Like a canine, he would sink his teeth into the calves of those he detested and then hold on for dear life! Sometimes he did the same to those whom he did not detest. But Voltaire was not always ferocious toward those on whom he heaped his deadly sarcasm. He was often mollified by a favor or a courtesy. He reached reconciliations with Trublet [a theologian] and Buffon [the naturalist]. He even bore no rancor towards friends and protégés who robbed and betrayed him, provided they were not arrogant about it. He feuded with his parish priest and his bishop, amusing himself by receiving communion from a notary just to scandalize the prelates. But basically he was not malicious, mean, or niggardly. He could be altogether obliging and bountiful, generous with his nieces and Marie Corneille, extending his hospitality, sheltering, aiding, defending, and patronizing I know not how many individuals.

He would reunite Champflour the son with Champflour the father or arrange transportation for little Pichon or see to it that a pregnant girl was provided with a husband. All this he would do with the same verve and dispatch he applied to more serious matters, to the Calas affair or the battle with Fréron, his critic and adversary. He was like a saucy Parisian street urchin and a spoiled child—all vanity, all nerves—harming no one by his follies so much as himself.[a]

From his little kingdom of Ferney he exchanged truths and barbs with Frederick; neither of them stood on ceremony with the other. He exchanged philosophical ideas and compliments with Catherine the Great, who succeeded in pulling the wool over his eyes on certain Polish affairs. He flirted with all manner of kings and princes. He carried on coquettishly with the French court, flattering la Pompadour as long as she lived without suspecting that he had once wounded her for life with a remark in his dedicatory preface to *Tancrède*. He exploited as much as he could his old and not too reliable friend marshal Richelieu as well as the ministers who dropped by. He lavished on them his flattery and adulation. There was "Babet the flower girl," as Cardinal Bernis was called; the duc de Choiseul [minister of foreign affairs]; the duc d'Aiguillon; Maupeou [the chancellor]; and finally Turgot,[4] the minister after his own heart—the only one he never praised without meaning every word of it. Voltaire asked them all not only for protection and favors for himself, for Ferney, and for the *philosophes*, but also for reforms, and he prevailed upon his friends to use their influence wherever possible, backing them in every effort they might make.

Such was the spectacle Voltaire produced, staged, and directed at *Les Délices* and Ferney for the entertainment of all Europe, a spectacle in which he, of course, played the leading role. His audience was fascinated by his performance. It could delight them or shock them, but it never failed to be entertaining. The show ran for twenty-three years and, miraculously, never grew stale. There was never a dull moment. It was always the latest topic of public conversation, the latest current event, whether

[a] Cf. Asse, *Lettres de Mme de Graffigny*, pp. 247–483, and *Bibl. nat.*, ms. 15 285, Voltaire's notebook, particularly p. 21.

serious or laughable, and it was always unpredictable. There were his Easter celebrations, his attacks of colic, *Tancrède* or *La Pucelle*, the adoption of Marie Corneille, a letter from Frederick of Prussia, or the dismissal or recall of Mme Denis. There were high-minded exertions on behalf of Calas or La Barre [victims of religious persecution], only to be followed by a withering barrage of wit and sarcasm leveled at La Beaumelle or Jean-Jacques Rousseau. It was either an exquisite display of common sense and concern for humanity or a deluge of pure rubbish and religious impieties. There was something new every day and never the same thing two days in a row. For twenty-three years Voltaire was the loudest bell ringer and the noisiest publicity seeker in all Europe.

There was no doubt about it. Gossip was music to his ears and popularity a necessity. He cared little that there were overtones of mockery in the laughter from the galleries. Voltaire lacked the moral armor, the hard shell of dignity that makes even the most vain and ambitious of men adopt a pose of decency and respectability. Renowned for his fine mind and his beneficence, Voltaire did not disdain an equal renown for contortions and grimaces. Yet in all his buffoonery and despite all his Harlequinades, he was possessed of an idea as tenacious as his ego. He wanted to improve the social order. From 1755 on, and especially after 1760 until his death in 1778, he wrote scarcely a page that was not a criticism of some abuse, a recommendation for a reform, or an appeal either to the government or the public on behalf of the latter or in opposition to the former. At 80 he was as angry as he had been at 60. A person would have to be very prejudiced not to perceive in Voltaire's inner being profound and unselfish convictions with respect to his fundamental attitudes.

He had returned from Germany at the moment when that most enlightened nation—France—was growing disenchanted with its king and court and impatient with its social ills. It was the country in which they were building a war machine known as the *Encyclopédie*.[5] Freethinkers, organized as a party, were about to man that machine. It was the country in which were drawn up, side by side, the old religious factions—Jansenists[6] and defenders of Catholic unity—and the newer breed of men dedicated to disseminating facts and ideas of all kinds and to improving the lot of the human race. These included philosophers, economists, and "patriots." It was the country in which every voice raised on behalf of reason and liberty was certain to produce prolonged echoes in all the states and provinces, the country where men who had the talent to express themselves were more and more carried away under the impact of the crowd who listened to them with ever-increasing applause and approval.

Conservative forces are powerful. Even more than the court, whose actions were sporadic and inconsistent, the Sorbonne and the *Parlement* of Paris opposed the movement of "reason." This opposition took the form of condemnations, one after the other. Among the works they banned were the abbé de Prades' thesis (1752) [which cast doubt on the credibility of Christian miracles]; *De l'Esprit* in 1738 [an ethical treatise by Helvétius which held that religion has failed as the basis of morality]; and Rousseau's *Emile* [a treatise on education] in 1762. They suppressed and suspended publication of the *Encyclopédie* in 1752 and in 1758. They condemned *Bélisaire* in 1767 [an historical romance by Marmontel which contained a chapter advocating freedom of opinion and toleration in religious matters]. Voltaire threw himself passionately into this mêlée. He was "the one who laughed at all frivolous stupidities and tried to rectify the ones that were cruel."[a] Disenchanted himself, he wanted to disillusion others, and he seethed with impatience at the thought that progress might take two or three hundred years to accomplish.[b] He fought, not at all heroically, but obstinately, trying to achieve the greatest possible results with a minimum of risk. He knew the terrain. He knew his enemy. And he proved himself a marvelous tactician.

He knew that no one could hope for privileges or tacit permissions for publication. Clandestine publication in France or abroad, especially in Geneva, removed the threat of censorship. But then one had all the dangers involved in contraband and the illegal movement of goods. Severe punishment threatened all authors, booksellers, and peddlers of books. And it was generally only the peddlers and retailers who were caught. These poor devils were thrown into prison, consigned to the galleys, and

[a] V. XLIII, p. 104.
[b] V. XXV, pp. 344, 318; V. XXVI, p. 95.

actually inflicted with the brand as criminals. If a writer were caught, he could usually get off with a humiliating retraction, but it would not be wise always to count on that strategy.

Voltaire would just disappear. If anonymity, pseudonyms, and disavowals of authorship were not enough to fend off French authorities, his location on the Swiss border enabled him to elude them. Legal actions were halted by denials and negations that fooled no one and greatly entertained the public at large. In order to immobilize his bitterest adversaries and to prevent the ever-threatening issuance of a *lettre de cachet,* and also to assure his pamphlets and brochures wider circulation, Voltaire cultivated his friends and contacts at court: Bernis and Choiseul, Richelieu, Villars, and La Vallière. He used them to restrain the zeal of their subordinates. He hardly needed Malesherbes, the supervisor of publishing houses and censors, but he tried to remain on good terms with police lieutenants, provincial administrators, and postal authorities. The countersignature of Damilaville, a revenue tax official. for years kept all Ferney correspondence away from the prying eyes of postal inspectors. Voltaire had as accomplices the public in general, all travelers returning from abroad, ambassadors and their retinues, and officers arriving in Paris with their bags full of Voltairian *rogatons,*[a] odds and ends of miscellaneous writings. This was before the man named Huguet and the woman known as Léger were entrusted with the surreptitious distribution of his writings.

As long as the public was on his side, Voltaire could be sure of outwitting all the powers spiritual and temporal. And he knew how to handle his public. It was an intelligent but fickle audience, curious and blasé, easily offended and easily amused. Its tastes were limited and refined. It would not concentrate long on any subject and had to be constantly courted and titillated. For twenty-three years Voltaire served his public a ragoût concocted of wit, satire, badinage, and saucy impudence, the spices with which he seasoned his ideas in order to make them palatable.

Above all, he was clear, concise, and to the point: No more great works, no more long volumes; instead, little brochures and pamphlets of no more than a few pages. Thinking of the huge

[a] *Ann. J.-J. Rouseau,* V. I, p. 129.

Encyclopédie, he remarked: "Never will twenty folio volumes bring about a revolution. Little books are the ones to fear, the pocket-size, portable ones that sell for thirty sous. If the Gospels had cost 1200 sesterces, the Christian religion could never have been established."[a] And so for twenty-three years Voltaire turned out at his Ferney factory all those "little *pâtés,*" those miscellaneous bits of writing, portable, easily concealed, easily digested, and always provocative. They came in all styles and varieties, on every conceivable subject: verse, prose, dictionaries, short stories, tragedies, diatribes; articles on history, literature, metaphysics, promissory notes underwritten by a gentleman, etc., etc. The truth is that no matter how dearly Voltaire cherished poetry and *belles-lettres,* from now on they became merely a means to an end. Tragedy and verses only served for the propagation of his ideas— the propaganda of the *philosophe.*[7]

He repeated and rehashed his material. He knew it, and he went at it again. For the public to become conscious of an idea, the idea must be repeated over and over. But the sauce must be varied to please the public palate. Voltaire was a master chef, a superb *saucier.* He had all the good qualities of a journalist as well as the corresponding vices. Above all, he had a flair for anything newsworthy. He had a voice that was heard, that could fix and hold public attention amid the confused clamors of the day. It is not enough to call Voltaire a journalist. He was a newspaper in his own right and a great one. He tackled anything and everything—serious articles, news reporting, the echoes of others, jokes and puns, and miscellaneous items. He kneaded and mixed all these ingredients into his *hors d'oeuvre variés,* his informal writings. He was not only a daily paper but also a magazine and an encyclopedia. All the functions of a popularizer, a propagandist, a polemicist, and a straight reporter were combined in him and practiced by his skilled hands. This lively old man was a public press and a public library at one and the same time.

Finally, he had an innumerable list of correspondents representing every station in life and almost every country on earth. He corresponded with Frederick of Prussia, the Empress Catherine, German princes, Russian and Italian gentlemen, English

[a] April 5, 1765.

thinkers, ministers of state, courtiers, people in the provinces, magistrates, actors, abbés, men of letters, administrators, businessmen, lawyers, and society women. And his epistolary art was exquisite. Virtually every letter contained a compliment to flatter the recipient's vanity, a bit of humor to delight and amuse, and finally a serious thought for the reader's reflection. With his thousands of letters, Voltaire aroused an interest in the success of his propaganda among countless individuals. He made his readers the willing disciples and disseminators of his ideas and did so without involving them in legal risks. Thus he increased the effect of his brochures and pamphlets twofold with the weight and power of his prodigious correspondence.

8

Voltaire's Art: Tales, Dialogues, and Miscellaneous Writings[a]

THOSE LITTLE, inexpensive, portable books with which Voltaire blanketed the public, in the hope of changing society, appeared in a vast assortment of styles and forms. Let us set aside his histories and poetical works. In the multitude that remain we find writings in which any pretense at literary art or invention had all but disappeared. There were dissertations, treatises, diatribes, newspaper articles, collections of plays, editions of texts, excerpts, and commentaries. Criticism and propaganda were their sole aim and intent, presented with no other disguises than the ironies and insinuations imposed by Voltairian humor and by the absence in France of a free press. The most important writings in this category took the handy form of a dictionary. There was the *Dictionnaire philosophique portatif* ("The Portable Philosophical Dictionary"), conceived during a supper at Potsdam and published in 1764, a small octavo volume with 73 articles in which Voltairianism was condensed into a light and nourishing consommé. There were the *Questions sur l'Encyclopédie*, nine volumes printed from 1770 to 1772, providing in 378 articles a vigorous reinforcement for the too often timid tomes of Diderot.[1]

"The most useful books," said Voltaire, "are those in which the reader does half the work himself. He develops the author's

[a] G. Lanson, *l'Art de la prose*, 1909, octavo.

thoughts if given the germ of an idea." Here are a few of the "germs" Voltaire planted, hoping they would take root and grow.[a]

Politics in all ages have retained the abuses that justice has always condemned.

It is not enough that a thing should be possible in order to be believed.

In general, the art of government consists in taking the greatest amount of money possible from a large portion of the citizenry to hand it over to another portion.

History is nothing more than the record of those who have availed themselves of the property of others.

Faith consists in believing what our reason cannot believe.

If a clergyman leads a scandalous life, he is asked: "Is it possible that you can dishonor the dignity of the clergy?" A judge is reminded that "he has the honor of being the king's counselor" and that "he must set an example." A soldier is told, by way of encouragement: "Remember that you belong to the regiment of Champagne." People ought rather to be saying to each other: "Remember your dignity as a human being."

A hanged man is useless.

The true charter of freedom is independence maintained by force. It is at the point of a sword that treaties are signed which guarantee this natural freedom.

Oh, philosopher! Experiments in physics, accurately recorded, together with the arts and crafts—these are the substance of true philosophy.[b]

It was just such brief, incisive remarks in the midst of factual data, anecdotes, jokes, and downright trash, that *impressed* themselves on the reader's rational mind. They stuck there. They gave him a basis for judgment, a principle of action. They threw a certain light on society. And they entered the reader's consciousness, one after the other, easily and effortlessly. It was not a philosophical system to be laboriously assimilated. It was a spirit, a state of mind that, little by little, penetrated and eventually dominated the reader's thoughts and attitudes.

In another department of the Voltairian factory for small, portable books we find ideas clothed with artistry and literary invention. These were his tales or short stories (*contes*), his dialogues, and his whimsical buffooneries (*facéties*). In these light

[a] V. XVII, p. 2. [Moland ed.]
[b] V. XVII, pp. 47, 253, 358, 417; V. XIX, p. 475; V. XX, pp. 54, 456, 553, 599.

and free prose forms, independent of literary rules, Voltaire revealed himself (more fully than in any of his poetic works) as a great, powerful, and original artist. And this sort of writing preoccupied him from the age of 60 until his death at 84. He gathered and sifted all the traditions and formulas for the various kinds of tales and short stories: philosophical, social, satirical, allegorical, oriental, and fairy tales, in French and in English. He was familiar with *Télémaque* ["Telemachus," the didactic tale by Fénelon] and *Gil Blas* [Lesage's picaresque romance], *Angola* and *Le Sopha* [satirical tales by Crébillon, the younger], *Les Mille et une nuits* ["The Thousand and One Nights," a French translation of "The Arabian Nights"], and analogous works. He was familiar with Hamilton[2] and Duclos[3] and the *Lettres Persanes* [Montesquieu's "Persian Letters"], the essays in *The Spectator* [Addison and Steele], *The Tale of a Tub* [Swift's religious satire] and *Gulliver's Travels* [Swift]. All sorts of artistic forms and elements were combined and concentrated in his short stories, to which he imparted a personal stamp of his own. *Zadig* was compounded of folklore materials reaching him from the most diverse sources: Ariosto and Boccaccio, Thomas Parnell, and Arabian, Persian, and Chinese tales. In *Micromégas* there are influences of Cyrano de Bergerac,[4] Swift, and more especially, Fontenelle.[5]

Voltaire's favorite technique was to write a travelogue combined with a biography. He recounted the story of a person's life as he trotted that life around the world. There were always countless episodes: abductions, pursuits, recognitions, enchantments, imaginary geography, travels through the lands of Asia, America, and Europe—fairies, genies, fanciful creatures, and talismans. He moved his action from antiquity to modern times, passing in review all civilizations and conditions of men. There were current events and fictitious events. His tone was mocking, bantering, and impertinent; his style was epigrammatic, brightened with buffooneries and racy commentary. The chapters were short and the titles piquant, whetting the reader's appetite and curiosity. His was a unique and savory mixture. At times he scattered his satire like buckshot, firing at all enemies, beliefs, and personalities encountered on the flexible trail of his fancy. So it was in *Zadig, Scarmentado, L'Ingénu,* and *La Princesse de Baby-*

lone. At other times he followed a predetermined plan with the intent of demonstrating or refuting a given idea. Such were *Micromégas, Candide,* and *L'Histoire de Jenni*. At such times the whole novel became a missile trained on its target, on the idea pin-pointed by its author. His imagination and invention, always controlled and disciplined, revealed only those characters, actions, and events that supported his thesis.

Candide is the model of this art. Voltaire enlarged the scope of his earlier *Scarmentado* and poured into it all his knowledge about life and history, from the days and memories of his travels in Westphalia to his present-day gardening at *Les Délices*—from his philosophical quarrels with Martin Kahle, a disciple of Wolf, to his extensive researches for the *Essai sur les moeurs*. He used it to demolish the idea of Providence when Jean-Jacques Rousseau[6] had dared come to the defense of the Providential view by addressing Voltaire a letter on the subject, after the latter had published his *Poème* on the disaster [the Lisbon earthquake: Nov. 1, 1755]. Voltaire's aim was to demolish optimism. The philosophy of optimism was therefore presented in its most ludicrous form, in the absurdity and the jargon of German metaphysics. He would single out Leibnitz[7] and not Pope, to whom Voltaire's thoughts naturally turned.[a] But artistic reasons ruled out the Englishman. He was too clear and too sensible.

Facts are the only things that prove anything. Consequently, the hero was to be either the victim or the witness of all the evils that afflict mankind: the evils of social institutions, the evils of human passions, and the evils of nature. There would be wars and autos-da-fé, rape and larceny, disease and earthquakes. Candide was to go from Europe to America to learn about wealth and poverty, to hear the cries of kings, monks, and women. Everyone was unhappy. Everyone was complaining. There was only one happy land (and it did not exist): the land of Eldorado.

Everyone was unhappy, but no one committed suicide. Then isn't life evil? No, since people put up with it. Life is mediocre and tolerable. There are a few good people and some good deeds in this world, some evidence of humanity, honesty, and even a little happiness, or at least a bit of sweetness and repose. But they

[a] V. XXXVIII, pp. 512, 513. (Besterman, 5939, 5941) (R.P.)

are rare and widely scattered in the unending procession of misery, wretchedness, and vice. Yet they are enough to block the road to pessimism without raising the flag of optimism. All philosophical and theological systems are false. There is no reason either for a benediction or for total despair. Life is not good, but it can be improved. How? By work, but by social work, by an effort in common in which each one will find his proper place. Reasoning about metaphysics is useless. Practical action must replace idle speculation. *Il faut cultiver notre jardin*: "We must cultivate our garden."

That is the reasonable, courageous, and clear conclusion for which Voltaire prepared his reader throughout the entire tale, a conclusion high-lighted by the final episodes: the encounter with the good Turk, the final reunion of the principal characters in their little farm on the shores of the Bosphorus, where even the monk becomes a useful member of the community. *Candide* is neither desolating nor desolate. Nor is it purely negative and critical. It is the principal parable of Voltairian philosophy, all of which tends toward greater human betterment and well being.

Not a single chapter, episode, or sketch fails to expose the snares and delusions of optimism and, as the dénouement approaches, the utility of social action. The facts are set forth so clearly that they themselves produce the ideas they symbolize. Their power of demonstration is in direct ratio to their picturesque or amusing clarity. It is a commonplace to say that one finds no evidence of psychology in Voltaire. That is true, if by psychology one means the inventiveness of Racine or Marivaux. Voltaire, like Lesage, was more the moralist than the psychologist. He used ready-made psychology to produce rather simple-minded characters composed of ordinary feelings or else driven by some intense mania required by the author's intent.

He was more the artist than the psychologist, and that is precisely where he enriched psychology. He did not analyze his characters; he drew silhouettes, cartoons. Each of his puppets in pursuit of happiness is caught in its most expressive attitude, revealing the mainspring of its action. Each has the standard mark and accent of his state or nation. Their names reveal their origins: the marquise de Parolignac; Vanderdendur, the Baron of Thunder-ten-tronckh, don Fernando d'Ibaraa y Figueroa y

Mascarenes y Lampourdo y Souza, etc. All of Voltaire's ideas about society and its component parts, his ideas about government, religion, and the manners and mores of different countries are etched into the many sketches and episodes that fill his short stories. They determine the choice of action and dialogue to reflect his characters. He gives a distinguishing trait to the Englishman, the Italian, the German, the Frenchman, and the Turk, as he does to the Anabaptist, the Calvinist, the Jesuit, and the Capuchin friar, as he does also to the military officer or the businessman. Ethnic psychology and the psychological attitudes of professional men were closely observed by Voltaire and given sharp delineation.

The action, like the characters, is not presented in general or abstract forms. Both are associated with particular places. We learn the menus of Candide's meals in every country of the Old World and the New. We learn about bread with beer in Holland, ham and chocolate in Paraguay, macaroni in Italy, the partridges of Lombardy, sturgeon eggs served with Montepulciano and Lacryma-Christi. In Turkey we are told about sherbet, *kaimak* (Turkish cream spiced with preserved citron peel), oranges, lemons, limes, pineapples, dates, pistachios, and Mocha coffee, not to mention the parrots and roast monkeys they sampled in Eldorado.

Voltaire's curious figures all pay their bills in the tender of the realm, in *écus, louis, sequins, piastres, maravedis, pistoles, moyadors,* and pounds sterling. In Spain their carriage is drawn by mules harnessed with ropes; in England they drive about in a poste-chaise; they go from Paris to Versailles in a *pot de chambre* ["a chamber pot"—so called because it was disagreeable]. The characteristics of a country are quickly indicated: the feudal patchwork of Germany and the hot, desolate Roman Campagna.

But Voltaire's picturesque realism was only a transposition of the senses into his art. His intention was to establish clear, precise ideas. The visual was merely handmaiden to the philosophical thought inspiring the work and, for that reason, remained profoundly symbolical. All such little details and circumstances served to sketch the thing itself, and, with it, the judgment of one's "reason" as applied to the idea in question. These casual sketches were caricatures. Pity itself, as well as indignation, was translated into sarcasm and buffoonery. The worldly art of presenting the ridiculous and the absurd was enlisted in the cause of philosophy. All man's miseries and those of society were arraigned before the court of human intelligence and made to appear as stupidities. That was deemed the best device, the surest technique for inciting clear thinkers to revolt against the causes of social suffering. Voltaire's novels were like mathematical demonstrations of progress by the use of the *reductio ad absurdum*.

The *dialogue* and *la facétie* (the broad jest) appeared in Voltaire's writings around 1750. It was in June 1751 that he discussed the merits of Fontenelle and Lucian. He wanted the dialogue to be simple, believable, and useful.[a] He brought back the dead to converse with the living: Cicero's daughter Tullia appears to Mme de Pompadour in her dressing room. He arranged conversations between people of every state and nation, even animals on one occasion—the hen and the capon.

The *facétie* was a monologue, letter, or dialogue, or else a series of monologues, letters, or dialogues, presented in a form of fictional whimsy or broad farce. Literary criticism, caricature, and social satire had created a vogue for these free-form writings. Following Saint-Hyacinthe, Desfontaines, La Mettrie, and others, Montesquieu[8] had dignified this kind of writing with his *Très humble remontrance d'une jeune juive de dix-huit ans aux inquisiteurs d'Espagne et de Portugal* ("A Very Humble Protest from a Young, Eighteen-Year-Old Jewess to the Inquisitors of Spain and Portugal"). Addison and Swift had been masters at this sort of humorous invention, and Voltaire had read them well. About 1759 he began once more to enjoy Rabelais, whom he had previously regarded with a certain disdain.[b] But he remained original. This part of his literary output resembles no one but Voltaire.

With inexhaustible zest and gaiety, with an astonishingly youthful imagination, he turned out those countless miscellaneous writings (*rogatons*) and those "little *pâtés*" which even the most jaded and fickle appetites found tasty and digestible. There were

---

[a] V. XXXVII, p. 284. (Besterman, 3907) (R.P.)
[b] V. XXII, p. 174, V. VIII, p. 577; V. XXVI, pp. 469, 491; V. XL, pp. 192, 350. (Besterman, 7806, 8108) (R.P.)

letters, speeches, sermons, pleas, resolutions, demands, briefs, newspaper clippings, reports, biographies, and anecdotes. Sometimes everything was mixed together in a peculiar fashion, as in his *Questions sur les miracles* or his *Pot Pourri* ("Miscellanies"). At times all Voltaire's fantasy was summed up in a provocative title. For the title was a matter of capital importance. It had to arouse the reader's curiosity and attract his attention. For example:

A Plea for Genest Ramponeau, Tavern-Keeper at La Courtille, Directed against Gaudon, Manager of a Theater of the Boulevards.

The Canonization of Saint Cucufin, Ascoli's Brother, and His Appearance to Sire Aveline, a Townsman of Troyes, Revealed by Sire Aveline Himself, in Troyes, at the Home of M. and Mme Oudot.

There is nothing more delightful from Voltaire's pen than items of this sort, exquisite bagatelles. They are a unique blend of reason and folly, of unbridled fancy and shrewdly expressed truths. The mask was worn or dropped with ease. Here his art was free and spontaneous, untrammeled by any literary rules. There remained only his sense of propriety, which kept his mockery, impudence, and even scurrilous writings within the confines of good taste and the tone of conviviality, the conviviality of 1760. His writing was lively and often brassy, but never slovenly; it was always elegant.

In his dialogues and broad humor, Voltaire's technique was to filter and simplify questions, reducing them to a few luminous facts, a few decisive formulas. Any difficulty or objection he encountered was vaporized into thin air and transformed into scathing ridicule. He excelled in finding the short phrase which could refute an argument while enunciating a truth, and he would make that phrase drop ingenuously from the lips of the very person whose pretentions were thereby destroyed or unmasked. For example:

We would be the masters if it weren't for those impudent men of wit. All these reasoning people are the downfall of a nation.[a]

We like to preach because people pay rent for their pews.[b]

[a] V. XXIII, pp. 272, 273.
[b] V. XXX, p. 451.

I would have fought that fellow if I felt I were stronger than he.[a]

There is nothing more proper than loving one's cousin. One can also love his niece. But it costs 18,000 pounds, payable to Rome, to marry one's cousin and 80,000 francs to sleep with one's niece in holy wedlock.[b]

In his short dialogues like *Le Plaideur et l'Avocat* ("The Litigant and the Lawyer") and *Les Anciens et les Modernes* ("The Ancients and the Moderns"), every word counts and every sentence drives its point home. In his longer conversations, such as *L'Intendant des Menus en exercice avec l'abbé Grizel* ("The Supervisor of Menus on Duty with the Abbé Grizel"), dealing with the practice of excommunicating actors, Voltaire's style is freer and seemingly more whimsical. From a description of Louis XIV's dancing and Maria Theresa's singing, he passes on to such subjects as the burials of Molière and the actress Lecouvreur, to magicians, to denunciations of financiers in the New Testament, to Church history and the excommunication of kings, to the intolerance of Jansenist fanatics, to the preponderance of civil power, and to contradictions in the manners and morals of *les Welches*[9] [Frenchmen]. He describes all their stupidities and maintains that their only real superiority among nations is their gift for theater, their dramatic art. He concludes by criticizing the president of the French bar association for having burned a memorandum submitted by members of the theatrical profession.

This kind of writing suggests a chapter from Montaigne. But with Voltaire the digressions all serve to shed further light on his subject, tying the particular question to larger, overriding issues, indicating their historical origins and putting the specific question into perspective with general social attitudes and mores. Everything was sprinkled with salt and pepper, with epigrams, jests, and current events. However, the interlocutors in his dialogues were always controlled and held back by the dominant idea, the thesis that each character incarnated. The actors in his *facéties,* those least formal of all his writings, were livelier, more vivid, and richer in reality. Voltaire imitated all accents, spoke English or Latin, sketched all nations and peoples. Here there was more verve and excitement. The color and atmosphere were

[a] V. XXIX, p. 369.
[b] V. XXV, p. 273.

always refined but warmer and more pervasive than in his novels. *Les Questions sur les miracles* were an album of Genevan caricatures. And here is a bit of Paris in the eighteenth century:

Brother Triboulet, of the Order of Brother Montepulciano, of Brother Jacques Clément, of Brother Ridicous, etc., etc., etc., and moreover, a Doctor of the Sorbonne, who had been designated to write a report of censure on behalf of the king's eldest daughter [the Church], known as the perpetual council of the Gauls, against *Bélisaire* [a novel by Marmontel], was returning to his monastery in a pensive frame of mind. He encountered in the rue des Maçons little Fanchon, his pupil, the daughter of the tavern-keeper who has the honor of providing wine for the *prima mensis* [the monthly meeting of the theological faculty]. Fanchon's father is a bit of a theologian himself, as are all the tavern-keepers in the vicinity of the Sorbonne. Now Fanchon was a winsome lass, and Brother Triboulet entered the inn . . . to . . . to have a little drink.

When Triboulet had drunk his fill, he began to thumb through the books of an habitué of the parish, the tavern-keeper's brother, a curious man who possessed a rather well-stocked library.

He consulted all those passages proving beyond any shadow of a doubt that all who had not lived in the vicinity of the Sorbonne as, for example, Chinese, Indians, Scythians, Greeks, Romans, Germans, Africans, Americans, whites, blacks, redskins, kinky heads, hairy heads, bearded chins, beardless chins . . . all were damned without mercy, as is just and proper, and that only some atrocious and abominable soul could ever imagine that God might take pity on any of these good people.

Brother Triboulet was compiling, compiling, and compiling, although it is no longer fashionable to compile; and Fanchon, from time to time, was patting his fat cheeks, and Brother Triboulet was writing, and Fanchon was singing. Suddenly they heard in the street the voices of Doctor Tamponet and Brother Bonhomme, a wealthy Franciscan, who were arguing vehemently with one another and attracting a crowd of passers-by. Fanchon put her head out the window. She was well known to these two Doctors, and they, too, went in . . . to . . . to have a little drink.[a]

The alert and lively movement, like a bird merrily hopping along, is a joy to the ear. At times we can even detect a definite musical pattern, nothing resembling a formal poetic and oratorical rhythm, but rather a musical fantasy, a tone poem marked

[a] *Pièces relatives à Bélisaire,* Amsterdam (1767), p. 9. (Moland XXVI, 169).

by repeated passages and parallel phrases. The tale of *Jeannot et Colin* is well known. The introduction is built entirely around the ever-recurring names of Jeannot and Colin. Replace the proper nouns by pronouns, and the effect is completely lost. Nothing remains. Here is a less well-known example:

It was on the 12th of October, 1759, that Brother Berthier went, to his misfortune, from Paris to Versailles with Brother Coutu, his usual traveling companion. Berthier had put in the coach a few copies of the *Journal de Trévoux,*[10] to present them to his patrons and protectors, such as the chamber maid of Madame the Wet Nurse, and an officer of the king's kitchen, and one of the royal apothecary apprentices, and several other lords who place a high premium on talent.

En route, Berthier suffered a few spells of nausea. His head grew heavy. He was overcome with frequent yawns. "I don't know what's the matter with me," he said to Coutu. "I've never yawned so much." "My reverend Father," answered Brother Coutu, "it's the same thing with me." "How's that? What do you mean 'the same thing with you'?" said Brother Berthier. "I mean that I, too, am yawning, and I don't know why because I haven't read anything all day long, and you haven't said a word to me since we started out together." Brother Coutu, on uttering these words, yawned more than ever. Berthier replied with a yawning that refused to stop. The coachman turned around and, seeing them yawn thus, started to yawn himself. The malady overtook all the passengers, and in all the houses 'round about everyone present was yawning—so great at times is the effect on men caused by the mere presence of a scholar.

Meanwhile, a bit of cold sweat came over Berthier. "I don't know what's wrong with me," said he, "but I feel a chill." "I can well imagine," said brother companion. "How's that? 'You can well imagine'?" said Berthier. "What do you mean by that?" "I mean that I, too, am freezing," said Coutu. "I'm falling asleep," said Berthier. "I'm not surprised," said the other. "Why so?" said Berthier. "Why, because, I, too, am falling asleep," said his companion. And they were both seized with a soporific and lethargic affliction. It was in this condition that they reached Versailles and stopped at the carriage gate.[a]

Voltaire's art consists in these finely wrought parallelisms. It would be a mistake to credit him only with *esprit,* wit, in the French sense of the word—a play on unforeseen relationships

[a] V. XXIV, p. 95.

between ideas. He also had *humor,* that *esprit* of the imagination which plays on the forms and distortions of reality. He also had a sort of musical *esprit* which delights the ear with its capricious interweaving of sounds.

But there was in Voltaire something superior still to his tales, dialogues, and buffoonery: his correspondence. Voltaire's correspondence brought together and united within itself all the rest of his work, all his biography, all his character, all aspects of his temperament, all his literary ideas, all his historical and philosophical curiosities, and all his humanitarian aspirations. In his letters he comes to life for us with a charming and saucy ingenuousness, parading his eccentricities and pretentions, but also his intelligence and generosity. No visitor to Cirey or Ferney has given us such a talkative Voltaire as the one he portrays in his own letters. And their artistic value is incomparable. They reveal all Voltaire's wit and taste in their most exquisite form. His classicism disappears. It becomes attenuated and lightened. There is no more pomp or cold solemnity. The only *noblesse* which the classicist never abandoned was his easy nobility of manners, an elegant grace and refinement of expression. Literary artifices and conventions have vanished. Of all the rules and proprieties of his time there remained only those that had become an inseparable part of his own nature. Voltaire's correspondence attained that perfection of the natural which Condillac defined as "art converted to a habit."

All the humors, passions, animosities, rancors, enthusiasms, and affections of the man burst open and bubbled up in his letters. But they were poured into molds prepared for them by the writer's taste and culture. Everywhere we encounter the fine, sensitive man of letters that Voltaire always was. Yet everything is alive, fast, light, and measured. His letters are never ponderous, labored, or contrived. Everything flows as from a spring, with sparkling clarity and sheer delight. Nature and civilized culture were fused into the most harmonious blend possible. And that is why the least contested and most widely read masterpiece of Voltaire today is his correspondence. And it is only by chance that readers of his own time were granted this enjoyable experience.

9

The Philosophy of Ferney

THE STATEMENT has often been made and repeated that
Voltaire's work was entirely negative. This is a very superficial
view and highly inaccurate. Undoubtedly, he criticized a great deal
and demolished many things. That fact is obvious. But Voltaire
aroused feelings in men's minds and formed convictions of a very
positive nature. He wanted to give men ideas that could be
translated into terms of human betterment and well being.

All social abuses had their historic bases and sanctions. A reexamination was in order. Error and evil had, as their justifica-
tions, interpretations of human development that had to be
replaced. Voltairian philosophy could not get along without historical support. The *Essai sur les moeurs* had given him this
historical basis for modern times. It was enlarged and completed
by various writings that shed philosophical light on the entire
field of past history.

1. Historical Criticism and Religious Criticism[a]

The conventional historical works that Voltaire composed
after 1756 are negligible for the purposes of our brief study. It

---

[a] *Des mensonges imprimés,* 1749. *Philosophie de l'histoire,* 1765. *La défense de
mon oncle,* 1767. *Examen important de Milord Bolingbroke,* 1767. *Le Pyrrho-
nisme de l'histoire,* 1768. *Fragments historiques sur l'Inde,* 1773. *La Bible
enfin expliquée,* 1776. *Un Chrétien contre six Juifs,* 1776. *Dictionnaire philosophique,* art. *Antiquité, Antiquité des Usages, Chronologie, Histoire, Incer-
titude de l'Histoire, Vérité,* etc. Dom Calmet, *Dictionnaire de la Bible,* 1722;
Histoire de l'ancien testament, 1737. Larcher, *Supplément à la philosophie de
l'histoire,* 1767; *Réponse à la Défense de mon oncle,* 1767. Guénée, *Lettres de
quelques Juifs portugais,* 1769.

Voltaire By Jean-Antoine Houdon
(1778)
Victoria and Albert Museum (London)

was not with them, but with his numerous pamphlets, that Voltaire developed an entirely new intellectual attitude and approach to the study of history. There was no period of history he failed to criticize nor any problem that he backed away from.

He had an astonishing degree of self-assurance. He would juggle with facts and texts. One could draw up an inexhaustible list of his flippancies, errors, inaccuracies, and fantasies. He had none of the careful methods and scrupulous severity of today's scholars. He worked too quickly. He formed snap judgments. He would pontificate on subjects in which his competence was questionable. He was consumed with prejudices and passions. He was an amateur and a journalist. But Voltaire had an inquiring mind, a desire for truth, an intuition for the problems that required attention, and a critical sense and awareness of the task that confronted him. He sometimes perceived what professional scholars were incapable of seeing or else preferred to ignore.

We smile today at his reflections on China and India. But he had consulted officials of the East India Company, Holwell and Dow, (as well as the French scholar, Le Gentil), for information on India. He made their assertions his own. What is more regrettable was his belief, shared by others, in the authenticity of the *Ezour Veidam* [a spurious Veda], which the Chevalier de Maudave had brought back from India. He was fired with enthusiasm for the wisdom and antiquity of the Chinese as described in the Jesuit accounts of Fathers Lecomte, du Halde, and Gaubil. Isaac Vossius, the English scholars of the *Histoire Universelle,* and De Guignes were no more dispassionate than Voltaire.

But whereas the majority of the scholars and popularizers were attempting to reconcile the annals of Indian and Chinese history with those of Holy Scripture, Voltaire took delight in their chronological contradictions and welcomed with glee all facts and figures increasing the antiquity of Far Eastern cultures and civilizations. Above and beyond his errors, Voltaire perceived, and was making his public perceive, a very significant fact: the existence of mankind and of powerful human societies that antedated the Bible and were outside the Biblical plan. He freed men's minds not only of religious prejudice, but also of the western prejudice that limited the search for civilization to those peoples who had received the dual heritage of the Judaeo-Christian and Graeco-Roman traditions.

His entire effort was directed toward breaking down the historical frames of reference that had satisfied everyone up to that time. He went at it with a bold spirit of adventure and was occasionally a bit scatter-brained. He had dealings with men of erudition, a prudent and meticulous breed who resent incursions by the layman into their private domains. For fifteen years he carried on a polite controversy with Foncemagne over *Le Testament du cardinal de Richelieu* ("The Last Will and Testament of Cardinal Richelieu"). Voltaire was the loser since he did not succeed in proving his thesis, namely, the falsity of the document in question. But what is not sufficiently recognized is that Voltaire's effort was not a loss, but a gain, for science. Before his inquiry, the *Testament de Richelieu* was presented to the public under dubious and deplorable conditions, among the highly apocryphal wills and testaments of Colbert and Louvois, with no kind of guarantee whatsoever. Voltaire established the rule that the editor of a posthumous work must "render a strict account of the origin and history of the manuscript." This rule astonished the scholars of his day. "The law is a new one," said the learned Ménard. Foncemagne won his controversy with Voltaire only because he satisfied the latter's requirements and curiosity. Thanks again to Voltaire, an affirmation of a will's authenticity changed its meaning. In order to resolve certain objections, Foncemagne was obliged to establish the fact that the cardinal had worked with collaborators and that the text was not entirely in the cardinal's own handwriting. In other words, Voltaire's doubts brought about a scientific approach to resolving the question of the *Testament de Richelieu*.

With Larcher it was a livelier skirmish and lacking in courtesy on both sides. Voltaire ridiculed him mercilessly, but Larcher had begun by calling Voltaire a "Capaneus"[1] and "a ferocious beast." He always added the harshest epithets to whatever corrections he made. There is no doubt that, in the matter of detecting errors in detail, Larcher was often right. It is sufficient to compare the second edition of *La Philosophie de l'Histoire* with the first in order to find proof of this in all the corrections Voltaire made. Errors in geography, grammatical slips (a certain

"Basiloi"[2]), inaccurate translations, the misuse of source materials: the precise scholar ferreted out all the mistakes that the brilliant man of letters, disdainful of verifications, had piled up pell mell. But once Larcher had done his little job of tidying things up, of rectifying these minor errors, his triumph came to an end. He was often wrong about the heart of the matter. He quibbled. He split hairs. He made extensive use of quotations that proved nothing. He was narrowly and childishly conservative and totally lacking in critical objectivity. He set himself up as the defender of religion and tolerated no skepticism in either sacred or secular history. For him, a Sarah at over seventy years of age inspiring love in an Egyptian king was an incontrovertible fact of history. He confirmed the authority of Scripture by a story of Ninon de Lenclos,[3] who at the same age, he believed, bestowed her favors on an admirer.

In his entire criticism there was only one important point where he had a definite advantage: that was on the question of sacred prostitution in Babylon. Here Larcher was right, displaying common sense as much as erudition, and the irony of it was that he defeated Voltaire tacitly using Voltaire's own weapon, a Voltairian principle that the philosopher had overlooked out of gallantry for the women of Babylon. "As soon as superstition has sanctioned a custom," said Larcher, "people no longer find anything repugnant in it, or at least they sacrifice their aversions and even find in it some new merit."[a]

Voltaire had made all Europe laugh at Larcher, but the abbé Guénée once gave pious individuals the consolation of laughing at Voltaire's expense in his *Lettres de quelques Juifs de Lisbonne* ("Letters from Several Jews in Lisbon"). Less erudite than Larcher, but sufficiently well informed to collect all Voltaire's "boners," the abbé Guénée possessed wit, sophistry, and a sharp tongue. Voltaire found him "mean as a monkey" and put up a poor defense. Guénée took the same view of controversy as Larcher. His victories were in the minutiae of erudition. But he was more of a lawyer than a philologist. He denied the most obvious contradictions in the Bible. He offered as authority,

---

[a] p. 88. Compare Voltaire, V. XXV, p. 120. "Men never feel remorse about things they are in the habit of doing." Cf. also V. XXIII, p. 440. [Moland ed.]

depending on the needs of his theses, either the Vulgate or the Hebrew text. To defend the story of the Golden Calf he made Moses into a remarkable chemist, one who had achieved the alchemist's dream of converting dross into pure gold and "the elixir of life." He was obstinate in arguing the most untenable thesis on the authenticity of the Pentateuch. With unabashed audacity he offered the most atrocious propositions in defense of Biblical massacres.

Neither Larcher nor Guénée had any general ideas or method. They fought over details. They were silent or vague on the great questions perplexing Voltaire. What is the Bible? How was it formed? Who wrote its constituent books and when? What were the relative value and authority of the various editions in the different languages? These erudite scholars had no desire to know anything about such matters, which were to become the concern of nineteenth-century historians. Voltaire, with his militant self-assurance, was closer to Harnack[4] or Loisy[5] than either Larcher or Guénée with all their meticulous precision.

Voltaire's virtue, not yet common at that time, was to have understood that there is no history, above all no ancient history, without criticism: criticism of the evidence, criticism of documents, and discussions as to the dates and authenticity of texts. He posed questions and entertained doubts that Montesquieu himself, more thoroughly educated than Voltaire, had not perceived. He had ideas on the nature of historical knowledge, on the degrees of certainty, and on the techniques for establishing historical truths. He drew distinctions between the age of *fable,* the *heroic* age, and actual *historical times:* "History was born very late." He wanted historians to seek out the source materials. He knew how quickly oral traditions become altered. He distrusted historians who were not contemporary with the events they described, and even with the contemporaries thereof, he was suspicious of their credulity, self-interest, and passions. He tried to evaluate the truth in Herodotus: "Nearly everything he reports, relying on faith in strangers, is mere fable; but everything he himself saw is true." He tried to discern the sources of Tacitus —Fabius Rusticus and Cluvius—and he was skeptical of being led astray by Tacitus' malevolence and style.

The farther one goes back into antiquity, the fewer certainties there are. One must search patiently for reliable indices.

An established etymology sometimes serves to prove the emigrations of peoples.

I regard an alphabet as an incontestable monument to the country from which a given nation acquired its first elements of knowledge.

In the dubious incoherence of traditions and theories, we must take as criteria plausibility and possibility. Whatever is rejected by the laws of physics, by reason, or by the nature of the human heart is unacceptable and must be rejected.[a] Now this is a vague and dangerous rule, too easily abused by passion and prejudice. Only physical impossibility is a reliable criterion. And even here we must remember that scientific development is constantly expanding the limits of what is physically possible. As for reason, we must regard it only as the principle of contradiction. Voltaire did not make such reservations, and more than once his rule misled him.

For their time, however, these rules marked a great step forward. They were new, at least for the general public. Voltaire gave the public an education in criticism, training it to demand proofs from its historians, to withhold credence whenever historians made traditional affirmations of fact contrary to the laws of nature, of reason, and of one's conscience. But with such doubts and such rules, Voltaire succeeded in achieving a positive objective. He established a framework for history that was destined to replace the naïve premises and attitudes of Bossuet,[6] Rollin, and Dom Calmet.[b]

Rejecting the doctrine of creation as outside the domain of science, Voltaire perceived, in the remotest times, diverse races of men grouped into rudimentary societies. These men—stupid, brutal, close to animality—slowly, and after a prodigious amount of time, fashioned for themselves an articulate language, clothing, and shelter. They worked with metals. Through ignorance of physics and out of fear, they produced crude religions. A thou-

[a] V. XXIII, p. 439. Cf. V. XXVII, p. 269; V. XI, p. 153, etc.
[b] *Hist. de l'anc. Test.*, I, 121.

sand bizarre notions and associations created their religious rites and forms of worship. Eventually great societies were formed, governed by theocracies or dynasties that issued from the gods. China, India, Persia, and Chaldea offered the first examples of civilization. Which of these was the oldest? It is difficult to say.

With civilization came the birth of science, astronomy, and mathematics; also true religion, monotheism—the worship of one God. That was the fruit of cultivated reason among certain philosophical priests, Brahmans, Magi, and wise men of China. Later came the Phoenicians, the Venetians of antiquity; later still the Egyptians, for whom it would be dangerous to claim greater antiquity, because of the proximity of the Jews.

Finally the Greeks appeared, civilized by the Egyptians and Phoenicians, to give the world a group of remarkable legislators. Then came the Romans—the last of the ancient peoples—a small, rude nation which acquired its laws and rituals from the Tuscans and the Greeks. Its history was obscure and dubious during its first four centuries. Voltaire had read, not Beaufort, but at least Levesque de Pouilly. Rome expanded through outright brigandage. She conquered the world through discipline and patriotism. But what were the Romans—pillagers of the universe—as compared with the Greeks—philosophers, artists, and civilizers?

This concept, this framework, Voltaire formed out of all the prejudices of the philosophy and all the errors of the science of his day. He alternated between over-skepticism and over-confidence. We smile when he reasons about Ogyges [the ancient king of Thebes] or religious mysteries or when he summarily reduces all religious phenomena to deliberate deceptions practiced by priests and legislators to hoodwink a gullible and stupid humanity. Yet it was the only possible explanation, as Hettner has said, the only *rational* explanation in the eighteenth century, given the state of the philosophical, medical, and social sciences at that time. It was the first step, and a necessary one, in the scientific study of religion.

In its day Voltaire's framework for the study of ancient as well as modern history—a flexible, adjustable format in which each writer could easily lodge his particular bit of information and which could be expanded or contracted at will—marked a most significant advance in historiography. It liberated the mind from theological history and from history of a naïve or childish character. Serving for one or two generations exactly as conceived by Voltaire, it was to remain the fundamental concept on which the entire development of historical research was predicated thereafter, with modifications, in varying degrees, from the time of Herder[7] and Niebuhr,[8] Michelet[9] and Quinet.[10] Its introduction into French and European thought was a moment of notable importance for culture in general.

But is it not necessary to make an exception for his religious criticism? There is nothing more vile and contemptible, nor more irresponsibly ludicrous in Voltaire's work, than what he wrote about the Jews and the origins of Christianity. Ernest Renan[11] has pronounced its final condemnation, and neither science nor contemporary notions of good taste permit us to reject this condemnation. But our task here is to understand Voltaire, not to vindicate him. We must make an effort to realize what this strident and impudent criticism meant to his contemporaries. It was more serious than one might suppose.

We cannot imagine today the naïveté, the childishness, the absurd lengths to which French commentators went in their efforts to justify the literal meaning of the Bible and the absolute infallibility of its inspired narrators. We must read Dom Calmet[12] in order to understand Voltaire. We must see him give an account of the "affliction" of Job. The position taken by Dom Calmet was an open invitation to the ridicule that Voltaire heaped on the Bible. It was tailor-made for exploitation. The Dom Calmets insisted that everything in the Bible was divine, true, profound, and respectable. Voltaire, with a sneer, paraded all the human weaknesses in the book, its contradictions, impossibilities, obscenities, and ignorance. The language and actions of the Prophets did not surprise him so long as they were human. They were the manners and customs of a small, uncouth tribe of people whose tastes were oriental. But when the orthodox insisted that God spoke through these symbols, Voltaire quoted liberally from Hosea and Ezekiel. The claim is made for the divinity of the Gospel: Voltaire presents the stories as the folklore of illiterate common people, credulous and fanatical.

Humanly speaking, the Bible is fascinating reading, like

Homer;[a] and Jesus is a rustic Socrates.[b] But the time to adopt this point of view had not yet arrived. The first task was to destroy in men's minds the prejudiced notion of divinity, the habit of blind respect that gave the Bible and the New Testament a place apart among the monuments of the human spirit. This explains the reason for the form of Voltaire's attack, and the fact is that it proved effective.

In substantive matters Voltaire popularized the problems and results of Biblical exegesis and critical studies on the origins of Christianity. He took his information from Bayle[13] and Spinoza,[14] from Englishmen, and also a few Frenchmen—Gaulmin, Levesque de Burigny, and Fréret. He failed to realize the importance of Astruc's book when Servan sent it to him in 1767. Voltaire had passed the age when one cares to reassess his positions or revise his arguments. He planted the idea that there is a criticism to be made of Biblical literature, that religious history follows the same laws and methods as nonreligious history, that we are confronted with the same difficulties, the same uncertainties, the same kinds of mistakes, and the same causes for error. These problems are compounded by further obstacles thrown in the way of the search for truth by religious piety and priestly authority. Voltaire made large numbers of people aware of what only a few had known before: the doubts and debates about the composition of the Holy Scriptures, their dates and authenticity, and the history of the Church during the first centuries of our era.

He put religious history into the orbit of universal history, not as the fount and center of everything, but as one wave in a vast ocean. Israel was a latecomer in Asiatic civilization, a small tribe of nomadic Arabs, coarse, ignorant, superstitious, and warlike. Jehovah was their tribal god, like Chamos, the god of the Moabites. Their judges and David were tribal chieftains. Solomon was a minor king. The Jews were influenced by the great societies surrounding them. They invented nothing. Everything they had came from Egypt, Assyria, the Phoenicians, and Persians, and even the Greeks, so Voltaire claimed, twisting and reversing the

[a] V. XL, p. 190. "This book informs one of the manners and customs of ancient Asia a hundred times better than Homer. Of all the monuments of antiquity, it is the most precious." (Besterman, 7806) (R.P.)
[b] V. XXVI, p. 353; V. XXVII, p. 69.

speculative views of Huet. At a very late date their legends and traditions were recorded in writing and were then collected by Ezra. What we call the Bible is an anomalous mixture in which we find morality tales, novels, chronicles, love poems, and rituals, not to mention the Apocrypha and spurious books. Conquered by every other people and often dispersed, the Jews, after Alexander, assimilated Hellenic culture. That marked the beginning of theology. Finally, during the period of Roman domination, Jesus appeared, a religious enthusiast around whom gathered large numbers of little people—a sort of George Fox [founder of the Quakers]. The facts of his life were completely obscured by legends. The Apostles went from synagogue to synagogue talking about him. Saint Paul, "the bald Jew with the big nose," traveled about the Roman world. But Saint Peter never went to Rome. The Gospels are simply the tales recounted by little groups of Jesus' followers. Each group had its own Gospel. Fifty-four are known to exist. The canonical laws were drawn up slowly. The fourth Gospel is the most recent.[a]

In the beginning there was no dogma or hierarchy. These developed little by little, reinforced by strained interpretations of Scripture and false or falsified documents. After several centuries a canon for the Gospels was fixed. From the faithful a special group emerged as priests who, in turn, became subordinate to bishops, and among the bishops there arose a number of patriarchs. Of the patriarchs, those in the two capitals of the Empire, Rome and Constantinople, achieved ascendancy over the others, while circumstances in secular history gradually increased the power and importance of Rome.

We must not believe pagan accusations regarding Christian manners and morals or the accusations of the orthodox directed against heretics. We must discount some of the legends concerning persecutions and the number of Christian martyrs. In these, especially, falsehood has flourished. Dogma was established through religious disputes and debates. Hellenism played a dominant role, and Platonic metaphysics furnished the materials for Christian theology. Thus Voltaire made the subject of Church history an element of his world history. Regardless of the validity

---

[a] Once Voltaire said Saint Luke instead of Saint John.

in detail of his portrayal, men of our generation find themselves more at ease with Voltaire's outlook than with the positions of a Bossuet or a Dom Calmet. Were it not for the tone of his re-marks, Voltaire's assertions, including those most offensive to the eighteenth-century defenders of the Church, would not be re-jected out of hand by certain Catholic scholars of our time.

Taking into account the state of historical knowledge in Vol-taire's day, he was, all things considered, a very remarkable popularizer, not only of facts, but of problems facing historical criticism. He was a man of bold common sense who tried to formulate an idea as to the way in which history could be written. A sense of history figured prominently in his intellectual make-up. An historical point of view dominated all his philosophy. He understood clearly that theological contradictions were historical in nature. Amid all sorts of prejudices and passionate *a priori* reasonings, we can discern in him a tendency in harmony with the experimental method: a habit of posing questions in tem-poral terms, a habit of looking for origins rather than principles. He resolved more than one problem, even making some of them disappear, by formulating the question in historical terms. Meta-physical notions, religious dogma, or social institutions—Voltaire verified first of all, accurately or imperfectly, the historical claims and bases of everything that commands our respect or demands our obedience. History was his effective weapon in the war he waged on all *absolutes*.

Voltairian Philosophy, Ethics, and Religion[a]

During his Ferney period Voltaire continued to prefer physics to metaphysics. But without *la divine Emilie*, this preference remained theoretical. It consisted of talking rather glibly, on occasion, about the great problems of science, the age of the earth, fossils, the earth's formation, the creation of life, and of cutting off a few snails' heads. He loved to publicize the suprem-

[a] Dubois-Reymond, Saigey, *op. cit.*: *Dictionnaire philosophique, Les singulari-tés de la nature, Le philosophe ignorant, Dialogues d'Evhémère, Profession de foi des théistes, Les adorateurs, Histoire de Jenny.*

acy of the experimental sciences and to make fun of "systems," but he would gladly intervene to defend the claims and attributes of God, "the eternal geometrician."

Pure metaphysics scarcely occupied him. It formed a negligible part of his work during his last twenty years. Only religion and ethical principles interested him, and of metaphysics he kept only what is inseparable from it. Metaphysics remained for him the domain in which it is hardly possible to do more than remain ignorant. The real philosopher is *le Philosophe ignorant*. He resolutely clarified his reservations on the question of freedom of the will, and eventually we find him completely deterministic, in the manner of Collins. He no longer knew anything about the soul. It was probably just an abstract word. He was a deist—obstinately, enthusiastically, and seriously: a deist against all the absurd dogmas of intolerant religions, a deist in the face of the dangerous negations uttered by reckless atheists. He fought d'Holbach[15] in his final years more than he fought the Sorbonne.

Actually, he avoided explaining fully his ideas on divinity. Whenever he tried to be specific, he tended toward pantheism. He took refuge in Malebranche[16] rather than compromise himself with Spinoza[17] whose abstract and rigidly systematic views Voltaire disliked. The world is eternal and necessary. God is everywhere in it, like gravitation. God made everything in us. "There is something of the divine in a flea."[a] He no longer reduced God, as he had previously, to the role of the first law of physics. He made God the basis of moral conduct. People have often quoted his reference to a God Who rewards and punishes, a statement he repeated many times in his writings. But with Voltaire this was only a temporary concession to popular belief. He accepted this belief, the error of which is not demonstrably provable. He regarded it as useful for society at its present stage of development. He did not make use of it for himself, and he admitted that at some future time enlightened generations would discard it.

In Voltaire's view, moral principles need God only as a basis and not as a sanction. All he asks of God, moreover, is to guarantee that the moral sense of justice and charity towards one's neighbor should belong to the true nature of man as divinely

[a] Art. *Idée.*

created. Voltaire wanted God to bestow a little of the prestige of His name on the sometimes painful efforts expended in behalf of moral principles. Morality is divine—meaning, for Voltaire, that it is natural. The morality Voltaire fashioned on this basis was in no degree a religious one. God had no place in it. He gave no commandments. Moral principles were not acts of revelation. Such principles, divine in the sense that reason is divine, evolved slowly, like reason, in the whole of mankind and in each individual, gradually working their way up from the lower, baser instincts of our primitive nature. Man emerged from animality by dint of his own actions, under the pressures of circumstances. Since there are no commandments, there is no forgiveness. Prayer is useless. The only prayer is submission. God is not an object of love. He communicates with man only by the inexorable necessity of things and events. God is a law that we know and to which we adapt ourselves. There is no duty that relates to God. Nor is there any duty binding the moral being towards himself. There is only a social duty. All virtue is a relationship of man to man. We can be guilty only with respect to our fellow man.

Religious dogmas differ because they were invented by men. But morality is universal since it comes from God. To be sure, we find all kinds of contradictions and differences in the laws and prejudices of different peoples. But everywhere, from Socrates to Jesus and from Confucius to Shaftesbury,[18] when man applies his reason to the conduct of life he finds the same moral principles—the principles of kindness and justice, and the social virtues which act as a counterbalance to our natural and deeply rooted self-love and self-centeredness. Voltaire's view of morality held out no promise of a visionary bliss. It authorized honest pleasures in moderation. Through social action and mutual agreements, it promised to enhance the collective well being of society and thereby multiply the pleasures of each individual. It neither astonished nor went beyond the minds of cultivated people in 1760. It invited them, in accepting man, in accepting themselves, to show a little kindness, gentleness, and consideration for others in the pursuit of happiness. It invited men to have a little concern, while living well themselves, for making life more agreeable for one and all. It neither frightened nor discouraged its adherents. It contained no irrational visions. It advocated only those actions so obviously useful, so clearly within the range of human possibility, that a refusal to accept them would be more an act of stupidity than of malevolence. It was this positive and independent morality which, with its affirmation of God's existence, was the natural religion, the only true religion, a monotheism that all the churches had enveloped with the ridiculous or inhuman fantasies of their dogmas.

The Voltairian Reformation of France[a]

If virtue resides only in social action, then the moral life is inconceivable without an involvement in politics, and the good man will be he who does good for everyone by working to improve society. And that is what Voltaire did, with unremitting fervor, during his last years at Ferney. Anxious for results, distrusting philosophical and theological systems, he did not apply himself, as Montesquieu and Rousseau had done, to the formulation of a political theory or to drawing up a plan for an ideal society. He did not refine on abstract principles. He was a realist to the highest degree, accepting France as she was with her social classes and her conditions so ripe for reform. He tried to discover what could be done immediately, what was within the realm of possibility, and limited his efforts to that end. He reviewed all phases of government and administration, criticizing them in the light of two or three moral principles of his own. He drew up a list of abuses and reforms, avoiding when possible any head-on collision with reality, the better to change it more effectively.

He regarded society as an established fact, a fact of life, and governments as the powers deriving from this fact. Governmental powers had, in the course of time, succeeded in disguising their rule by force as rule by law. But there is no law, save in the free

[a] *Dictionn. phil. Mélanges,* Moland, ed. V. XXII–XXXII. Ed. Hertz, *Voltaire und die französische Strafrechtspflege,* 1887. Masmonteil, *la Législation criminelle dans l'œuvre de Voltaire.* E. Faguet, *Politique comparée de Montesquieu, de Voltaire et de Rousseau.* L. Robert, *Voltaire et l'intolérance religieuse.*

The following pages are the résumé of a more comprehensive study in which all the references will be given.

consent of men,[a] for men are by nature free and equal. There is no divine right. Democracy is the most rational kind of government. But because it can survive only in small countries, and also because monarchy is the most ancient form of government in France, a concern for peace and order requires the Frenchman to be a royalist. A constitutional, representative régime is good in itself, but, for France, feudal anarchy had made a régime of absolute monarchy both useful and necessary. The force of royal power saved the people from petty tyrants. Yet one must require a respect for laws on the part of absolute royalty itself, and these laws must have as their object the preservation of freedom, the only "fundamental law of all nations."[b] But general freedom, in practice, consists of a number of individual freedoms which must be guaranteed to each citizen through laws.

Here is Voltaire's list of required freedoms: (1) *Freedom of person:* slavery is against nature. (2) *Freedom of speech and the press,* even in matters of politics and religion. This freedom is the safeguard and basis of all others. Character assassination, outrages against authority and laws, even seditious libel, must be punished. (3) *Civil liberty: habeas corpus* should be introduced. (4) *Freedom of conscience.* (5) *Security of private property:* if required for reasons of public utility, private property may be expropriated with compensation for the loss sustained. All citizens must have the right to possess private property, but there shall be no law enforcing an equal distribution of goods. (6) *Right to work* and to sell one's work or product to the highest bidder. Work is the property of those who lack property.

Property ownership confers an obligation to hold public office and the right to participate in public affairs. In the present state of France an enlightened bourgeoisie governs both the weak and powerful and controls public opinion. Finally, there is no other guarantee for liberty and freedom than the will of the governed. One is free when one so wills it, and only to the extent that one desires freedom. There is little need to recall that Voltaire hated war, but he doubted that it would soon disappear from the earth. Armies were therefore a necessity. The best sort would be a

[a] V. XXVII, p. 197.
[b] V. XXVII, p. 388.

militia. A professional and permanent army is constantly tempted to embark on external conquests, or else it poses a threat to the people's freedom. Since it is impossible at the present time to do without a military establishment, we must limit its size and strength in accordance with the needs of self-defense. It is folly for a nation to ruin itself under the pretext of self-preservation. With fifty thousand married soldiers, well paid, to be retired at half pay at age 50, France would have all the army she needed and have it with a minimum of social disruption or inconvenience.

Patriotism in the eighteenth century had nothing to do with war and the military. Voltaire was patriotic because, like Montesquieu and Rousseau, he was interested in the public weal. In the English manner, he linked his country, his *patrie,* to the concepts of liberty and property, and it seemed to him that only those who possessed private property could really claim a native country. He felt that such people were bound by common interests and would intervene in one way or another in the preservation and development of those common interests. He believed that in large nations millions of people still had no *patrie,* no country they could call their own.

In theory he would make education a function of the state, but in practice he accepted freedom, that is, the University and the religious schools and congregations brought under state control. He did not think it either possible or desirable that the masses, the common people, should be educated.[a] Otherwise, who would perform the disagreeable and difficult chores that must be done? But his concept of the masses, *le peuple,* was restricted to the lowest class of manual laborers. He desired through education to enlarge the middle class. He wanted manufacturers, artisans, masons, carpenters, blacksmiths, and farmers to become educated and enlightened. He wanted them to look beyond their trade or profession and acquire a knowledge of public interests. Voltaire's school would thus be essentially a citizens' school.

Voltaire did not seek separation of Church and State. His ideal

---

[a] He meant by education what we would call the secondary level, the one enabling a pupil to read "the best chapters of *The Spirit of Laws.*" He opened an elementary school at Ferney.

was the English system. In France *Catholicism* would be *the state religion,* but the Church would be subordinate to civil authority and respectful of civil law. There would be an end to Roman jurisdiction and the abolition of all taxes paid to the Roman chancellery. Church property would be subject to taxation just like the property of every other citizen. The state would supervise these funds and intervene in their distribution to ensure all priests an adequate income. In this sense Voltaire was moving toward the idea of a clergy paid by the state, thereby permitting the state to limit the number of priests and to dispose, as it saw fit, of excess ecclesiastical profits.

Voltaire advocated civil marriages; state control over all rites, catechisms, and educational and devotional books; and state supervision of the pulpit. Civil authority would not intervene in matters of dogma, but it must ensure respect for public order, laws, and morality. Priests would retain the right to teach faith and morals and the practice of charity. Voltaire would discontinue burial within a church edifice, and he would reduce the number of religious feasts observed as public holidays. He would have religious communities supervised and permit the renunciation of monastic vows at the age of twenty-five. He favored a progressive reduction in numbers leading to the eventual abolition of monasteries, convents, and religious communities. He would transfer their wealth to charitable institutions.

He wanted freedom of conscience but not an equality of religions. Voltaire said nothing about freethinkers and atheists. Their beliefs he regarded as individual matters of no concern to the state. But churches, other than the Roman Catholic, would not be officially recognized. *Tolerance and test*; it was the English example Voltaire wanted France to follow. For Protestants, Voltaire demanded freedom for private worship, recognition of the validity of their marriages, the right of Protestant children to inherit family property, freedom from any sort of physical harassment, and the right to engage in business or to practice any profession. To the Jews, whom he despised, he offered personal safety and a status as resident foreigners, and he invited them to rid themselves of their uncouth manners and become a cultivated people.

Instead of an ambitious policy of conquest and military glory, Voltaire preferred a peaceful, economy-minded government. He wanted, not great cabinet ministers, but good administrators. The government should devote itself, above all, to promoting conditions favorable for work and population growth. He found that, unfortunately, most governmental regulations impeded work and caused a decline in population. The financial system of France was detestable. Taxation should be proportional without restriction or regard for social privilege. The exclusive system of the physiocrats was as absurd as tax exemption for the clergy and nobility. Taxes should bear most heavily on the wealthy. It is despicable to take from a wage earner part of the bread he earns.

The farm system of taxation[19] was a bad one. Direct taxes would be less burdensome on the treasury and less vexatious and ruinous for the people. Changing the value of money, abolishing *rentes* [interest from stocks and bonds], creating offices, lotteries, and salt taxes, and collecting internal customs—all these were just so many abusive or detestable means of taking money from the citizenry. Free trade for wheat, at least within the country, was essential. Taxes must be levied where the money is. Tax receipts must be increased by lowering the tax rate. Taxes must be collected with the least possible expense. The tax structure must be organized in such a way as to promote, rather than paralyze, the nation's economic activity. Feudal taxes, forced labor, and tithes must also be abolished.

As for agriculture, commerce, and industry, everything could be summed up in one word: freedom—that is, freedom from hindrances of all sorts, from onerous or tyrannical regulations, from the *jurandes* and *maîtrises* [the corporation of craftsmen, which restricted the liberty of industry], from the requirement to sell only at the market, and from the prohibitive taxes on wine, etc. Voltaire's liberal policies nevertheless allowed for protection against foreign competition, but in such a way that wheat, that is, bread, should remain inexpensive. He recommended the establishment of standard weights and measures.

Voltaire was thinking primarily of commerce and agriculture as practiced by the large property owner and the wealthy businessman. He was hardly aware of industrial problems although he had created factories himself and was acquainted with the unhappy plight of the Lyonnese weavers. So far as the worker's interests were concerned, Voltaire limited his demands to advocating the worker's right to sell his service or his product to the highest bidder and to earn a salary permitting him to live and to bring up his family. To enable the worker to earn more, he proposed merely an increase in the number of work days. And yet he believed that factory work was stultifying and degrading. His whole economy was basically tied to a theory of affluence, *la théorie du luxe*. To spend one's income was a social obligation. The wealthy man, both in his needs and in his pleasures, provides a livelihood for the poor man. His expenditures stimulate business, industry, and agriculture. All his delights and pleasures trickle down into the populace in the form of wages and salaries and thereby promote general prosperity.

Prosperous and well-run nations can afford to pay heavy taxes, but taxes are not meant to be squandered by the court and used to nourish parasites. Taxation is first of all a guarantee, serving to establish order and security. It must also be a cooperative venture intended to subsidize enterprises of public utility. Money would be better employed for water and markets in the cities, for canals and highways across the country, than for waging wars. Productive expenditures are those that protect public health and facilitate business and agricultural activity.

Of the postal system Voltaire asked only for freedom from censorship, a respect for the secrecy of private correspondence. In this matter there was no requirement more urgent. In welfare matters, Voltaire regarded public assistance as a duty of the state. He wanted to end public begging. He urged hospital reforms, the creation of new hospitals, particularly maternity hospitals, foundling homes, and homes for the aged and infirm workers. To provide for these necessary establishments, one must use "the poor tax" levied on theatrical entertainment, and available funds of the clergy and monasteries.

Lastly, the administration of justice needed a thorough reorganization. The worst abuses of all were in the judiciary. Voltaire was to applaud the abolition of the *Parlements*,[20] for he hoped this would result in two capital reforms he had long advocated: the termination of the right to acquire judicial office by purchasing it, and the separation of judicial powers from political powers. He also desired a reduction in legal costs for litigants and fewer delays in the administration of justice. He wanted a single body of laws, a civil code and a penal code, that would put an end to contradictory and arbitrary judgments in legal decisions.

Into civil law he would introduce divorce. But for criminal law Voltaire demanded sweeping reforms. Criminal justice was atrocious, absurd, blind, and ridden with theological ideas. It struck hit or miss. While severe on little people and lesser crimes, it was lenient with those committing great crimes, with persons who happened to be powerful and influential. One should punish only those felonies that directly affect men and harm the social order. Offenses against God, sacrilege, sorcery, suicide, heresy, and sodomy are not within the province of the judiciary. One must carefully define cases of legal repression, distinguish misdemeanors from more serious offenses, make the punishment fit the crime, and not abuse the use of sentences to the galleys or, above all, the death sentence. One must remove from the death sentence the refinements of cruelty which men have added to it. Punishment must be a purely personal matter, not be extended to an innocent family by the confiscation of its property, or otherwise.

Legal procedures continued to disregard the rights of the individual. An accused man must not be treated as guilty. Innocent people must not be thrown in jail frivolously only to be released after many long months, ruined, demoralized, and with no indemnity whatsoever. Voltaire wanted the abolition of *monitoires* [secret ecclesiastical informers]. Such testimony appealed only to witnesses for the prosecution and encouraged secret denunciations. He advocated the abolition of torture and secret trials. Witnesses must not be intimidated or disregarded. The accused must be allowed to confront his accusers. He is entitled to legal assistance in both criminal and civil cases. One must abandon the barbarous and puerile system of partial proofs—half-truths and quarter-truths. There must be an end to this accumulation of uncertainties twisted into a legal certitude. Motives for arrest must be clearly established, whether in criminal or civil cases.

And so we have given a very matter-of-fact summary of the reforms Voltaire sought over a twenty-year period. He did so with an indefatigable zeal, alternately sarcastic and indignant, trying to win over to his views human reason and public conscience. Their collective effect is not that of a fine philosophical treatise developed in the abstract to the glory of the human intellect. It was a series of corrections, of repairs to the old social structure, not to be judged apart from the realities on which they had an immediate bearing. Voltaire asked himself what modifications and retouches were demanded in every phase of government and administration in the name of liberty, equality, and humanity, those principles which, in his eyes, expressed the social conscience and national views of his age.

We are tempted today to underestimate and to belittle the importance of this criticism because it was not organized into a system, and because the majority of the reforms called for have either now long since been realized or else have become outdated and irrelevant through the evolution of our institutions and our society. But his contemporaries were grateful to Voltaire for his realistic and precise analyses indicating what improvements were possible of attainment in all parts of the body politic.

And if we will just think of it for a while, if we pause to visualize the France of Louis XV with all its many abuses and shortcomings: the capricious despotism of its government, the self-centered and extravagant court, the powerful clergy and judiciary, more concerned with their own special privileges than with the welfare of all, the financial disorder and its oppressive fiscal system, the poverty of the parish priest, the chaotic conditions of the laws, the conflict and confusion between various authorities and their jurisdictions, the intolerance that condemned Protestants to concubinage or hypocrisy and consigned their pastors to the galleys, the multitude of rules and privileges that were just so many sources of vexation and misery for the masses—if we apply to those conditions the reforms Voltaire advocated, and if, into this France of the Old Régime, a France Catholic and monarchical, if we introduce tolerance, freedom of the press, proportional taxation, a uniform code of laws, reforms in criminal procedure, a submissive and salaried clergy, a program of public assistance, liberal and peaceful principles of government and of honest, conscientious administration, one truly concerned with the public interest—then, and only then, can we realize the extent of the transformation that Voltaire's criticism was bringing about. Only then do we realize how wide of the mark it is to regard Voltaire's work as negative and timid. His criticism was in process of producing a new and different France, a France disengaging herself from an old feudal and monarchical chaos that was Roman and ecclesiastical, anarchical and tyrannical. It was a new France that was becoming, under the very Christian Bourbon king, somewhat like the France that emerged during the peaceful moments of the Consulate or the Second Empire. More precisely, the Voltairian reform, in its main outline—except for the two Chambers [the Chamber of Deputies and the Senate] was the design for the bourgeois government of Louis-Philippe [1830–1848]. It is the France that would have come into being had Turgot[21] been able to stay in power for twenty years and been permitted to do what he wanted. Broadly speaking, Voltaire was the journalist and propagandist for the work of which Turgot was the statesman.

We would also be wrong about Voltaire's spirit or intentions if we believed that they did not go beyond the reforms he championed. He was not a revolutionary or a visionary. He was an opportunist and a realist. He indicated what could be accomplished immediately, under the pressure of public opinion. Having achieved a certain limited objective, he did not give up asking for something else. He did not claim to be a republican. He did not call for a constitution on the English model. He did not expressly ask for the direct participation of property owners and industrialists in the management of public affairs. He did not ask for the right for Protestants to hold public office or be given the freedom of public worhsip. He did not demand that all professors be nominated by the state. But these were matters he regarded as altogether reasonable. He contented himself with declaring the right of the state to supervise religious communities. He did not demand their immediate dissolution, though he desired and hoped for it.

Voltaire was, beyond any doubt, a conservative. But he was conservative in the manner of any true liberal. He did not want a violent upheaval. He did not try to abolish social classes or the unequal distribution of wealth. He put France into the hands of the enlightened bourgeoisie, whose limits he would expand to include greater numbers of common people through the process of education. But his program, precisely because it was a practical one, contained nothing absolute or definitive. He maintained the constant attitude of seeking certain limited and realizable reforms, towards which he bent every effort, and then anticipating additional improvements made possible by having accomplished his first objectives. And thus it would continue to be so long as we find evil in the world and, with the aid of human reason, can conceive of something better. Thus it would always be so long as humanity and justice are, in one place or another, wounded and suffering, and so long as society remains imperfect and men unhappy.

10

The Rise of the Voltairian Legend:
His Last Years and Death[a]

THE SALIENT feature of Voltaire's life was his determination to be more than just a man of letters. In this respect he differed from Montesquieu, Diderot, and Rousseau, who were content to enlighten or inflame men's minds through their writings alone. No sooner was Voltaire quietly settled down in his canton of Gex and safe from harassment, or virtually so, than he became involved with others, not with mankind in general, but with specific individual cases which he regarded as either a result or a symptom of social abuses.

First, in 1759, it was the little affair, not widely publicized, of the six Crassy brothers whose inheritance Voltaire retrieved from the Jesuits of Ornex. Then in 1762 there was the Calas affair. It was on the 10th of March that Jean Calas, a textile merchant on the Rue des Filatiers in Toulouse, was put to death by being broken on the wheel after a long trial conducted first by the municipal magistrates and later by the *Parlement* of Toulouse. Calas was accused of murdering his eldest son, Marc-Antoine, who

[a] Desnoiresterres, V. VIII. Eug. Asse, *Lettres de Mmes (de Graffigny . . .), Suard,* etc., 1883. Voltaire, *Recueil des particularités curieuses de sa vie et de sa mort* (by Harel), 1782. (Longchamp and Wagnière, *Mémoires sur Voltaire et ses ouvrages.* Ath. Coquerel, *Jean Calas et sa famille,* 1858 (2nd ed., 1869), C. Rabaud, *Sirven, étude historique sur l'avènement de la tolérance.*

was found hanged in his father's shop October 13, 1761. The crime was attributed to the Calvinist family's horror at the thought that Marc-Antoine wanted to become a Catholic. Jean Calas died protesting his innocence.

Informed of this event on the 22nd of March by a businessman named Audibert, Voltaire first considered it an instance of Huguenot fanaticism. But further inquiry soon convinced him that he was in the presence of a judicial error. Thereupon Voltaire took personal charge of the case. He ran headlong into the indifference, skepticism, or open hostility of ministers, courtiers, and parliamentarians. So he turned to the public. With all kinds of writings, discussing the charges and facts in the case and developing his ideas of tolerance, Voltaire aroused and set in motion the great force of public opinion. He supported and directed from Ferney all the moves made by Mme Calas. He assisted the lawyers Elie de Beaumont and Loyseau de Mauléon. On March 7, 1764, came the Council's first decree ordering a judicial review of the trial. On June 4, 1764, the judgment of Toulouse was reversed. On the 9th of March 1765 the forty appellate judges of the Town Hall of Toulouse unanimously exonerated Calas, thereby clearing his name and restoring his family's civil and property rights.

From time to time thereafter, whether prompted by Catholic fervor, a concern for the honor of the magistracy, or simply by hatred for Voltaire, attempts have been made to invalidate this judicial reversal. Nothing has been produced that would indicate Calas's guilt. Neglecting all evidence in favor of the accused, opponents have succeeded only in producing certain circumstantial evidence which, without justifying the sentence, makes clear that a number of prejudiced judges, who were by no means scoundrels, had found sufficient cause to put an innocent man to death. Nothing, absolutely nothing, constituted proof against Calas. The public was convinced of his innocence and enthusiastically applauded the family's rehabilitation. That moment marked Voltaire's transfiguration in the minds of his contemporaries. He was "the defender of Calas." People began to see in him something more than a clever wit. To his *gloire*, tremendously enhanced by this affair, were now added feelings of warm devotion and respect such as Voltaire had never before inspired.

After the Calas case came that of the Sirven family. Again it was the same story. A young Huguenot girl had thrown herself into a well and was drowned. The father was condemned by the fiscal attorney of Mazamet in southern France (1764). Fortunately, he was able to escape by fleeing with his wife and two surviving daughters. With his sharp, practical judgment, Voltaire chose not to move on behalf of Sirven until the Calas affair was terminated. Then he took hold of the case with the zeal of a crusader. He finished it by having Sirven and his wife fully cleared in 1771 by *La Tournelle de Toulouse* [a special bench of the *Parlement* dealing with criminal cases] which included some of the judges involved in the Calas affair.

Then there were a number of Protestants he wanted to have freed from galley sentences or whose marriages he sought to have legalized. There was the La Barre case. A crucifix had been mutilated at Abbeville (August 9, 1765). Several youths were suspects. The Chevalier d'Etallonde had fled. The Chevalier de La Barre was arrested and convicted. He was convicted only of not baring his head during the procession of the Holy Sacrament, of having sung some impious and obscene songs, of having recited *La Pucelle* [Voltaire], and of having in his possession such books as *La Religieuse en chemise* [a rather licentious novel, published anonymously] and *Le Dictionnaire philosophique portatif* [Voltaire]. For these offenses, aggravated by private grudges, the Seneschal's court of Abbeville condemned him to have his tongue torn out and then be beheaded. The sentence was upheld by the *Parlement* of Paris. La Barre was spared only the mutilation of his tongue. His body and head were burned on a pyre on which they also threw the *Dictionnaire philosophique* for good measure. Voltaire was thunderstruck. He appealed to the public. He befriended Etallonde and secured him a post in the service of Prussia. He tried later to quash the arrest warrant which condemned Etallonde by default. He was unsuccessful. He could only curse the judges of Abbeville in all his writings. And this he did not fail to do.

On May 9, 1766, the comte de Lally, former commandant in Pondichéry, was beheaded in the Place de Grève, gagged so that no one could hear his cries of protestation. Voltaire was disturbed by the vague terms of the charges in the arrest warrant. He made inquiry and became convinced of Lally's innocence. He used his pen and popularity on behalf of the son of the condemned man. He lived to see Lally's name cleared and the family restored to good repute. In 1769 he was to be engaged in another such effort. This time it was Martin, a farmer in Barrois, broken on the wheel for an assassination later confessed to by the actual assassin. In 1770 it was a miscarriage of justice in Arras. A drunken old woman was killed, allegedly by her children. Montbailli was broken on the wheel. His wife stated she was pregnant. Voltaire succeeded in having her, as well as the man whom they had put to death, declared innocent.

In 1772 he took charge of the case of Mlle Camp, a Protestant girl whom the vicomte de Bombelle had married quietly in a remote rural area [Protestants were forbidden to meet in churches]. The wedding rite was performed by a Protestant pastor. The vicomte later abandoned her and their child in order to marry a wealthy Roman Catholic. He maintained that the first union was null and void. Voltaire was successful only in obtaining financial aid for the victim.

He was less fortunate and less astute when he undertook to defend the comte de Morangiés against his creditors. This time the public was unsympathetic. It was merely a question of money, and, if the creditors looked like rogues and cheats, the debtor was certainly no paragon of virtue. Moreover, he was completely ungrateful to his overly solicitous defender. Although Voltaire denied he was "the Don Quixote of all the broken and hanged men," he was hardly able to stand idly by at what appeared to him cruelty and injustice. He raised his voice in protest, and he caused others to do the same.

When he learned that there were still *main-mortables* [serfs without property rights] in France, and that only a short distance from Ferney some 12,000 men were held in serfdom by twenty priests of Saint-Claude, Voltaire was horrified. From 1770 on, he besieged the king's councillor, Turgot, with pleas and petitions. He supported the lawyer Christin de Besançon, who had decided to act on behalf of the serfs in the Jura mountains. Although he stirred up public opinion, his clients were not to win their freedom until the French Revolution.

Unsuccessful in ridding France of the salt tax (*la gabelle*), he undertook with the same ardor the task of freeing his own community of Gex from this oppressive levy. The peaceful citizenry of Gex were no less plagued by smugglers and tax officials than the rest of France. He negotiated long and patiently with the chief tax collectors (the farmers general), to secure a fixed levy on salt and tobacco. He enlisted the aid of Trudaine[1] and Turgot. He persuaded the abbé Morellet, Dupont de Nemours,[2] and one Mme de Saint-Julien, whom he called his "Butterfly-philosopher," to act on his behalf. He alternately angered and mollified the craft unions and the Estates [representatives of the three social orders] of Gex. He urged them to make necessary concessions. Finally he succeeded. He offered the tax collectors a payment of 20,000 pounds per annum. They wanted 60,000. It was settled for 30,000.

A remarkable scene occurred when the representatives of the Estates of Gex convened at the Town Hall to discuss the agreement. Voltaire arrived December 12, 1775, "all bundled up." He was given a seat. He made "a good speech," and read some letters from Turgot and Trudaine. The delegates of the three orders approved the treaty. "Then he opened the window and cried: *Liberté!*" He was answered by shouts of *Vive le roi! Vive Voltaire!* ("Long live the king! Long live Voltaire!").

A letter by Mme de Gallatin gives this account:

There were twelve dragoons from Ferney standing in the public square outside the assembly hall. The dragoons held their swords in hand as a tribute to our friend, who left at once and came back for dinner. As he drove through four or five villages, people threw laurel wreaths into his carriage. He was covered with them. All his subjects stood in line to welcome him and greeted him with fireworks displays, etc. He was very happy and took no note of the fact that he was 82 years old.[a]

These warm-hearted actions on behalf of others, the increasing prosperity of Ferney, the unending output of letters and pamphlets dedicated to public causes—all these activities supplanted, little by little, in the minds of his contemporaries, the earlier impressions Voltaire had created by his irascible humor, his un-

[a] Letter of Mme de Gallatin (*Zeitschrift f. fr. Sp. u. L.* VII, 207). Cf. the letter of M. Hennin (Desnoiresterres, VIII, 76).

dignified quarrels, and his degrading and deplorable antics. Despite the irreconcilable hostility of the Church and its faithful, despite the ill-disguised antipathy of atheists, the great majority of the public were aligned with Voltaire. They venerated the Old Man of Ferney. In 1770 Mme Necker took the initiative by launching a subscription drive to raise funds for erecting a statue to Voltaire. But Pigalle [the sculptor], upon modeling his living skeleton, produced a masterpiece of anatomical realism bearing little resemblance to the idealized image conceived by Voltaire's admirers. In 1772 Mlle Clairon, in her home and in the presence of friends, crowned the philosopher's bust by reciting an ode composed by Marmontel. Even in Geneva he was triumphant. He could not appear there without immense crowds gathering about him. In 1776 he was almost crushed to death by the throng of well-wishers. His defense of Calas had superseded his *Guerre de Genève* ["The War of Geneva," a satirical poem which had displeased the Genevans].

Nothing gives a more vivid picture of the legendary transfiguration of the patriarch of Ferney than the letters of Mme Suard. This young woman of twenty-five experienced in the presence of this shrewd old man with a scintillating wit "the joyous raptures of Saint Theresa." When near him she felt a surge of emotions, feelings of tenderness, pity, and ecstasy. She asked him to bestow his blessing upon her. She describes for us a kindly Voltaire, good, indulgent, gentle, and compassionate, a Voltaire for sensitive souls. He was consumed with a desire to enjoy his *gloire*. But the government was still unrelenting. After a report had circulated concerning Voltaire's illness (July 1774), the governor of Burgundy received an order from Versailles to seize all his papers the moment he died. But they did not dare touch him as long as he was alive. The queen wept at a performance of *Tancrède* and expressed a desire to "embrace" the author. D'Argental and the marquis de Villette summoned him to Paris. Mme Denis was anxious to go back.

On the 5th of February, 1778, he left Ferney in his *dormeuse* [sleeping coach], which was equipped with a small heater. He arrived in Paris February 10th, about half past three in the afternoon, and lodged with the marquis de Villette on the Rue de Beaune at the corner of the Quai des Théatins. The rest is well known. He became intoxicated with so much public adulation and glory. Indeed, it killed him.

If the overly pious king did not allow the queen to see him, Paris offered ample consolation. Visitors flocked to the Rue de Beaune: friends, writers, delegations from the French Academy and the Comédie Française, Gluck, Mme Necker, the comtesse de Polignac, Mme du Barry, the English ambassador, the Masonic Lodge of the Nine Sisters, and Benjamin Franklin, whose grandson he blessed with the words "God and liberty." On the 16th of March his tragedy *Irène* was performed in the presence of the queen and the comtesse d'Artois. Having just recovered from an illness that had kept him confined and without visitors for three weeks, Voltaire ventured out in his carriage in the midst of an enthusiastic throng shouting its acclaim for "the hero of the Calas case." He went to see Turgot. On the 30th of March he appeared at the Academy, and from there, dressed in magnificent attire, wearing his large wig and wrapped in the fur coat given him by the Empress of Russia, he went to the Comédie to attend the sixth performance of *Irène*. One of the actors placed a crown of laurel on his head. At the end of the play, with the entire cast on stage, his bust was crowned by Brizard, wearing a monk's robe, and it was kissed by all the actresses. He went out on foot. He paid visits to the princes of Orléans, to Sophie Arnould [a famed opera singer], and the marquise de Gouvernet, that pretty Suzanne de Livry who had been faithless to him fifty years earlier.

In the midst of all this activity he kept working. He had induced the Academy to adopt a new plan for its dictionary and had immediately set himself to the task of preparing it. He was consuming twenty-five cups of coffee a day, losing sleep, filling himself with opium, and growing delirious. On the 25th of May he was near death. He recovered long enough to congratulate Lally-Tollendal on the Council decree that reversed the judgment brought against his father. Doctors Lorry and Tronchin gave up hope. Tronchin was slyly watching to see how the philosopher would react to the approaching "nasty moment." The philosopher wanted to live. He was furious with himself for not having taken the advice to return to Ferney. He begged Tronchin "to pull him out of this." He was suffering dreadful pain. He was afraid of what they would do to him after his death. He remembered the fate of Adrienne Lecouvreur.[3] He did not want his remains tossed into a public dump. Some priests were already active, notably a certain abbé Gautier, the priest of that particular parish, which was Saint-Sulpice. He signed a confession of faith and a retraction which was later deemed insufficient. They brought him another declaration. "Let me die in peace," he said.

Voltaire had placed his true confession in the hands of his secretary Wagnière, after the first warning on February 28th:

I die adoring God, loving my friends, not hating my enemies, and detesting persecution.

It would appear that he recovered his equanimity when he learned there was no hope for him and that he accepted the inevitable with resignation. He died May 30, 1778, about eleven at night.

The Archbishop of Paris and the parish priests of Saint-Sulpice refused him a Christian burial. The king said, or is alleged to have said: "Let the priests handle this." Neither the ministry nor the *Parlement* would intervene.[a] Voltaire had chosen as his last resting place the center of his arbor in Ferney. But Ferney was far off. And there was the Bishop of Annecy to fear. One had to act quickly to prevent ecclesiastical vengeance. The abbé Mignot [Voltaire's nephew] placed the body in a carriage, wrapped in its dressing-gown and wearing a night cap. He took it to the Abbey de Scellières in Champagne, over which he held jurisdiction as *abbé commendataire*. There Voltaire's remains were placed in a coffin and buried (June 1–2). The prior, who had permitted the interment, was dismissed from his post by the Bishop of Troyes.

Voltaire did not have to wait long for his revenge. The Revolution brought him back to Paris in July 1791. A triumphant cortege—city officials, deputies, magistrates, Academicians, young women dressed in white, cannoneers, and opera singers—conducted his earthly remains to the Panthéon, there to be enshrined amid universal acclaim and enthusiasm. The political evolution of France was already leaving Voltaire behind. But the people had not forgotten this defender of humanity. It was Calas who led Voltaire to the Panthéon in an apotheosis of glory.

---

[a] The ministry did intervene; see *Commentary*, p. 194. (R.P.)

11

Voltaire's Influence

THAT VOLTAIRE influenced his own century as well as the nineteenth century is an indisputable fact, but it is impossible at the present time to ascertain with any degree of accuracy the precise extent of his influence. I am not sure that it will ever be possible to do so. Voltaire very definitely received from his own age, and from the intellectual currents of his time, the majority of the ideas and suggestions that he reflected and re-echoed. His influence in many instances was that of a transmitter, a relay-station, as it were, adding the enormous energy of his contagious passions and seductive power to an output of ideas that had originated elsewhere but would never have reached so vast an audience without the tremendous boost Voltaire provided. It is difficult to distinguish and dissociate his personal role and influence from the collective tendencies and individual efforts of others moving in the same direction.

Perhaps he served his age primarily as a kind of executive officer, drawing up the "Order of the Day" for public opinion. By the bells he rang and the fireworks he set off, he rallied the minds of the century and made all available forces converge on a single target. He disciplined his troops and coordinated their common objectives. It is not easy to decide whether he was always the general in command of the army of progress or simply its drum major. The difficulty is compounded by Voltaire's aversion to any systematic organization of his ideas. The presence of a

Montesquieu or a Rousseau in any given plan of action is quickly discernible from the traces of doctrinal views held by these philosophers. Voltaire often did little more than whip up certain sentiments without imposing any dogmatic preference of his own.

Perhaps these difficulties will some day be resolved. For the present, at any rate, it would be vain to pretend to have done so. The history of ideas, their formation, and their modes of propagation in the eighteenth and nineteenth centuries have not as yet been sufficiently studied and analyzed. We have not yet accurately determined the relationship of social and political facts to moral and literary facts. It would be necessary to take a close look at the intellectual training and development of many individuals, distinguished or mediocre, illustrious or obscure. But as of now, we have not collected an adequate number of such observations to permit formulating any general conclusions. And it will be only after this work is completed that the question of Voltaire's influence can be answered with some degree of accuracy.

Therefore, without laying claim to any precision or certainty on a subject that is still illusory, I shall offer a few observations on what seem to me the most plausible facts of the matter. In the first place, while we cannot establish with accuracy the detail or extent of Voltaire's influence, we can scarcely question its reality. Voltaire was the intellectual nourishment of many minds for several generations, and consequently he affected to some degree the thoughts of multitudes. Almost no one escaped his influence among the last generation of the eighteenth century. And Christians, like Joseph de Maistre[1] and Chateaubriand,[2] often did no more than oppose Voltaire with the very facts and opinions they had acquired from him.

It would be interesting to know how widely Voltaire was read at various moments of history. Bibliography can give us some help on this point. From 1740 to 1778 there were nineteen collections of his complete works, not counting the separate editions of his principal writings, which were very numerous.[a] From 1778 to 1815 Quérard indicates six editions of his complete works, not including two that were incomplete but still sizable. Finally, for the twenty-year period from 1815 to 1835, Bengesco has found 28

---

[a] Bengesco, V. IV, Nos. 2122–2141.

editions of Voltaire's complete works.[a] Then nothing from 1835 to 1852. From 1852 to 1870 there were five editions, including the propagandistic one sponsored by the daily newspaper *Le Siècle* ("The Century"). After 1870 there were two or three editions, only one of which, that of Louis Moland, is important. The Moland edition [1877–85] is of a purely literary and historical nature, entirely free of any intent to preserve or spread Voltairian ideas.

Generally speaking, there was great interest in his writings down to the outbreak of the Revolution, then a falling off and lull until 1815. A prodigious renewal of interest during the Restoration [1815–1830] was followed by another decline and then an appreciable upturn during the Second Empire [1852–1870]. This curve corresponds rather closely to the waves of liberalism in France. Voltaire was printed or reprinted particularly during those periods when liberal movements encountered their greatest opposition and consequently became more militant. Yet we must recognize the fact that, with so many editions of Voltaire's works already available—the special edition of 1775 (with each page framed in decorative lines), the two Kehl editions prior to the Revolution, and the 28 consecutive editions prior to the reign of Louis-Philippe [1830–1848]—there could very well have been a glut in the Voltaire market. The public needed time to absorb the publishers' output. Moreover, the extensive offerings by the publishers indicated a considerable demand from readers of liberal persuasion.

We need to know the number of copies of each edition. The Restoration government tried to compute the number of "bad books" that were distributed. From an official report, analyzed by the newspapers of the day,[b] it was estimated that between 1817 and 1824 there were twelve published editions of Voltaire's works, comprising a total of 31,000 sets and 1,598,000 volumes. At the same time thirteen editions of Rousseau totaled 24,500 sets and 480,500 volumes. Separate editions of the writings of one or the other put 35,000 sets and 81,000 volumes on the market. In all, there were 2,159,500 volumes of philosophical writings launched against the royalist and clerical reaction over a seven-year period,

---

[a] V. IV, Nos. 2145–2174.
[b] *L'Etoile,* Thursday, June 9, 1821.

and of this frightening number of projectiles, Voltaire accounted for more than 75 percent.

Let us try to discover some of the ways in which this powerful force was utilized. Voltaire acted as both artist and philosopher, the one usually supporting the other. Yet there were times he could be the one without the other. Hence, the two roles must be studied separately. He influenced literature mainly by his discriminating taste and choice of language: first as a propagandist and initiator, but very soon, and down to the time of his death, as the guardian and defender of classical precepts. The intellects he trained had limited and refined principles of taste coupled with a clear, colorless style of writing. They were meticulous about linguistic purity and accuracy. They were frightened by any novelties or bold, unfamiliar imagery. They were quick to heap ridicule on expressive or stylistic details if the inherent thought or idea startled or shocked them. Voltairians shuddered at Chateaubriand, and they detested Romanticism. His devotees, in matters of taste, flourished throughout the nineteenth century, particularly in the University and the magistracy. Thiers[3] exemplified this spirit quite well.

As for tragedy, Voltaire was ranked by his contemporaries alongside Racine and Corneille. A whole generation of writers of tragedy, mediocre, alas, were to follow in his footsteps: Marmontel, La Harpe, Lemierre, etc. His best disciples were foreigners, and we may legitimately include among them the *misogallo* Alfieri who appropriated the Voltairian concept of tragedy. But his influence was to be checked, on the one hand, by the partisans of English drama and the bourgeois *drame*, which went beyond Voltaire's experiments, and on the other hand, by the pure classicists of the Revolutionary and Imperial era who, in the name of Racine and the Greeks, reacted against Voltairian innovations. Meanwhile, the moderate experimentation which occurred during the Restoration, incorporating certain Romantic elements into the writing of tragedy, as with Casimir Delavigne, continued the Voltairian tradition.

Voltaire was the undisputed master of light verse, but Delille replaced him as the authority for didactic poetry, and Jean-Baptiste Rousseau remained, with Malherbe, the arbiter of the ode. The influence of Voltaire's clear and ironic genius was offset, above all, by the vogue for melancholy literature and Ossianism which struck a dominant elegiac note in poetry between 1770 and 1820. Yet despite the effects of Delille and Roucher, Voltaire's fluid, even, monotonous verses retained all their seductive charm to find renewed expression even in the poetry of Lamartine.

In the writing of history, Voltaire's influence radiated outside France. He created a school of philosophical historians who were accused of having sacrificed facts for opinions and critical research for dogmatic philosophical premises. There is truth in these accusations, and neither Mably nor Raynal can satisfy us today as competent historians. But here we must make an exception for Montesquieu and his *Considérations*. Voltaire, for all his flippancies and hasty judgments, for all his passions and prejudices, nonetheless advocated a serious examination and a truthful expostion of historical facts. He had given the world models of composition and simplification and had written narrative masterpieces. We find his precepts and techniques emulated by the English historians Robertson and Gibbon. And the same is true for the best works of French historians who preceded the Romantic Movement or were uninfluenced by it. Many tried to copy his clear methods of exposition and expression while eschewing his philosophy or surpassing him in erudition. If Ruhlière[4] is completely Voltairian, he communicated something of Voltaire to Anquetil,[5] Daunou,[6] Daru,[7] and Thiers.[3] Even Michelet,[8] who had read Voltaire carefully, remembered him in his youth when he wanted to make a clear, concise *précis* of modern history. He even incorporated in his work an entire chapter, intact, from Voltaire's *Essai sur les moeurs*, certain he could not improve on it.

Voltaire's philosophical tales were imitated in the eighteenth-century novel. But *La Nouvelle Héloïse* [Rousseau] and *Werther* [Goethe], and the torrent of sensibility heralding the Romantic Movement, arrested Voltaire's influence on the development of this literary genre. Even in the short story, people wanted something more than sarcasm. It was necessary to write for sensitive souls. Marmontel himself forsook Voltaire.

In the nineteenth century, Chateaubriand, George Sand,[9] and Balzac[10] led the novel into paths ever more remote from *Candide* and *L'Ingénu*. Stendhal,[11] who had an unmistakable affinity for the eighteenth century, is closer to Laclos[12] and Duclos[13] than to

Voltaire. And perhaps Mérimée's[14] artistic sobriety owes nothing to Voltaire. However, traces of Voltaire persisted in the short story writers of a lively, piquant style, like Mme de Girardin[15] or Tillier,[16] the Nivernais author of *Mon Oncle Benjamin,* who is not yet sufficiently well known in France, or again, like Edmond About[17] and his friend Sarcey.[18] Toward the close of the nineteenth century the Voltairian novel had an unexpected revival in the work of a great artist, Anatole France,[19] and in a certain number of younger writers who, between the movements of Naturalism, Lyricism, and Symbolism, tried to preserve Voltaire's qualities of light, witty, trenchant writing, a bit dry and colorless, but always perfectly clear. Among these I would mention Veber,[20] Hermant,[21], and Beaunier.[22]

But where Voltaire's influence was immense, obvious, and still persistent is in the field of journalism, pamphleteering, and all forms of polemical writing. He was the master of militant irony and murderous ridicule. He taught the art of cunning devices, ingenious inventions of plot and incident, and ludicrous or saucy transpositions that tantalized the bored or inattentive reader. He demonstrated how a ponderous question could be deflated, simplified, and reduced to a few truths of common sense. He showed how an opponent's arguments may be transformed into propositions so absurd as to require no refutation whatever. He taught the art of repetition in such a way as to implant an idea in the reader's mind without wearying him, always restating the idea in an unending variety of clever situations and amusing symbols. He was a great artist in forms of writing not usually noted for their artistic merit. He was the forerunner of nineteenth-century polemicists who dramatized current events with imaginative artistry. Among his disciples were Paul-Louis Courier[23] during the Restoration and Tillier under Louis-Philippe. Prévost-Paradol[24] studied him and so, no doubt, did Henri Rochefort.[25] Edmond About and Francisque Sarcey were as Voltairian in style as in wit in their periodical *Le XIXᵉ Siècle* ("The Nineteenth Century"), written during the Third Republic. And when Anatole France, in his latter years, moved away from the pure novel into social and political satire, he again accentuated the Voltairian spirit of his work in his exquisite dialogues *L'Orme du Mail* ("The Elm Tree on the Mall") and *L'Anneau d'améthyste* ("The Amethyst Ring"), in which dramatic action is relegated to the background by philosophical criticism.

Setting aside his controversial writings, we may say that in the nineteenth century Voltaire was the principal arbiter of style for literate Frenchmen whose temperament was disinclined to assimilate the Romantic or Parnassian schools, who avoided lyrical effervescence, pictorial intensity, or the sculptured, plastic effect in poetry. Wherever the style was primarily intellectual without being oratorical and dialectic (I make this reservation for Brunetière,[26] who surely borrowed nothing from Voltaire), we can easily discern Voltairian elements in the style of these cultivated Frenchmen. Cherbuliez,[27] Boissier,[28] Lemaître,[29] Faguet,[30] and many university people furnish ample proof. Voltaire confirmed, without creating it, the French need for ease, lightness, clarity, finesse, and a bright "gaiety" of expression. His prose became the symbol for qualities we consider typically French, and it imposed on others the obligation to emulate these qualities. One may add to them whatever one pleases, but they remain the indispensable prerequisites. Flaubert[31] did not disavow Voltaire while admiring Chateaubriand[32] and Hugo,[33] and although he achieved in his own style a beauty that was hardly Voltairian, he took care to avoid the faults Voltaire deemed unpardonable. There is also a bit of Voltaire (of Voltaire's taste, that is) to be found in Ernest Renan.[34] It is reflected in his vibrant and colorful prose amid the bold interplay of subtle metaphysics and mystical imagery, revealing that luminous smile of an alert common sense, ever wary of dangerous extremes and ever anxious to avoid the heavy-handed or the obscure. More than one Voltairian has been converted to the Christian faith while remaining a disciple of Voltaire in matters of style and intelligence. And more than one Catholic has found an affinity of taste with Voltaire.

But for a long time, and oftener than not, Voltaire's seductive literary charms were the vehicle for his ideas and opinions. It is especially difficult to analyze this question insofar as the eighteenth century is concerned. To a very large degree, Voltaire's strength resided in his talent for bestowing the beguiling form of his inimitable wit upon the opinions and aspirations of his contemporaries. The duchesse de Choiseul has clearly explained what it is that makes his precise influence as difficult of analysis as it was undoubtedly significant and widespread. On September 21, 1779, she wrote:

Whatever faults may be attributed to Voltaire, he will always be for me the writer whom I shall read and reread with the greatest pleasure because of his taste and his universality. What does it matter that he tells me nothing new if he articulates and develops my own thoughts, and if he tells me better than anyone else what others have already told me? I have no need for him to teach me more than what everyone knows, and what other author can tell me, as he does, what everyone knows?

There is a bit of self-deception in this observation, and it was part of Voltaire's art to be able to make his reader believe that everyone, including the reader himself, already knew and thought precisely those things Voltaire wanted him to know and to think. Nevertheless, there is a great deal of truth in Mme de Choiseul's remark. We may consider Montesquieu,[35] Rousseau,[36] Buffon,[37] and Diderot[38] as greater geniuses, but Voltaire was, in the broadest sense, the most representative mind of his age, the one in whom the brilliance of eighteenth century French society was summed up most completely and brought to its most exquisite perfection. He embodied its good and bad features, its graces and blemishes, its breadth of view and its limitations, its impulses and enthusiasms as well as its hesitations and timidities.

The memoirs of Bachaumont[39] show clearly the extent of this harmony between Voltaire and the age in which he lived, and they indicate the strong hold that Voltaire had on eighteenth-century society. Cultivated and sophisticated people paid little attention to Voltaire's violent anti-Christian tirades. They were too indifferent to the truth, too unconcerned about articles of faith to become excited over questions of dogma. As good Frenchmen, it cost them nothing to go to mass, to be married by the parish priest, and to have their children baptized: ceremonial acts of little importance but socially respectable.

Voltaire de-Christianized many minds without inoculating them with the virulence of his hatred. In the eighteenth and early nineteenth centuries there were even Voltairian women, quietly, serenely agnostic, who managed quite well to do without religious faith or fervor: the duchesse de Choiseul, the vicomtesse d'Houdetot, Mme Quinet, Mme Dumesnil (Michelet's friend), etc. I do not know if the species was ever very numerous. Doubtless Rousseau made more converts among women than Voltaire. But all France, or almost all, applauded and followed Voltaire when he championed deism and rejected atheism, when he fought ecclesiastical abuses and the financial privileges and tyranny of Rome, when he sought to subject the clergy to taxation, to reduce the number of monks or even eliminate them, and when he became indignant over fanaticism and religious persecution. In these matters Voltaire found support even among many of the clergy, as well as among the less serious-minded elements of society.

The people were still marching behind his banner when he accepted the principle of an absolute monarchy, provided it used its power and authority in the nation's true interests. They were behind him when he denounced all the abuses of the judiciary and came to the aid of its victims, when he fought governmental abuses and called for practical reforms, when he voiced his contempt for war, and when he advocated a peaceful monarchy that would create public prosperity through wise legislation in favor of commerce and agriculture.

Generally speaking, Voltaire acted upon his age by developing its critical faculties, by creating a public with an *esprit critique*. He brought to the court of public opinion every question concerning government and administration, as well as religious, political, judicial, and economic questions. He accustomed public common sense to regard itself as competent in all matters, and he turned public opinion into one of the controlling forces in public affairs. To be sure, this movement did not begin with Voltaire and was not confined to him and his influence. In the affairs of the Constitution *Unigenitus*[40] and in parliamentary and ministerial conflicts, since the time of the Regency, one had heard the same appeals to the public, the same voices of opinion. Every *philosophe* used as his main weapon in the battle for men's minds this same technique for manipulating and arousing the nation's collective thoughts and feelings. However, it is here that Voltaire seems to have played the most active and conspicuous role. It was he who, as I have said, served *par excellence* the function of a newspaper and of an entire press. With his innumerable writings he formed a spirit and attitude designated

in his day as *patriotique* or *républicain*. It could be defined as
the interest that the ordinary citizen, the private individual,
took in all matters concerning the public welfare and in all the
means of achieving general prosperity. It involved the individual's participation in the affairs of state, even under an
absolute monarchy, by engaging in constant criticism of social
abuses and by endeavoring at all times to bring about practical
reforms and improvements.

It was in large measure Voltairianism that disarmed the nobility in 1789 and handed it over to the Revolution, an accessory,
in its thinking, to its own dispossession. Montesquieu favored a
social élite. Rousseau was too paradoxical and extreme. Voltaire
gave the privileged classes what they wanted, both of good and
evil, and thus he indoctrinated and molded them so well that he
furnished them with a rationale that was allied, from the outset,
to the intentions of their enemies. They would be forced to
emigrate in order to recreate a nobility with a conservative,
Catholic outlook, suspicious of criticism or new ideas.

Obviously, Voltaire's influence was halted by the Revolution.
Events moved at such a pace that all his ideas were quickly outdated. The abuses he had denounced were uprooted along with
the institutions Voltaire would have retained. The reforms he
thought realizable around 1760 or 1775 were either rapidly en-
acted or found to be no longer applicable to the new France.
Perhaps he helped in defining the new relationship between
Church and State, the establishment of civil marriages, the
standardization of weights and measures, and the unifying of the
legislative processes. The Declaration of the Rights of Man[41]
was no more his handiwork than anyone else's. It was a product
of the entire movement of the eighteenth century. We can only
observe that if Montesquieu appears prominently in article 16,
articles 7, 9, 10, and 11 correspond to the objectives most strongly
advocated by Voltaire. But once again, the various credits cannot
be accurately allocated.

During the Revolution itself, the Voltairian mind was no
longer fashionable. It was a time when the public demanded
enthusiasm, passion, oratory, and emotional excesses. Rousseau,
better than Voltaire, spoke in tones that suited the occasion and
touched men's souls. But the Consulate and the Empire recalled

Voltaire to active duty. A substantial portion of Voltaire's ideas were unquestionably ignored under Bonaparte, particularly his views on the control and criticism of public authority and his hatred of war. But in the man who had served as "the journalist of the opposition," as Voltaire had done under Louis XV, there were the makings of a Prefect[42] of the Empire: an enlightened skepticism, a hatred of metaphysical ideologies and political systems, a conception of benevolent and active despotism which develops a nation's resources, a materialistic philosophy of government administration dedicated to practical improvements and an increase in social well being, and unequivocal views on the subordination of the Church to civil authority. The Concordat,[43] with its several amendments, was not at variance with Voltaire's aspirations.

But it was from 1815 to 1830, during the Restoration, that Voltairianism triumphed. It led the struggle against legitimist and Catholic reaction. It furnished arms, a strategy, arguments, and an arsenal of facts, views, and witticisms for liberal journalists and pamphleteers. It was the favorite reading matter for the liberal bourgeoisie which found Voltairian ideas within its grasp and a spirit pleasing to its taste. As the Church had made herself the protectress and directress of the monarchy, so liberalism tended to identify itself with Voltairianism. And from the Voltairian spirit emerged a portion that eventually came to be considered Voltairianism in its entirety; namely, a hatred for the Church and a contempt for religion. Moreover, after the Revolution almost all of Voltaire's politics was useless except his pleas for freedom of the press. The new France of the Restoration reduced Voltaire to little more than his anticlericalism. That was to be his function throughout the rest of the nineteenth century, a supply depot, as it were, for anticlerical ammunition. Consequently, Voltaire's popularity would reflect those moments in which clericalism appeared to pose the greatest threat to liberal forces. Voltairianism governed after 1830 and educated the youth of the nation in the university. Mme Ackermann, born in 1828, was imbued with Voltaire under her father's influence. The great revolution of 1848 rejected Voltaire, who was no longer sufficient for the situation. But during the Second Empire and the Third Republic we discover him again in the polemical writings of such newspapers as *Le Siècle* ("The Century") and *Le XIX*ᵉ *Siècle* ("The 19th Century").

From 1850 on, however, Voltairian influence continued to decline, losing itself in the mass of eighteenth-century traditions which likewise thinned out and exhausted themselves. The Revolution had lost Voltaire his following among the nobility. In the nineteenth century the Falloux education law[44] and a rising fear of socalism rallied the bourgeoisie to the cause of religion, thereby depriving Voltaire of those very readers who appreciated him most and for whom he was the writer *par excellence*. The more anticlericalism filtered down among the masses, the less readily it could draw sustenance from Voltaire or arm itself with Voltairian wit and irony. Common people demanded simpler reading matter and cruder weapons.

Among the literate class which the Church had failed to win back Voltaire lost ground. The rich and powerful literature of the nineteenth century gave us new requirements in taste and an artistic ideal that Voltaire no longer satisfied. His influence on us decreased with every new position taken by the Romantic Movement, the Parnassian school, the Symbolists, and contemporary writers. But more especially, an educated man in our day and age, knowing the requirements for scholarly research, will no longer draw his information from Voltaire. Apart from material errors and inadvertencies which rigorous modern standards no longer condone, the progress made in philosophical and historical sciences, psychology, and Biblical exegesis has brought to light aspects of problems that Voltaire had never suspected. If Renan, who replaced him, had already made him obsolete, all the more reason for our not adopting at face value Voltaire's views of religious phenomena and religious history. We can no longer discuss these matters in Voltaire's *terms. Accordingly, while aware that we are continuing in our time the work he undertook in his day, we now find in all Voltaire's anti-Christian polemics, whether in their argumentation or form of presentation, nothing more than an historical museum. It was serviceable in combating the Church in 1770. It has scarcely any relevance to the twentieth century.

The Church, moreover, is no longer what it was. It has, to a certain extent, revised its apologetics, abandoned certain theses, and reformed its scholarship. Even against conservative theologians, those, for example, who still defend the authenticity of the Pentateuch, we need other arguments than those of Voltairian polemic. The result of all this is that Voltaire is read less frequently today, or else he is read for different reasons. Outside the circle of cultivated readers there are a certain number who, in reading Voltaire, make no distinction between form and substance and are not in the least troubled by a concern for historical perspective. They apply everything Voltaire wrote to the world we now live in. There are such. But how many are there? What role do these Voltairians play in the intellectual movement of our time?

It seems to me beyond question that if Voltaire still has an influence to wield in the France of today, it should be, above all, a literary and intellectual influence of pure form. His definitions of good taste, and his enslavement to those definitions, will never again be taken as infallible authority. But as Romanticism fades into the distance, it is possible that there will be a rebirth of the desire for clear, carefully winnowed thoughts and ideas, and a renewed love of the simple, refined expression. It is possible that there will be a demand for lessons in literary style and analysis such as are found in those parts of Voltaire's work least bound by rules and classical ornamentation, in such writings as his *Mélanges* ("Miscellanies"), *Romans* ("novels"), and *Correspondance*. It would appear that, since the passing of Naturalism and the crisis in Symbolism, the evolution of prose writing has been in the direction of clarity and simplicity, which is to say, toward the Voltairian qualities of the eighteenth century.

Shall I say a word about Voltaire in countries outside France? Here again, it would be easier to write a history of his reputation than of his influence.[a] We need to know the precise extent to which French civilization influenced the rest of Europe in the eighteenth and nineteenth centuries in order to claim credit for clearly distinguishing the part that Voltaire played. If I venture to suggest what seems to me probable as of the present moment, I would judge Voltaire's influence very weak in England, except

[a] V. Rossel, *Histoire des relations entre la France et l'Allemagne*. Eug. Bouvy, *Voltaire et l'Italie*.

in the area of historical writing. Philosophical thought in England was well ahead of Voltaire and had little, if anything, to gain from him. Also Voltaire shocked the English conscience and English notions of decency. And finally, the age in which France's classical forms made their imprint on English literature was drawing to a close while Voltaire was just on the threshold of his career and England was taking cognizance of her own genius. It is not that Voltaire was unappreciated in that country. Indeed, he was perhaps better appreciated there than in France. But England studied and judged him more than she followed him.

On the other hand, in every continental country, even in Spain and Portugal, there were a considerable number of Voltairian minds in the second half of the eighteenth century. They included princes, noblemen, and members of the bourgeoisie, all imbued with Voltairian skepticism, fond of trenchant mockery, and alien to feelings of respect or reverence, who delighted in a style of writing that was deft and clear in expression and elegantly casual in tone. Frederick II was the most illustrious representative of this category of men in whose intellectual development Voltaire played what seems to have been the preponderant role. The same intellectual type can be discovered among men of all backgrounds: Germans, Hungarians, Russians, Italians, etc.

The birth and development of a national literature in Germany barred the road to Voltairian influence in that country and, by its extension, prevented the spread of Voltairianism in other parts of eastern Europe. It was Voltaire whom "the bards" of Goettingen despised in Wieland.[45] Then came Romanticism to add new obstacles. As in France, liberalism and the need to counteract ecclesiastical power prolonged Voltaire's influence in certain countries. It was strong in Italy where aspirations for social reform, for liberty and unity, and a hatred for monks and priests found nourishment in Voltaire. In varying degrees and in different ways, and despite all sorts of divergent views, such men as Gorani,[46] Beccaria,[47] Pietro Verri,[48] and later on in the nineteenth century, Foscolo,[49] Monti,[50] and a number of writers and journalists received and transmitted Voltairian thoughts and ideas. We find in Spain, among the liberal *afrancesados*, controversialists molded in the school of Ferney, writers who cultivated the neatly turned phrase and the pithy, caustic comment. I mention only Mariano de Larra.[51]

In general, in countries outside France, to the extent that historical circumstances moved further away from the conditions that obtained in France when Voltaire's work first appeared, his influence is not easily discernible except among certain clear-thinking minds at odds with their social group or in revolt against its demands and prejudices. In Germany it was the skeptic Wieland and later on the ironist Heinrich Heine,[52] who called himself "a German nightingale nesting in Voltaire's wig." And is there not also a bit of Voltairian humor in the sarcasm of Lord Byron? He would allow no one to criticize Voltaire, "the greatest genius of France, the universal Voltaire." He dedicated to him a stanza of his *Childe Harold* in which he drew a sympathetic portrait that attests to a precise and first-hand knowledge of the man as well as his work.

> The one was fire and fickleness, a child,
> Most mutable in wishes, but in mind
> A wit as various,—gay, grave, sage, or wild,—
> Historian, bard, philosopher combined;
> He multiplied himself among mankind,
> The Proteus of their talents: but his own
> Breathed most in ridicule,—which, as the wind,
> Blew where it listed, laying all things prone,
> Now to o'erthrow a fool, and now to shake a throne.
>
> (I, 106)

COMMENTARY

by René Pomeau

Translator's note

The following commentary (translated from the French) first
appeared as an Appendix to the 1960 edition of Lanson's *Voltaire*
published by Librairie Hachette, Paris, "reviewed and brought up
to date" by the French scholar René Pomeau. M. Pomeau states in
his prefatory remarks to the same edition: "Gustave Lanson's *Voltaire* is by way of becoming a classic. We did not feel we had the
right to change a word in the text except for a few dates or chronological details. Wherever the results of half a century of Voltairian
studies imposed a correction or modification, we have added a note.
Where the question necessitated a fuller discussion, we have dealt
with it in the Appendix."

This "Appendix" by René Pomeau (which I have chosen to call
a "Commentary"), coupled with Peter Gay's *Introduction* to this
volume, effectively updates the Lanson biography from the standpoint of recent Voltairian scholarship and, in particular, the newly
discovered Voltaire correspondence published by Theodore Besterman at the Institut et Musée Voltaire in Geneva, Switzerland.

R.A.W.

If the value of a work is measured by its resistance to the erosion
of time, the little book on Voltaire by Gustave Lanson will remain as one of those rare critical works enshrined in the storehouse
of a literature. More than half a century has passed since this
essay first appeared, but it has not aged. Solidly and finely written,
consistently accurate in tone, precise without losing itself in endless
detail, carefully balanced in its judgments, this work demonstrates
the power of an objective critical method based on seriously established documentation.

Yet Lanson's very method prepared the reader to expect that
the portrait sketched in 1906 would eventually require some re-

touching. Today we must take into account documents brought to light during fifty years of research. Letters by Voltaire or relating to Voltaire have continued to be published in large numbers. The Moland edition of his *Correspondance* having become increasingly inadequate, Mr. Besterman finally undertook the immense critical task that this great work of French literature has long deserved. His edition, begun in 1953, brings together letters neglected by Moland or else published since the Moland edition [1877–85]. Following the manuscript or the most reliable text available, Besterman restores those letters that had been truncated, amalgamated, or reworked and were copied by Beuchot from the Kehl edition and by Moland from the Beuchot edition. But more importantly, Mr. Besterman has located many hitherto unpublished letters that are sometimes quite remarkable. At the same time many studies appearing since 1906 (some by Lanson himself) have thrown light on little-known aspects of Voltaire's life and works while, with the passing of time, there have also been changes in the over-all view of the Age of Enlightenment. By a fortunate coincidence, this progress has gone hand in hand with an enrichment of the psychological understanding on which literary studies are founded.

The result is that Voltaire appears more complex now than in Gustave Lanson's time. Beginning with the very first lines in the essay, new documents oblige us to reopen a debate in which the psychologist is soon involved. A mystery surrounds the birth of François-Marie Arouet. In his *Vie de Voltaire* [1786], Duvernet indicates two persons who "took a great interest" in the child: the abbé de Châteauneuf, his godfather, about whom the biographer gives abundant details, and M. de Rochebrune, whom he is content simply to mention. Apparently Duvernet knew more than he reported, for this much is now an incontestable fact: Voltaire was persuaded that his true father was this Rochebrune "of an old and noble family from upper Auvergne," "a musketeer, officer, and author" (Best., 6283). At *Les Délices* in 1756 Voltaire declared before his nieces, while discussing D'Alembert, that he, too, was an illegitimate child (*ibid.*); three years earlier he had attributed to heredity the "dropsy" from which he suffered. Rochebrune had died of this disease (Best., 4832, letter to Mme Denis). Contrary then to the opinion of Desnoiresterres, it is in the literal sense one must interpret Voltaire's mention of the "bastard of Rochebrune" in a letter dated June 8, 1744 addressed to Richelieu, to that Richelieu whose family had long been associated with the family of Arouet the notary (the duke was godparent to Armand Arouet) and who presumably knew whereof he spoke when referring to Voltaire's birth.

It is therefore reasonable to ask whether we are not obliged to reexamine the question of Voltaire's date and place of birth. Voltaire repeatedly maintained that he was born February 20, 1694 "despite *those* engravings which contain the printed falsehood indicating *his* date of birth as November 20th" (letter to Richelieu, Feb. 27, 1765; and the same declaration to Damilaville, Feb. 20, 1765; and also to d'Argental, Jan. 1, 1777; and in the *Commentaire historique*). People said that these were fantastic statements. But Condorcet and Duvernet, who gained their information from Voltaire and his friends, also report that he was born on the 20th of February at Châtenay, a neighboring village of Sceaux; he was so weak they thought he would soon die like the two children of Mme Arouet who had preceded him. Because he insisted on living, they had to have him baptized. But according to Duvernet, they concealed from the priest of the church of Saint-André-des-Arcs in Paris the fact that the child had been born nine months earlier in another parish. This is a plausible account if we assume that Mme Arouet had been obliged to give birth in secret. As for the documents deemed decisive, the baptismal register and the letter from a cousin to relatives living in Poitou, these contain only the official version of the event.

The question offers more than just anecdotal interest. Voltaire was never frank about the proofs he had of his illegitimacy. Was his conviction not based, then, on any serious evidence? If not, it may be regarded as highly revelatory of some hidden psychological intention. But if the opposite hypothesis is true, it is clear that Voltaire's certainty that he was not the son of his alleged father undoubtedly had a profound influence on his conscience. He felt he was smuggled into the world "as contraband" (to quote the old man of Ferney on returning to Paris in 1778)! André Delattre has proposed, with necessary circumspection, a psychoanalytical interpretation: Voltaire lost his mother at the age of seven; he did not like François Arouet, his father; he continually quarreled with his "Jansenist brother," a hard and insensitive boy of strange, unstable character. Little is known about Voltaire's childhood. This new fact, the conviction of his illegitimacy, would reinforce the psychoanalytical explanation of an element by no means unimportant, assuming, at least, that we grant that little Arouet was informed of the fact at an early age. In any event, at the age of sixty-two he was rejoicing to friends over his mother's preference for a Roche-brune in place of Arouet the notary, "who was a very common man to have produced genius." He always "flattered himself on being under obligation for his birth" to that witty individual, Rochebrune (Best., 6283).

In view of these considerations we shall have to revise certain opinions about Voltaire as a young man, the Voltaire before 1726. This entertainer of the Regency, whom Lanson sees diverting him-self with light verses and witticisms, is indeed a real person. But it is not enough to say "he was neither respectful nor docile" (p. 34). There already appears another and harsher Voltaire, a young *révolté,* an angry young man: no sooner out of school, having shaken off the Jesuit hold on him and likewise resisting the will of his father, he affirms from the very outset his general attitude of opposition and dissent. Lanson perceives the rebel in Voltaire, but closer attention should have been given to the two major works of the young writer, works that fall just short of being masterpieces but are fraught with significance: *Œdipe* and *La Henriade.*

Œdipe is not one of the kind of tragedies Voltaire was to turn out later on, the ones he would improvise in a couple of weeks. He worked on it for years and put a great deal of himself into it. Care-fully pondered by Voltaire, the philosphy of this traditional drama deserves close scrutiny. Over and above his satirical epigrams against the clergy, it contains an accusation against an unjust deity. Voltaire, like Oedipus declaring his innocence in the fifth act, rises up in protest against a cruel God. Again in 1722 (for this appears the likely date of the essential contents of the *Epître à Uranie*) Voltaire apostrophizes the Supreme Being: "I am not a Christian, but it is to love Thee better." In his *Henriade* the strongest pas-sages are those satirizing the working agents of a sanguinary deity: the assassins of the Saint Bartholomew's Day Massacre, the fanatics of the Ligue [the Catholic party formed in 1576 to combat Cal-vinism]. He begins his assault on oppressive intolerance and the official doctrines of the day. At an early date he is in contact with the English embassy, only recently in open hostility to France. He associates with Bolingbroke, writes to Pope, reads Locke's *Essay Concerning Human Understanding;* he is learning English and has scarcely disembarked at Greenwich when he begins keeping his *Notebook* in the English language. Here again we must not seek explanations based on minor incidents. Even without the drub-bing administered by the Chevalier de Rohan, he would have made his journey to London. Before the year 1726 Voltaire was already becoming a *philosophe* in the English manner. Beneath the outward appearance of a man of the world, advanced to the status of a court poèt, the essential Voltaire was already fashioned, the only one with a future before him. Playful and waggish, he could muster powerful forces of indignation nourished by deep emotional resources. But he preferred to appear as a cold, cynical mocker. A sense of decency made him choose an indirect form of expression, thereby restraining the savage emotions within him.

It was well known that he seldom listened to the dictates of his conscience and that on occasion he could play the most reprehensible sort of tricks. To the list of his dishonest deeds we must now add the following, which has come to be better known: the dedication of *Mahomet* to Pope Benedict XIV. Actually, it was not a question of a "dedication." The simple fact is that, after the banning of his tragedy, Voltaire had the audacity to address the text to the Roman pontiff. He counted on this stratagem to override the opposition of the *dévots* [religious zealots] who had blocked his admission to the French Academy. So on the 17th of August, 1745, he dispatched five letters to Rome. Two were for the pope (Best., 2949, 2950). In one of these he expressed his thanks for five holy medals he had obtained by means of a diplomatic maneuver. The other letter accompanied *Mahomet* and requested the protection of His Holiness for this work directed "against the founder of a false and barbarous sect." At the same time he sent to Leprotti and to Cardinals Passionei and Quirini his *Poème de Fontenoy* (Best., 2951, 2952, 2953). Benedict XIV answered, September 15, 1745, with prudence and finesse. He thanked Voltaire for his "very beautiful new poem," that is, *le Poème de Fontenoy* which Cardinal Passionei had presented to him. Of his *Mahomet*, not a word. Such is the authentic text of the papal brief reproduced in Besterman 2967 from the original. Obviously, a harmless reply of this sort could not serve Voltaire's purposes. Accordingly, he circulated a falsified copy whose manuscript is described in the catalogue of bookseller Jacques Lambert for the year 1957 under the number 185. It attributes to the pope a sentence which translates as follows: "Several weeks ago there was offered to us on your behalf your most beautiful tragedy of *Mahomet* which we read with the greatest pleasure. . . ." This forgery was printed in the Dresden edition (1748) as a prefatory comment to *Mahomet* along with the Besterman letters 2949 and 2980, a reply to Benedict XIV in which Voltaire declares he is "forced to recognize the infallibility of the pope in literary decisions as in more respectable matters." No one at the time suspected the hoax. Neither Benedict XIV nor the papal nuncio offered a word of protest.

In Voltaire's biography a reexamination is required of those mid-century years 1745–1750. Since Mr. Besterman's discovery of the *Lettres d'amour,* we now know the role played by Mme Denis. Certain contemporaries of Voltaire, his secretary Collini and Mme d'Epinay, had insinuated there were intimate ties between the great man and his niece. He himself had uttered imprudent remarks which his enemies seized upon. The *Lettres d'Alsace,* published by G. Jean Aubry (1938), have confirmed these rumors and accusations. Should one call it incest? That was not the view commonly held in the eighteenth century. As Nancy Mitford has emphasized, it was not rare for an uncle to marry his niece. The court of Rome granted the necessary dispensations, and Voltaire was informed of the cost.[1] Perhaps he envisaged an eventual marriage with Mme Denis. When was this liaison formed? Certain details suggest that it antedated the death of Mme du Châtelet, a hypothesis confirmed with the publication of the *Lettres d'amour.*

Marie-Louise Mignot, married to the *commissaire des guerres* Denis, became a widow in May 1744. Back in Paris in the month of August, Voltaire consoled this niece, for whom he always felt a special affection. Soon their relations began, interrupted in 1750 by Voltaire's departure for Prussia. Mme Denis dominated the final years of what is customarily called "the Cirey period." Why did Voltaire, who already knew English, begin to learn Italian around 1744–1745? It was for Mme Denis, who wrote fluently in this "language of love." It was in Italian that the lover, cheerfully defying social convention, composed his most ardent letters. To be sure, he remained officially linked to Mme du Châtelet. He appeared at court with her, and with her he gambled at the queen's table. She continued to be his intellectual partner and confidante. But the other ties were broken. Was she duped by her lover's efforts to conceal his infidelity? It would seem so. Yet some *Réflexions sur le bonheur* ("Reflections on Happiness") that she put in writing several months before her death testify to great emotional disturbance. How can one harbor resentment against her for having sought consolation in the somewhat ridiculous passion she felt for Saint-Lambert? After her tragic disappearance we are inclined to believe that in Voltaire's profound grief there entered

[1] See the Voltairian quip quoted by Lanson, p. 133. (R.W.)

a measure of remorse for not having sufficiently loved this truly superior woman who was too often the target of calumny.

She had known him well. "He is in love with love," she used to say. A capricious, sensual, and sensitive Voltaire, such in effect is the man revealed in his love letters. Voltaire: a name that too often evokes the old man of 83, sculpted by Houdon. Mme Denis: one conjures up the picture of a dumpy matron whom Mme d'Epinay laughed at on her visits to *Les Délices*. For this image let us substitute the attractive portrait by Van Loo reproduced on the first page of the *Lettres d'amour*. It is not surprising that Voltaire succumbed to the voluptuous charms of this young widow, easygoing and fond of pleasure . . . and by no means stupid. In her mind as in her person she exhibited a suppleness, a graciousness and playfulness of nature that Voltaire always loved. Her fickleness merely added to her charms. As Voltaire's mistress she did not deny herself a few flirtations. She even thought of remarrying. But she also knew how to be tender, thus assuring her power over a lover who was already growing old. That great polemicist affected a pitiless pose in his public writings, but in his secret correspondence he revealed himself a vulnerable human being.

He underwent a critical period from 1745 to 1750. As a member of the Academy and historiographer, he had achieved worldly success. These *Lettres d'amour* give a glimpse of the official writer working for the court. But these same letters disclose, above all, the dissatisfaction he experienced in the wake of apparent success. To the fatigue accompanying the life of a courtier were added the complications of his double liaison and his anxieties about his health. His digestion was worse than ever. He had "to die of hunger in order to live." He would have liked to escape from all these worries and end his days "unknown to anyone," alone with Mme Denis. It was at this time he wrote his *Epître à Mme Denis sur la vie de Paris et de Versailles,* that anti-*Mondain*. It was at this time the Voltairian short story was born. His correspondence from 1747 to 1748 quivers with a nervous, overwrought excitement to be transmuted into *Babouc, Zadig,* and *Memnon*—all satires on that Parisian life as charming and deceitful as "la belle Denis."

Were they "sterile," "wasted" years as Gustave Lanson wrote (p. 70)? Not at all. Voltaire experienced the crisis of a man reaching fifty. At this turning point in life what direction was he going to take? Would he, like so many others, look back on the past? Age fifty, the age of conversions. A Gresset, who until that age had been something of a mocker and a freethinker, became a devout Christian. And had not Voltaire assured Father de la Tour of the fervor of his Catholic sentiments? True, it was for the purpose of being admitted to the Academy. But no matter; the good Fathers, his former teachers, were waiting. He had only to say the word. He would be well received.

The Fathers were to be disappointed. As a philosopher and man of action he resolved the crisis by moving forward into the future. He emerged from his trial convinced of his mission of human emancipation. It was the date 1749 that he was to inscribe at the head of his *Sermon des cinquante,* a virulent indictment of that religion on which rested an entire social order or disorder. This unusual "gentleman-in-waiting of the king's chamber" is incensed that society is not doing "all that could be done." The best of Voltaire is present therein, and posterity was to be unaware for many years of the lover of Mme Denis. But after the discovery of a Voltaire *tenero amico,* the man and his work became suffused with a more human warmth, while at the same time the living source of his philosophy became apparent. A heartless, bloodless mocker, this swashbuckling foe of hypocrisy? Assuredly not. In love with women, in love with life, it was from the same depths of his being that he despised all manner of joyless oppressors.

When he left France to enter the service of Frederick the Great, it was agreed that Mme Denis would join him shortly. From the banks of the Spree he wrote to her letters that were at times very melancholy. But another woman then found a place in his life. At Berlin he reencountered the Countess Bentinck, related to the highest aristocracy of England and North Germany; she was residing at the Prussian court to conduct a lawsuit against her husband, from whom she was separated. A *grande dame,* as distinguished for her wit as for her high birth, she was a Sanseverina of the North with whom Voltaire formed an intimate friendship.

They exchanged letters two or three times a week. In these communications, recently published in the large edition of Voltaire's *Correspondance,* there are many new details. We discover, for instance, a secret cause of the conflict that set Voltaire against Maupertuis. The countess had quarreled with the austere president of the Academy of Berlin. There was an oppressive atmosphere around the king. Friendship with the charming woman helped Voltaire to put up with this gloomy atmosphere, permitting him, moreover, to uncover and frustrate many plots and machinations. Were it not for Charlotte-Sophie, Countess Bentinck, he would have perhaps deserted the court at Potsdam sooner. Less harsh and egotistical than he was reported, Voltaire delighted in the ambiance of pleasure and refinement created by the presence of a woman. Having lived with Mme du Châtelet and Mme Denis, he could not have survived in the isolation of an exclusively masculine society.

On his return trip he was joined in Frankfort by his niece, whom a good German called "Madame de Voltaire," unaware he had said anything humorous (Best., 4710). In the aftermath of the royal affront, Voltaire accused Frederick of having wanted to insult, through his agents Freytag and Schmidt, a woman whose relations with Voltaire were well known to the king. He would never forget those painful days. From then on he felt firmly attached to Mme Denis, who would never again leave him except for a few months' quarrel in 1768–1769.

Accordingly, we would be guilty of making a rash and hasty judgment to oppose a certain "femininity" in Rousseau to the masculine character of Voltaire and his work. The frivolous gaiety of his *Contes* and *Facéties* is no less "feminine" than the sentimental warmth of the *Héloïse*. However different he was from his great rival, he knew, like Rousseau, how to please women. And like Rousseau, he loved them. Throughout his life there was always an intimate woman friend at his side, and others whose smiles brightened his everyday existence: Mme du Deffand, Mme d'Epinay, his "belle philosophe," Cornélie-Chiffon, Belle et Bonne, Mademoiselle Quinze-Ans. . . .

These recent disclosures, filling in, as they do, a hitherto sketchy chapter in the life of Voltaire, should put an end to a long debate. The contemporary school of character analysis has, not without reason, considered Voltaire a case study illustrating the effectiveness of its methods. His alleged traits of character, an extensive documentation of his actions, certain facts about his life, the dominant qualities of his writing, and his antithetical position *vis-à-vis* Rousseau—all of this seemed to promise a particularly uncomplicated analysis, one that would explain Voltaire's life and works in terms of his character. For that matter, whoever has dealt with one or the other has felt intuitively the importance that had to be given to the man's originality. It was an unwitting character analyst who, in 1734, drew a portrait of this "ardent person always going and coming"—an image destined to have a long career. A character study is implicit in each of the various essays on Voltaire, with Lanson's study no exception.

Yet on putting it to the test, difficulties were encountered in fitting the Protean man into any one of the given categories devised by Heymans and Wierzma. That he was an *actif* no one has ever denied. It is likewise conceded that he most frequently acted in a manner remarkably *primaire,* that he reacted with astonishing rapidity, and that he loathed all types of systematic theories. Yet here we must make certain reservations. Not only did he harbor resentments for a long, sometimes a very long time, but he generally conceived and executed his plans with carefully calculated forethought. In the presence of personalities as richly endowed as Voltaire's, we must be wary of schematic simplifications. He was flexible enough to give evidence, should the need arise, of reactions opposite to those that were habitual with him. . . .[1]

Concerning the Ferney period of Voltaire's life, neither the *Correspondance* nor recent studies have produced anything to contradict Lanson's presentation. We note only that the anti-Voltairian reaction set in before the death of the patriarch. As the years passed, the influence of Rousseau and, to a lesser degree, Diderot counteracted the influence of Voltaire. After 1770 he sensed that his influence had waned. He remained attached to a period that had ended and which appeared remote to the new generation. Irritated over the vogue for Shakespeare, regretting that he himself had given the public a taste for melodramatic spectacles, Voltaire returned to a strict classicism in his final tragedies. But *Sophonisbe, Irène,* and *Agathocle* were not very successful. Against the attacks of the new school of physiocrats he defended the memory of Louis XIV and the "great age" of the Sun King. One of his last projects was a reply to the *Mémoires* of the duc de Saint-Simon, portions of which he had read. His own age had not fulfilled his expectations. He had hoped to inter *l'infâme,*[2] but he saw that the "monster" had a tenacious hold on life. Disenchanted, he devoted more attention to local affairs in the region of Gex. It was a semi-retreat from which he suddenly emerged to return to Paris to die.

He had committed a serious indiscretion. The Archbishop of Paris and M. de Tersac, his parish priest, had decided to refuse him a Christian burial, failing a retraction according to established

---

[1] Several lines couched in the technical jargon of characterology have been omitted here. (R.W.)

[2] *Ecrasez l'infâme!* ("Crush the Infamous One!"); this was a Voltairian "war cry" generally interpreted as referring to religious fanaticism of any sort but especially Catholicism and its priesthood. (R.W.)

procedures. Voltaire succeeded in eluding this requirement by manipulating the abbé Gauthier, a good man who was well intentioned but rather naïve and maladroit, as the authentic text of his letters reveals. Still, nothing had been settled when the death agony of the old man began on the 20th of May. Fortunately, his nephew, abbé Mignot, acted in Voltaire's behalf. One week before his death the abbé concluded an agreement with Tersac, a fact we have learned from recently discovered correspondence. After his death Voltaire was to be transported, as though he were an invalid, to his estate at Ferney where his remains were to be interred. In the meantime the ministry intervened. M. de Maurepas decided that the corpse would be conveyed, fully dressed, outside the city limits. After a journey of several miles they were to stop at an inn to have the body embalmed. Then they would continue on to Ferney. But Mignot preferred not to run the risk of such a journey. This sly individual provided himself with two documents signed by M. de Tersac: a certificate attesting the authenticity of Voltaire's profession of faith, dated March 2nd (and judged inadequate); and a permit to move the body, obtained *in extremis*. He was thus able to proceed with the embalming in the house of the deceased. Then he had the corpse clothed and placed in a carriage. But he did not head directly for Ferney, where the village priest was under orders to prevent interment. He reached Scellières, where he was the abbé in charge. Presenting the two documents delivered by M. de Tersac, he took the authorities by surprise and secured the desired burial rites. An interdiction coming from the Bishop of Troyes arrived after the ceremony had ended.

This death, preceded by a painful agony that gave rise to absurd rumors, was used as a basis for attacking Voltaire's religion. But the subject deserves to be examined in its fullest dimensions. Lanson does so on two occasions: "God, a necessary hypothesis," we read on p. 58; and on p. 149: Voltaire "was a deist . . . obstinately, enthusiastically, and seriously." Between one judgment and the other there is a notable difference, based on the evolution of Voltaire's thought. The first refers to the philosopher of Cirey, the second to the one of Ferney. After 1760 his declarations of faith became more numerous and more heartfelt. But prior to that time his God was already more than a mere hypothesis. He made the God of Newton his God, one whose existence is revealed by the irreducible element inherent in the law of gravitation. His was a God mathematically demonstrable, whose presence could be sensed by contemplating the *cosmos*. All his life long Voltaire repeated his faith in such a Being, maintaining, against the temptation of Spinoza's pantheism, that God is personal and distinct from Nature.

Consequently, several charges of conflicting beliefs have been leveled against Voltaire. According to some, his deism was merely a suppressed Christianity. Albert Chérel, and, much more emphatically, Alfred Noyes are persuaded that he was a Christian in spite of everything. This is an unacceptable proposition based on only a handful of declarations (even omitting their implications), and overlooks all that Voltaire wrote against the doctrines of the Incarnation and the Redemption. Others suspect him of being a clandestine atheist, the opinion yesterday of Daniel Mornet and today of M. Henri Guillemin. On the one hand they note his deism—Voltaire's official doctrine, hence untrue—which is expressed in all his writings. And on the other hand they uncover his secret thoughts which are expressed. . . . But here we come upon a serious difficulty. The adherents of this thesis have yet to produce a text in which Voltaire confesses to some reliable confidant that his professions of faith are pure comedy, that he really places no credence whatever in the God conceived by Newton and that he finds the atheists, whom he has been combating, clearly in the right: Meslier, La Mettrie, Diderot, d'Holbach, and the whole "coterie." He has left written evidence of other confessions, however embarrassing, which, while not intended for posterity, have nevertheless become common knowledge. Where, then, is the hidden proof by which an entire life and work will stand convicted on the charge of imposture? M. Henri Guillemin replies: in the jests about Brioché. But this is not so. The Brioché of the *Pot-Pourri* (Chaps. I, III), the father of Punchinello, represents Joseph, the father of Jesus. Certainly it is a blasphemous farce, but it is by no means a negation of the God of Newton, the only one Voltaire ever professed to acknowledge.

The question can be clarified insofar as one eliminates passion and prejudice. On the one hand, it will be admitted that Voltaire was not the unbeliever some would wish him to be. He was a deist, a bigot (so Diderot complained). On the other hand, we must recognize that to write off as an atheist whoever refuses the Christian concept of divinity is to jump too quickly to a conclusion. It was a need for grandeur that moved Voltaire toward the idea of a God Who is remote and Who is all the more sublime for avoiding involvement in wretched human affairs. He exalted this pure

Being with all the aversion he felt for the sectarian followers of a God too human in concept. Whenever he reflected on "the crimes of priests," and he thought of these very often, a veritable frenzy took possession of him. On each anniversary of the Saint Bartholomew's Day Massacre[1] he took to his bed, shaking with fever. And let it not be said that he was putting on an act, that he was playing to the galleries. These strange scenes, experienced behind closed doors, were disclosed after his death by the confidential remarks of intimate friends. These must be added to the data in Voltaire's psychoanalytic dossier.

But considered in eighteenth-century terms, this deistic philosophy was not unique or unusual. In Voltaire's day atheism was espoused by only a few thinkers, and these were generally second-rate, whereas the entire thinking of the age, even Christian apologetics, inclined toward a "natural" religion. Montesquieu and Maupertuis were deists. Voltaire offered only the particular spectacle of opposing tooth and nail what others were content to treat with polite scorn.

On one point, however, we may speak of a cleavage between the private philosophy of Ferney and its public expression. The patriarch had strong doubts about the immortality of the soul. Without reaching any definite certainty in the matter, he was rather inclined to believe that everything perishes with the body. But in that case what becomes of his references to a God "Who rewards and punishes," an affirmation important to preach to the common people? The wise man will do well to keep his doubts to himself. Assuredly, God exists: but that He would stoop to punish or reward creatures as insignificant as we are is something which seems unlikely. Yet this useful doctrine should be instilled in the minds of ordinary people as well as in the minds of tyrants who can be restrained only by fear of the hereafter. Is this the expedient calculation of a rich bourgeois? Then so be it. And likewise "the postulate of practical reason."

A God threatened to the point of being deprived of His attributes of Supreme Judge recedes into a metaphysical background. By the same token, the crushing weight of ancient terrors is diminished. But tragedy dies. The failure of Voltaire, the playwright, author of *Zaïre* (at least a failure in the long run) acquires its meaning from a philosophical history of the theatre. R. Naves explained this curious phenomenon of Voltairian tragedy as the creative

[1] See Chapter VI, note 2. (R.W.)

activity of a critical mind. It was the man of good taste, the devotee of letters and the connoisseur, who produced *Zaïre, Alzire, Mérope, Sémiramis,* and *Tancrède,* proving thereby the inadequacy of such qualifications. It is a thesis that completes, without contradicting it, the analysis offered by Lanson in his *Histoire de la Tragédie:* "for Voltaire there was no fatality; his philosophy of tragedy, like his philosophy of history, is the philosophy of chance" (p. 148). Tragic emotion, in its pristine purity, is born of the immediate presence of an angry God. That vision of humanity, bending under the might of transcendent wrath, Voltaire evoked once more in his *Œdipe,* but did so to challenge forthwith a divine judgment accused of injustice. With his first dramatic work Voltaire, the novice, ended the era of tragedy. From that moment on he was rather ill at ease. He sensed that tragedy is nourished by religious emotion (cf. Best., 3374). But no service was to be rendered by a divinity as geometrical as the deity of a "natural religion." Voltaire then made use of pretense. In *Zaïre* and *Alzire* he speculated on the reputation of a faith that he scorned. Or else he resorted, with no greater conviction, to the supernatural resources in Shakespeare. The ghost of a murdered father, the "machine" of *Eriphyle* and *Sémiramis,* seems a parody of *Hamlet.* Just as vainly he attempted romantic pathos in *Tancrède*—a melodramatic plot, introducing some lyrical scenes. As Lanson observed, this formula was to be adopted by Hugo the dramatist. Voltaire stands on the threshold of the crisis created in the theatre by the divorce alienating the modern spirit from the spirit of tragedy. Like the various experiments that followed, Voltairian tragedy was in search of its soul. It died from its failure to find one.

From time to time revivals have been attempted. As *Zaïre* had not been played at the Comédie Française since 1936, Jean Hervé gave a performance on April 4, 1952, at the Théâtre de la Porte-Saint-Martin before a group of *lycée* students. In 1958, at Le Petit Théâtre de Paris, Michel Dubosc staged *Le Dépositaire* under the title of *Ninon de Lenclos.* Mr. Henry Carrington Lancaster has advanced the idea of a film adaptation of *Tancrède.* But is not *Mahomet* the Voltairian play most likely to appeal to a contemporary audience? As drama "it is often ahead of its time," to quote R. Naves. It presents a military chieftain, the prophet of a new faith, a faith of his own invention, to be used as an instrument of psychological conquest. At his side is Séide, a young man of generous impulses and blind devotion, filled with love for his Chief and motivated to commit a criminal act. Standing before somber altars he takes an oath to kill. And he does kill. When his eyes are opened, it is too late. It is unfortunate that with ineffectual devices (lost children, "my mother's cross," slow poisoning) Voltaire weakened this great drama of deceit whose pathos he sensed better than anyone else.

Between the philosophy of tragedy and that of history a connection existed that Lanson did not fail to indicate. But his chapters on Voltaire the historian and Voltaire the politician have now aged considerably. Despite his remark that he would disregard "the preoccupations of the present," the essayist could not achieve total detachment from the views and attitudes of his own time. Yet now, on rereading Lanson, we discover how much the world stage has changed since 1906. A reevaluation is in order and justifies the abundance of works devoted of late to the history and politics of Voltaire, the two questions being interrelated.

With regard to the serious elements in Voltaire's method of historical research, as evidenced in works like *Charles XII* and *Le Sièele de Louis XIV*, Lanson's judgment remains entirely valid. With regard to the polemical parts of his writings, such as those dealing with the Bible, a fair estimate of wherein Voltaire was right and wherein he was wrong will be made possible only by comparative studies once the great subject of Biblical criticism in the eighteenth century, still very unclear, has been thoroughly examined and clarified. Let us simply point out that Voltaire had surmised the important role of the Essenes in the origins of Christianity. He did not believe that Jesus was an Essene (see article *Essénien* in the *Dictionnaire philosophique*), but Essenism and Christianity struck him as comparable phenomena. Amid the Palestinian anarchy of the Roman era, virtuous men joined together to lead a virtuous life. This is the point of view of the historian who cannot think of Christianity as an event without a cause or as something having an absolute beginning in itself.

That Voltaire stands as "the first historian of civilization" (p. 100) is confirmed by the studies in recent years, notably in Italy. That he undertook to write the first modern universal history starting with the idea that "humanity has produced itself" (p. 108) and "rendering justice to all nations" (with the exception of the Jews), therein lies the outstanding achievement of his *Essai sur les Moeurs*, in our judgment as well as Lanson's. But in dealing with Voltaire's political philosophy, the little book of 1906 stressed, above all, those views corresponding to the liberal policies of the Third Republic at the height of its power. The notion of "enlightened despotism," important in Voltaire's thinking, and toward which the tide of events was to draw the political thought of our own day, is only briefly touched upon by Lanson. I doubt that the ideal government envisaged by Voltaire was realized "during the peaceful moments of the Consulate or the Second Empire" (p. 159). Those were the moments of a stabilized Counter-Revolution. Now Voltaire praised his "despots" for their innovations (or alleged innovations). His ideal would be a Peter the Great without Peter's cruelty. He portrays the great man as having created a modern state almost *ex nihilo*, for he simultaneously exaggerates Russian barbarism during the previous reigns and the changes brought about by the revolutionary Czar. In the same manner he writes that the French nation was "formed in some measure by Louis XIV" (*Siècle de Louis XIV*, chapt. 29). A political idea may be defined by the date at which it sets in motion the state of things currently prevailing. We assign the eighteenth century to the Old Régime, but Voltaire, as J. Dagens has pointed out, designated the year 1640 as the great dividing point in French history. With the "age of Louis XIV" a revolution had begun which Voltaire saw developing in his own day.

Voltaire long believed, and never wholly abandoned, the idea that sovereigns were the indispensable agents of social progress, sovereigns whose absolutism was to be commensurate with their degree of enlightenment. This view was slightly modified, however, on Voltaire's contact with Geneva. Peter Gay has shown that his prejudices against *la canaille*, the riffraff, were lessened by the dealings he had with workmen and craftsmen in that city during the troubles of 1765–1767. In a series of moves, Voltaire first deserted the camp of the *négatifs*, the party of the patrician aristocrats; then he deserted the party of the *représentants*, bourgeois citizens enjoying certain privileges, among whom Rousseau exercised considerable influence. He allied himself finally with the *natifs*, workers who were deprived of any political rights and were legally exploited by the upper classes. In associating with these workers, watchmakers for the most part, whose education was acquired through the practices of their trade, he came to admit that he "could adjust himself fairly well to a democratic form of government":

I like to see free men make the laws under which they live just as they make their own houses. It is a pleasure for me that my mason, my carpenter, and my blacksmith, who have helped me build my house, my friend the farmer and my friend the manufacturer, all rise above their trade and are better informed of the public interest than the most insolent Turkish emissary. . . . To be free, to be one among equals, is the true life, the natural life of man. . . . There are peoples who have been blinded in both eyes like the sorry old steeds that are made to turn the millstone. I want to keep my eyes. I suspect that they gouge out one eye in an aristocratic State and both eyes in a Monarchy. (*Dialogues entre A.B.C.,* 1768, *6ᵉ entretien*).

With an optimism which the future did not justify, Lanson considered this kind of liberalism outdated as a matter of course. Writing at a time when the twentieth century had not yet really begun, he thought the society of his day was established on firm foundations. Regarding this question, for instance, he passes it over with a discretion that does honor to his time: "The abolition of torture"—a reform that had become "outdated and irrelevant through the evolution of our institutions and our society" (p. 158). But now that wars and revolutions have restored the practice of this "strange manner of interrogating people" (*Dictionnaire philosophique,* article *Torture*) such a reservation is no longer admissible. Voltaire was combating institutionalized torture included in the normal judicial processes, a practice already on the way out. Frederick II had abolished it in Prussia on coming to the throne. Twentieth-century torture is at the other end of the cycle: a rebirth of torture that is practiced clandestinely, secretly prescribed or hypocritically condoned by the authorities. The psychology of the torturer differs according to the case. In Voltaire's day this person was "a solemn magistrate who purchased for a sum of money the right to make experiments upon his fellow man," and "who tells his wife at dinner time what happened during the morning." What remains ever constant is the despicable nature of these practices and, in the presence of such scandal, the apathy and inertia of well-meaning people. It was this that aroused Voltairian wrath.

With the rights of man that Voltaire championed currently annihilated, curtailed, or at least threatened to some degree in almost every part of the world, we will not say, as Lanson does (p. 181) that henceforth Voltaire has no other influence to wield save that of "a literary and intellectual influence of pure form." Lanson failed to recall an essentially modern aspect of society that he himself had so well defined in his *Histoire de la Littérature* (1894):

"Voltaire is the philosopher who has perhaps done the most to fashion the form of contemporary civilization: he would have applauded the marvelous progress of our utilitarian and practical-minded age, the inventions of every description which have made life easier, more pleasant, more active, and more intense at the same time. . . . He is the philosopher *par excellence* for a world of bureaucrats, engineers, and producers."

This modernity of Voltaire explains the international audience he continues to enjoy and his popularity among readers who, knowing him only in translation, can hardly appreciate the formal qualities of his prose. A journalist recently discovered that the book most frequently requested in the railroad station of Oport, Siberia, on the Chinese frontier, was *Candide*. As an enemy of all illusions that befog men's minds, Voltaire teaches people to see clearly. Fundamentally healthy and vigorous, his work tends to dispel the clouds of mystery. Yet we must be careful not to attribute to his genius a solely negative character. His clairvoyance is conducive to action. A prophet of the technically minded society, he preached a gospel of "enlightenment," a mystique our civilization has lived by for some two hundred years. Therein Voltaire represents a decisive orientation in the history of the world.

Let us conclude by saying that we have not yet finished with Voltaire. As he wrote to his niece (*Lettres*, Plon, 1957, No. 60):

"They wanted to bury me. But I outwitted them. Bonsoir."

TRANSLATOR'S NOTES

In annotating Lanson's biography, an effort has been made to keep constantly in mind the general North American reader whose mother tongue is English and who cannot reasonably be expected to have a background in French literature and history comparable to "the general reader" for whom Lanson's work was originally intended.

Consequently, although I have not sought to annotate every literary or historical reference in the Lanson text, care has been taken to clarify items that seemed particularly important for the average reader. Hence the inclusion of information concerning many well-known French writers and historical figures as well as those less well known but having specific relevance to the life and times of Voltaire.

By the same token, I have attempted to summarize certain facts and events in French history and culture familiar to every educated Frenchman but not necessarily familiar to every literate American: such matters as "the farm system" of taxation, Jansenism, the French *parlements*, the Regency and the System, the *Encyclopédie*, etc. All these items have been placed in the Appendix to avoid cluttering up the text itself. Only the briefest of notes have been bracketed within the printed text, and, with very few exceptions, only the footnotes that the author himself had included are given at the bottoms of pages. Like Frank Sullivan, the humorist, most of us abhor "a garland of ibids." We quail at the sight of endless notes and forests of fine print. Such erudite underbrush, inevitably rampant in monographs and dissertations, must not be allowed to proliferate in books for the general reader. Accordingly, I have tried to confine the extensive annotations to their own private preserve which the reader can explore or ignore as he chooses.

Among the standard reference works consulted, none was more frequently drawn upon than *The Oxford Companion to French Literature* (edited by Paul Harvey and Janet E. Heseltine, Oxford University Press, 1959), a truly invaluable "companion" to any English-language reader of French literature. Roughly half the following entries are adapted or condensed from the *Oxford Companion* and reprinted by permission. Grateful acknowledgement is also made to the publishers of *The Columbia Encyclopedia* (Columbia University Press, New York); *L'Encyclopédie Larousse* (Librairie Larousse, Paris), and *The Reader's Encyclopedia* (Thomas Y. Crowell Co., New York).

R.A.W.

CHAPTER 1, PP. 13–36

1. THE CHATELET. Ancient fortress of Paris which served as a tribunal and prison. Seat of criminal law courts. Demolished in 1802.

2. "PAYER OF SPICES." It was a French judicial custom in medieval times for a litigant who had won his case to make a small voluntary gift to his judge or attorney, consisting of such things as *dragées* (sugar-coated almonds), *confitures* (preserves), or *épices* (spices). The voluntary nature of the offering had become obligatory by the beginning of the 15th century and was subsequently converted into an outright tax. Because of the venality of judgeships under the Old Régime, the "spice tax" was much abused by magistrates who, having purchased their positions at great cost, kept increasing the amount of this source of revenue. The detestable practice was not abolished until the French Revolution. Condorcet, in a note to his biography of Voltaire, states: "Voltaire's father ... (who took his oath of office in 1701) became the alternate and triennial collector of spices, legal fees, and fines in the Chamber of Accounts in Paris." (Moland, I, 190, n.1)

3. BOILEAU-DESPRÉAUX, NICOLAS (1636–1711). Leading French literary critic of the 17th century. Friend and supporter of Molière, Racine, and La Fontaine, he formulated in his *Art Poétique* (1674) neo-classical literary principles which prevailed during the 17th and 18th centuries. He was an advocate of reason, common sense, and moderation, and attacked all forms of pedantry and affectation.

4. ROUSSEAU, JEAN-BAPTISTE (1671–1747). A leading poet of his time (not to be confused with the famed philosopher Jean-Jacques Rousseau). He wrote many odes and poems of a panegyrical nature and religious inspiration and was banished from France for years because of some defamatory verses attributed to him.

5. SAINT-SIMON, LOUIS DE ROUVROY, DUC DE (1675–1735). Author of celebrated *Mémoires* in which he gives a vivid, candid picture of life at the court of Louis XIV and during the Regency.

6. JOURDAINS AND TURCARETS. Characters created by Molière and Lesage,

respectively. Both are prosperous members of the middle class aspiring to social acceptance by the nobility. Jourdain is the ingenuous social climber in *Le Bourgeois Gentilhomme* (1670), and Turcaret, the cynical, ruthless parvenu who makes a vulgar display of his wealth, is the principle character in a play bearing his name (1709).

7. CORNEILLE, PIERRE (1606–1684). Famous French dramatist whose play *Le Cid* (1637) inaugurated a great era in French theatre. His dramas are noted for their psychological conflicts, as between love and honor in *Le Cid*, with the human will emerging triumphant over the emotions and desires of the heart. He wrote several great tragedies, *Horace* and *Cinna* (1640) and *Polyeucte* (1641), and is remarkable for the heroic stature of his tragic heroes, the grandeur of his style, and the high ethical quality of his dramas.

8. COLLÈGE. The French *collège* does not correspond to the American college. It is a secondary school maintained by a local authority, but more commonly by the Roman Catholic Church.

Early medieval *collèges* were founded in Paris and subsequently in the provinces as hostels for needy students attending courses at the University. Later on, in order to exercise more control over the students, teaching was organized within the *collège*. By the middle of the 14th century several famous *collèges* were already in existence, e.g., the Sorbonne, and the Collèges de Navarre and de Montaigu. Some 60 *collèges* were founded before 1500. From the 16th century onwards, secondary education was greatly developed and many teaching institutions were founded by the religious orders, particularly the Jesuits and the Oratorians. These, together with the *collèges* of the University, were for the most part suppressed during the French Revolution.

Education in France, a bulletin published in 1963 by the Office of Education (U.S. Dept. of Health, Education, and Welfare) makes the following observations:

"At the time of the French Revolution more than 75% of the women and 50% of the men were still illiterate.... Schooling was not free nor did the State have sufficient funds to provide free education. Children of the poor often went to work at the age of eight.

"There were some secondary schools called *collèges* which provided education to a few, mostly under the direction of the Catholic order of Jesuits. The willingness of the government prior to the Revolution has been explained as follows: 'The Jesuit *collèges* insisted on the kind of classical scholarship that suited the French sense of Roman heritage; they also took care of good and formal manners; they provided knightly sports and games, and theater, and a highly competitive spirit with unquestioned authority. What more could the absolutist government demand of a school system that cost so little?' (Ulich, Robert, *The Education of Nations: A Comparison in Historical Perspective*, Cambridge, Mass., Harvard Univ. Press, 1961).

"In the field of secondary education, Napoleon established a system of public secondary schools (*lycées*) supported and controlled by the national government. Within a short time similar secondary schools (*collèges*) were established by local communities.... As the 19th century proceeded, the national government gradually took an interest in education of the people, and a public school system free of religious control eventually was established against much opposition from the Catholic Church."

9. JANSENISTS. Adherents of a Roman Catholic movement inspired by the doctrines of Flemish bishop Cornelius Jansen (1585–1638). Their headquarters were two convents. One, southwest of Paris, known as *Port-Royal des Champs*, was an old Cistercian convent reestablished in 1608 by Jacqueline Arnauld, known as Mère Angélique. In 1625 the nuns migrated to premises in Paris which were designated *Port-Royal de Paris*. In 1634 the abbé de Saint-Cyran became director of the convent and introduced the austere moral and theological concepts of Bishop Jansen, concepts drawn from the works of St. Augustine.

Jansenist doctrines approximated Calvinism in repudiating the efficacy of the human will and asserting predestination and the sole virtues of divine grace, as against the Pelagian doctrine of salvation through good works. Jesuit teachings tended to take a less pessimistic view of human nature and to attach greater importance to the human will.

When the Jansenist nuns moved to Paris, *Port-Royal des Champs* became occupied by a group of solitaries (*solitaires*) holding Jansenist views. Here and in the vicinity they founded small schools (*Les Petites Ecoles de Port-Royal*) which became famous for their education and began to rival the more numerous and powerful Jesuit schools. Racine and Pascal were among their famous pupils.

By the end of the 17th century Jansenist influence permeated the court, the society, and the literature of France. Of the great writers of the period only Molière and La Fontaine escaped its influence, according to the critic Brunetière. Jansenism was strongly condemned by the Jesuits, who led the effort to have it eradicated as a heresy. They were successful in having certain doctrines condemned by several popes, notably Innocent X in 1653, who censured five propositions in Jansen's *Augustinus,* and by Clement XI in his Bull *Unigenitus* (1713). The Jansenists had a powerful intellectual spokesman in Blaise Pascal, who attacked and discredited the Jesuits in his writings. Louis XIV was also hostile to Jansenism, fearing, no doubt, possible political dangers like those Calvinism had posed for royal and religious absolutism. The abolition of Port-Royal was decreed by papal bull in 1708, the nuns forcibly expelled in 1709, and the buildings razed to the ground in 1710. The importance of Port-Royal seems to have resided less in its Jansenist doctrines than in the spiritual zeal with which it combated irreligion and the worldliness of society.

10. CAS DE CONSCIENCE (1704). Literally, "a matter of conscience." The reference here is to *le cas de conscience par excellence* of 1701 which reopened the long and bitter theological quarrel between Jansenists and Jesuits concerning five allegedly heretical propositions in the writings of Bishop Jansen. Pope Innocent X and Pope Alexander VI renewed the ecclesiastical condemnation. French bishops had forced communicants of suspected Jansenist sympathies to sign a prescribed form condemning the propositions Jansen claimed to have found in St. Augustine's writings as well as Jansen's interpretation thereof. The supreme *cas de conscience* of 1701 propounded the question: "Should the sacraments be administered to a man who had signed the form but who believed at the bottom of his heart that the Pope and even the Church might be mistaken in the facts?" In 1705 Pope Clement XI issued the Bull *Viniam Domini* ordering the faithful to accept the facts as set forth by the Church. Jansenists who refused were denied the sacraments. (*Cf.* Voltaire, *Siècle de Louis XIV,* Chapt. XXXVII.)

11. NINON DE LENCLOS (1620–1705). A celebrated leader of Parisian society, famed for her wit, beauty, and *amours.* Her salon was frequented by leading writers of the day, including Racine, Molière, La Fontaine, Mme de La Fayette, Mme de Maintenon, and Mlle de Scudéry.

12. CAMISARDS. Protestants of the Cévennes region in central France who revolted after the revocation (1685) of the Edict of Nantes. They were so called from the white canvas shirts (*camisa*) they wore over their other clothes. They were subjugated by marshal Villars.

13. DORANTES AND CHÉRUBINS. Characters in plays by Marivaux and

Beaumarchais, respectively. The Dorante in Marivaux's *Les Fausses Confidences* (1737) is the traditional lover, timid and awkward, but sincere and good-hearted. Chérubin in *Le Mariage de Figaro* (1784) is an adolescent page boy, bewildered by his budding amorous desires, in love with the countess, alternately shy and aggressive, ever ready to begin a flirtation.

14. LETTRES DE CACHET. Letters sealed with the king's privy seal and usually directing the imprisonment or exile without trial of the person named therein. They were used especially to confine persons whose conduct was likely to bring discredit on their families. The practice was much abused during the 17th and 18th centuries.

15. LA MOTTE, HOUDAR DE (1672–1731). Poet and critic, author of odes, fables, and dramas. He formulated avant-garde poetic theories but generally conformed to the classical rules of the day. He suffered most of his life from paralysis and partial blindness.

16. THE REGENCY. The regency (1715–1723) of Philippe, duc d'Orléans, nephew of Louis XIV, during the minority of Louis XV. It was a period of profligate reaction to the moral austerity of the latter years of Louis XIV and of liberal reaction to his political absolutism. It was marked by the disastrous System of John Law (see note 28).

17. VILLARS, LOUIS-HECTOR, DUC DE (1653–1734). Maréchal (Marshal) de France; celebrated French diplomat and military commander. He was defeated at Malplaquet (1709) by Marlborough and Prince Eugene, but triumphed over the latter at Denain (1712) ending the War of the Spanish Succession. He was admitted to the French Academy (1714) and is remembered in literary connection for his friendship with the youthful Voltaire, who frequented the château de Villars from 1718 to 1724. He left many *Mémoires*.

18. BOLINGBROKE, LORD HENRY (1678–1751). Prominent English political figure in favor with Queen Anne but dismissed by George I. He had served the Pretender and helped plan the Jacobite uprising in 1715. Restored to favor in 1725, he opposed Robert Walpole. After Walpole's political success in 1735, Bolingbroke spent most of his remaining years on his estates in France. He was a friend of Voltaire and Alexander Pope.

19. PIRON, ALEXIS (1689–1773). French poet, author of many witty songs and satires, often licentious. An anecdote illustrates the character of the man. The wealthy Voltaire expressed regret over the fact that Piron was not rich. Piron replied: *"Cela est vrai, mais je m'en moque, et c'est comme si je l'étais."* ("That is true, but I scoff at

the idea, and it's as if I were rich.") He was said to have worsted Voltaire in exchanges of repartee.

20. DUBOIS, GUILLAUME, CARDINAL (1656–1725). Minister during the Regency (1715–23) (see note 16). He was of venal character but a skillful diplomat. He served as Prime Minister in 1722.

21. DU DEFFAND, MARIE, MARQUISE (1697–1780). Celebrated French-woman whose salon was frequented by the highest society and by numerous *philosophes*. At 68 she formed a strong affection for Horace Walpole and ultimately left him all her papers. She was also an intimate friend of *Président* (Presiding Judge) Hénault of the *Parlement* of Paris. She left a remarkable correspondence that reflects the social and intellectual life of her period.

22. CONTI, LE PRINCE DE (1717–1776). Member of the house of Bourbon-Condé; Grand Prior of the Society of the Temple; a distinguished soldier and patron of the arts; protector of Jean-Jacques Rousseau, Beaumarchais, and others. His salon was frequented by the best society including men eminent in art and literature. Mozart gave a performance there.

23. CHAULIEU, GUILLAUME AMFRYE, ABBÉ DE (1639–1720). Poet, born in Normandy; attached himself to the two sons of the duc de Ven-dôme (the younger duke and the prior of the Temple) becoming manager of their affairs. An easy-going genius, enjoying pleasures with refinement, he was designated the Anacreon of the Society of the Temple. His later poems show a melancholy disillusion-ment and contain some of his most delicate work.

24. LA FARE, CHARLES-AUGUSTE, MARQUIS DE (1644–1712). Author of light, epicurean verse and memoirs. Following a distinguished military career he spent the last 30 years of his life in idleness and dissi-pation; a member of the Society of the Temple (and close friend of Chaulieu); translated many Latin verses. His *Mémoires* contain interesting portraits and criticism of his age, including a severe judgment of Louis XIV.

25. RACINE, JEAN (1639–1699). Generally regarded as the greatest French writer of tragedy. Famed for intense psychological con-flicts in which (unlike the tragedies of Corneille) a vacillating human will succumbs to passions and emotions. He was strongly influenced by Greek tragedy and the austere religious doctrines of the Jansenists (see note 9). His most striking characters are women. Among his best known tragedies are *Andromaque* (1667), *Britan-nicus* (1668), *Bérénice* (1670), *Iphigénie* (1674), and *Phèdre* (1677). After *Phèdre* Racine decided to abandon the theater (which was

strongly disapproved of by the Jansenists), repented of his dramatic writings, and was reconciled with Port-Royal. Thereafter he wrote only two religious dramas: *Esther* (1689) and *Athalie* (1691).

26. RONSARD, PIERRE DE (1524–1585). Famed poet of the French Renaissance; leading member of a literary group calling themselves *La Pléiade*; wrote many graceful, amorous verses, notably odes and sonnets under the influence of Petrarch, Horace, Pindar, *et al.* His famous *Mignonne, allons voir si la rose* was written in 1553. He occupied the position of court poet; was protected by Charles IX and honored by Queen Elizabeth and Mary Stuart, Queen of Scotland, where he served during the reign of James V. His *Sonnets pour Hélène* include some of his finest poems.

27. CHAPELAIN, JEAN (1595–1674). The leading French literary critic between Ronsard and Boileau; esteemed by Cardinal Richelieu; one of the original members of the *Académie Française* (founded in 1635 under Richelieu's auspices); first to conceive the idea of the Academy's dictionary.

28. THE SYSTEM. The System was a disastrous fiscal experiment by John Law (1671–1729), a Scotsman who had obtained the favor of the Regent. He persuaded the French government to adopt the use of paper money issued through the medium of a *Banque Générale,* which Law founded in Paris in 1716. The bank notes proved successful and Law extended his operations by creating the Mississippi Company to exploit colonial commerce in Louisiana. This scheme was a notorious fiasco subsequently known as "The Mississippi Bubble." Law was named comptroller general of finance in 1720. Frenzied speculations to which his operations gave rise collapsed the same year causing widespread ruin. Law's System is frequently mentioned in French literature.

29. VADIUS AND TRISSOTIN. Literary phonies in Molière's comedy *Les Femmes Savantes* (1672). Both are vain, affected fops; the former an egotistical pedant, the latter a sorry wit who fancies himself a poet.

30. BRUNETIÈRE, FERDINAND (1849–1906). Literary historian and critic. He was Professor of French Language and Literature at the famed Ecole Normale Supérieure in Paris from 1886 and editor-in-chief of the influential *Revue des Deux Mondes.* An admirer of 17th-century literature and opponent of 19th-century theories of "art for art's sake," he believed in the need for a moral purpose in art. He made many valuable studies of literature and history.

31. LESAGE, ALAIN-RENÉ (1668–1747). Dramatist and novelist; spent a

life of unremitting literary work. He was the author of *Turcaret* (1709), a play satirizing the world of the financiers; and several picaresque novels including the famous *Gil Blas* (4 vols., 1715–1735).

32. MARIVAUX, PIERRE CARLET DE CHAMBLAIN DE (1688–1763). Dramatist and novelist; best known for his plays dealing with love and especially the trifling psychological incidents of courtship, the reticences and mutual testings of couples attracted to each other but reluctant to declare their feelings outright. Among his best plays are *La Double Inconstance* (1723), *Le Jeu de l'amour et du hasard* (1730), and *Les Fausses Confidences* (1737).

33. LAMBERT, ANNE-THÉRESE, MARQUISE DE (1647–1733). Author of works of moral instruction; famous for her salon, where twice a week from 1710 until her death she received members of the aristocracy and the literary world. She was noted for her high principles and refined judgment.

34. MLLE DELAUNAY (LAUNAY, MARGUERITE CORDIER DE) (1694–1729). A learned woman, friend of Fontenelle, Chaulieu, and Mme du Deffand; long employed by the duchesse du Maine. Lacking independent means, she had to endure selfish exploitation by her employer. She wrote *Mémoires* and letters, one of which describes a visit by Voltaire and Mme du Châtelet to the duchesse du Maine's court at Sceaux.

35. SAINT-EVREMOND, CHARLES DE SAINT-DENIS, SIEUR DE (1613–1703). Man of letters who at first followed a military career but was obliged to leave France in 1661 for criticizing Mazarin's treaty with Spain. Most of the remainder of his life was spent at the English court. A distinguished freethinker of skeptical and epicurean temperament, he wrote essays on many subjects and exercised considerable literary influence in England.

36. LOCKE, JOHN (1632–1704). Famed English philosopher, known as "the Father of English empiricism;" educated at Christ Church college, Oxford, and thereafter, employed by the First Earl of Shaftesbury, a prominent English statesman with whom he was long associated. He spent four years in France (1675–79), where he met leaders in science and philosophy, and later spent several years in Holland, where he completed his famous *Essay Concerning Human Understanding* (1690). This work was published in complete form after his return to England upon the accession of William of Orange to the English throne; thereafter he held various minor offices and served as occasional state adviser. He

became known in England and on the Continent as the leading philosopher of freedom. He made important contributions to philosophy in almost every field, but is remembered chiefly as a champion of the experimental method. He stressed the necessity of tolerating opposite opinion, maintaining that each man can honestly and reasonably see truth in differing aspect. His system was practical, anchored in human experience, and expressed in concrete details. He seemed distrustful of metaphysical speculations; believed that matter had primary and secondary qualities, the primary being the stuff of science, the secondary the source of men's perceptions; denied any independent existence to abstractions, and regarded the mind of each person at birth as a blank slate, a *tabula rasa* on which personal experiences inscribe themselves; and held that man can reason only with these experiences, thus anticipating the associational doctrines of modern psychology. Locke thus rejected the notion of innate ideas and placed the source of knowledge in sense experience.

In his *Letters on Toleration,* which appeared from time to time, he advocated an established church with broadest possible toleration, except that he would legislate against atheism and Roman Catholicism as inimical to religion.

Locke is also renowned for his political theories. Contradicting Thomas Hobbes (1588–1679) who believed man in a state of nature to be selfish, "nasty, brutish, and short," Locke regarded the original state of nature as happy, reasonable, and tolerant and the establishment of the state as a social contract to protect men from those who lived outside the law of nature. He proposed the policy of checks and balances followed by the United States Constitution and argued that revolution in some instances is not only a right but an obligation. He greatly influenced both Rousseau and Voltaire and the theorists of the American Revolution, especially Thomas Jefferson.

37. Fontenelle, bernard le bovier, sieur de (1657–1757). Miscellany writer of wide curiosity and learning. His famous *Entretiens sur la pluralité des mondes* ("Conversations on the Plurality of Worlds") (1686) awakened a general interest in astronomy and popularized the scientific system of inquiry. In other writings he analyzed the causes of human credulity and rejected popular assumptions of supernatural causation. In general he was a precursor of the attack which, before long, science was to make on religion, unostentatiously encouraging freedom of thought by substituting the play of mechanical forces for Providence in explanations of natural phe-

nomena. He was a member of the French Academy and the Royal Society of London.

38. SPINOZA, BARUCH (1632–1677). Famous Dutch philosopher of Portuguese-Jewish parentage. He developed a system of religious rationalism and in his *Ethics* (1677) carried the Cartesian method to its extreme—a rigorously geometrical form. His system is still regarded as the most eminent exposition of the doctrine of pantheism.

39. MALEBRANCHE, NICOLAS DE (1638–1713). Theologian, scientist, and philosopher. A disciple of the Cartesian method and physics but not metaphysics, he held that divine reason surpasses imperfect human reason. He resolved the Cartesian dualism of mind and matter by regarding God as the source of our ideas of the material world and as the sole and universal cause of movement of both external objects and ideas. His doctrines tended toward pantheism and involved him in much theological controversy.

40. COPERNICUS, NICOLAUS (1473–1543). Polish astronomer who demonstrated that the earth and planets revolve about the sun. Medieval cosmology held that the sun and planets revolved about the earth, a system formulated by the Alexandrian astronomer Ptolemy in the 2nd century A.D. Destroying the notion of the earth's centrality in the physical universe inevitably carried disquieting implications for the theological view of man's place in the cosmos.

41. GALILEO GALILEI (1564–1642). Italian astronomer whose observations confirmed the Copernican system. He was condemned by Rome as a heretic (1616) and was forced by the Inquisition to recant his views publicly.

42. DESCARTES, RENÉ (1596–1650). French philosopher and mathematician whose *Discours de la Méthode* (1637) is a cornerstone of modern philosophy. He substituted deductive reasoning for scholastic syllogisms and arrived at a rational and purely mathematical conception of the universe. His famous point of departure was *Cogito ergo sum* ("I think; therefore I am"). He held a dualistic view of spirit and matter, regarding man as a mechanical body inhabited by a spiritual soul capable of thought and will. He carefully separated the realms of science and faith and affirmed existence of God both by intuition and deduction. Descartes exerted a powerful influence on the philosophic thought of Europe.

43. BAYLE, PIERRE (1646–1706). Lexicographer, philosopher, and critic, often considered "the bible" of 18th-century rationalists. A Protes-

tant who became a Catholic and reverted to Protestantism, he was a champion of toleration in opinion, for if religion, he held, is irrational, reason on the other hand leads to no certain conclusions. His condemnation of superstitions, his view that morality is independent of religion (for a man may be an atheist and yet have all the moral virtues) and his doctrine of toleration are set forth chiefly in his *Pensées sur la Comète* ("Thoughts on the Comet") (1682). His *Dictionnaire historique et critique* (1697) became an arsenal from which the *philosophes* drew much of their ammunition.

44. LA BRUYÈRE, JEAN DE (1645–1696). French moralist, employed as tutor in the household of the prince de Condé. His *Caractères* (1688) contain maxims, character observations, and portraits, many of living people under disguised names. Written in terse, rapid style with vivid touches of detail, they are generally pessimistic, critical, and often scornful of human vanities and frivolities. He expressed sympathy for the plight of the poor.

45. VAUBAN, SÉBASTIEN LE PRESTRE, SEIGNEUR DE (1633–1707). Military engineer and marshal of France; renowned for his many successful military sieges and for fortifying the frontiers of France.

46. FÉNELON, FRANCOIS DE SALIGNAC DE LA MOTHE (1651–1715). French theologian, archbishop, and man of letters. For the education of the Duke of Burgundy he composed a didactic poem, *Télémaque* (1699), which contained passages interpreted as criticism of the government of Louis XIV. This, together with his espousal of a religious movement known as "Quietism," incurred the disfavor of Louis XIV and of the influential Bishop Bossuet and brought about his banishment from Paris to Cambrai, where he devoted himself to episcopal duties and produced many literary works of distinction.

47. JURIEU, PIERRE (1637–1713). Protestant pastor and theologian, famous as an adversary of Catholic Bishop Bossuet. He went to Holland after the revocation (1685) of the Edict of Nantes.

48. PARLEMENT. The French *parlement* is quite different from the English "parliament," a distinction to be kept in mind as Lanson refers to the *Parlement* of Paris and other French *parlements*. The *parlements* of France were judicial, not legislative bodies. Originally, the royal *Parlement* was the supreme judicial assembly, next after the *conseil d'état* or king's council. In time there came to be eight *parlements,* those of Paris, Toulouse, Bordeaux, Rouen, Aix, Grenoble, Dijon, and Rennes; Pau and Metz were added later.

The *Parlement* of Paris was the most ancient, and had developed from the days of Louis IX (1215–1270); its jurisdiction extended over half of France and comprised 200 magistrates who sat in general assembly only to consider the gravest questions of State, such as verifying and registering royal edicts, a procedure required to give them force of law.

The *Parlement* was divided into separate benches to deal with ordinary suits and with appeals from lower jurisdictions. A special bench, known as *la Tournelle,* dealt with criminal cases. The *parlements* of other cities comprised fewer magistrates but were organized on the same plan as the *Parlement* of Paris. They had control of the police, and their officials were irremovable. Their offices were hereditary and might be purchased. As a political institution the *Parlement* exerted a most unfortunate influence in the 18th century, stubbornly opposing reforms in administration and new ideas in philosophy. Nevertheless, as the chief seat of opposition to a corrupt court it enjoyed popularity. Suppressed by Chancellor Maupeou in 1771, the *parlements* were reconstituted amid general rejoicing by Louis XVI on his accession in 1774.

49. SAINT-PIERRE, CHARLES-IRÉNÉE, ABBÉ DE (1658–1743). Economist; born in Normandy of a noble family. He was author of many projects for political and economic reform, some visionary, some practical. Among them was a *Projet de paix perpétuelle* ("Project for Perpetual Peace") (1713), of which J.-J. Rousseau wrote an abstract and critique. His projects were all designed for human welfare; he was esteemed by Montesquieu but was generally treated as an impractical dreamer.

50. MASSILLON, JEAN-BAPTISTE (1663–1742). Celebrated preacher; bishop of Clermont-Ferrand; noted for his subtle psychological analyses and greater concern for ethics than for dogma. His sermons were gentle and persuasive, avoiding oratorical thunder. He pronounced the funeral oration on Louis XIV, and was approved by the *philosophes.*

51. MONTESQUIEU, CHARLES DE SECONDAT, BARON DE (1689–1755). Political philosopher, born near Bordeaux. His *Lettres Persanes* ("Persian Letters") (1721), a collection of letters supposedly written and received by two Persians who visit Paris, contain a satirical review of French contemporary society, ranging over a wide variety of subjects. His *Considérations sur les causes de la grandeur des Romains et de leur décadence* ("Considerations on the Rise and Fall of the Romans") (1734) is an interesting example of early scientific nonreligious history in which events are traced to natural

causes without reference to a guiding Providence. Montesquieu's chief title to fame is his *Esprit des Lois* ("Spirit of Laws") (1748) introducing a new method in the study of social institutions and setting forth the ideal of a liberal and beneficent government and the removal of the abuses of the French monarchical system. Its doctrine, of which it has been said that it changed the thought of the world, was prominent in France in the political experiments of the Revolution and in the parliamentary constitution of 1815. It had a notable influence on the framing of the American Constitution in the idea of federation of states and the principle of separation of powers.

52. FLEURY, ANDRÉ-HERCULE, CARDINAL DE (1653–1743). Chief minister of Louis XV. Fleury was a careful administrator who, with the English minister Walpole, labored for peace; but in 1748 he allowed France to be drawn into the War of the Austrian Succession.

CHAPTER 2, PP. 37–48

1. "THE KING." It is unlikely that this "English gentleman" was the king. According to L. Foulet, it was the banker, Mendez da Costa, whose bankruptcy had left Voltaire in financial straits. Cf. Besterman No. 294. (Note by René Pomeau).

2. WALPOLE, HORACE, 4TH EARL OF ORFORD (1717–1797). English author, son of Robert Walpole, friend of poet Thomas Gray. He is best remembered for his "terror" novel, *The Castle of Otranto* (1764), which had an important influence on the Gothic revival in the arts. It is considered an ancestor of the modern detective novel. On his estate at Twickenham, which he named Strawberry Hill, Walpole built "a little Gothic castle" and also operated a private printing press. He wrote many essays and letters on a variety of subjects providing an invaluable picture of Georgian England. He was a member of Parliament from 1741 to 1768 and visited Paris in 1765 where he gained the close friendship of Mme du Deffand (see Chapter 1, note 21). He traveled widely, collected works of art, and always professed to be an amateur in literary affairs.

3. WALPOLE, ROBERT, 1ST EARL OF ORFORD (1676–1745). A leader of England's Whig party; twice prime minister and chancellor of the exchequer. An advocate of peace between France, England, and Spain, he studied finance and commerce and laid the basis for free trade.

4. LECOUVREUR, ADRIENNE (1692–1730). Celebrated French tragedienne; made her début at the Comédie Française May 14, 1717, in Racine's

Mithridate; broke away from prevailing over-declamatory style of acting in the direction of greater naturalness. Her fine personal qualities helped to raise the social position of actresses in France. She was a friend of Voltaire, who dedicated an epistle to her (1723) and wrote an elegy on her early death, indignantly censuring the Church for refusing her a Christian burial.

5. LETTRE DE CACHET. See Chapter 1, note 14.

6. TRÉVOUX. A small town on the Saône near Bourg. It became one of the famous 18th-century centers for books printed outside Paris. The *Journal de Trévoux* was a literary and critical monthly founded in 1701 by the Jesuits at Trévoux. Well written and well informed, it was especially directed to the defense of religion and the discredit of the doctrines of the *philosophes.* It continued until the expulsion of the Jesuits from France in 1762.

7. CYTHERA. In general, an enchanted isle, allegorical land of love. Actually it was an island off the southern coast of Laconia on which Aphrodite was said to have landed after her birth in the sea; subject of a famous painting by Watteau (*L'Embarquement pour Cythère*) (1717).

8. DESCARTES. See Chapter 1, note 42.

9. PASCAL, BLAISE (1623–1662). Philosopher, mathematician, and physicist, regarded by many as the most profound genius France has ever produced. He made remarkable mathematical and scientific discoveries, is credited with founding the modern theory of probabilities, invented the mathematical triangle, helped formulate the laws of atmospheric pressure and the equilibrium of fluids (Pascal's Law), and invented the adding machine. Pascal is equally renowned as a religious thinker and psychologist; embraced Jansenism (see Chapter 1, note 8) and became its most eloquent defender by discrediting the ethical code of the Jesuits. He intended to write an *Apologie de la religion chrétienne* ("Apology for the Christian Religion") but died before its completion, leaving his now celebrated *Pensées* ("Meditations"), written down in preparation for the apology. He sought to win over the rational skeptical mind (the disciples of Montaigne) to an acceptance of the Christian faith. He depicts man's reason as suspended between two infinities which it cannot grasp but only seize "some appearances in the midst of things." Pascal regarded faith as not contrary to reason but above it. He made a searching and eloquent analysis of the yearnings of the human heart: *C'est le coeur qui sent Dieu et non la raison.... Le coeur a ses raisons que la raison ne connait pas.* ("It is the heart

which feels God and not reason. . . . The heart has its reasons which reason knows not.") Pascal became a religious mystic. His writings combine the style of a philosopher with that of a lyric poet. Both by the profundity of his thought and the beauty of its expression he was one of the greatest of French prose writers. (For a good biography, see Morris Bishop's *Pascal, Life of Genius:* Reynal & Hitchcock, 1936).

10. A PHILOSOPHE. The term *philosophes* is a broad one used to designate French literary men, scientists, and thinkers of the 18th century all of whom, however widely they differed in their individual tendencies, were united in their belief in the sovereign efficacy of human reason and in their desire to undermine or overthrow institutions and beliefs that offered obstacles to its effective supremacy.

The term is generally left in its original French since the word *philosopher* usually suggests a person preoccupied with epistemology, the science of knowledge, or more especially in our time, the logical analysis of science in terms of modern mathematics. The 18th-century *philosophes,* unlike most modern philosophers, were concerned with every phase of life and society, with science, literature, the arts, religion, government, economics, politics, metaphysics, ethical principles, human rights, education, etc. Their interests ranged over every conceivable subject. Voltaire, for instance, has been compared to Aristotle for the breadth (if not the depth) of his knowledge. Broadly speaking, they applied the rational, scientific method elaborated by Descartes in the 17th century (see Chapter 1, note 42) to *all* beliefs and institutions. They sought to examine the entire spectrum of human knowledge and human values in the light of "reason." The movement was moderate and restrained in the first half of the 18th century, a period dominated by Montesquieu (see Chapter 1, note 51) and Voltaire. It gained momentum in the second half with the emergence of Diderot (see Chapter 8, note 1), Rousseau (Chapter 7, note 3), Buffon (Chapter 3, note 7), Condillac, Turgot (Chapter 7, note 4), Condorcet (Chapter 3, note 8), and an increasingly militant Voltaire. Other prominent *philosophes* included D'Alembert (Chapter 7, note 2), Morellet, d'Holbach (Chapter 9, note 15), Helvétius, and Raynal. The *Encyclopédie* (see Chapter 7, note 5) gathered together all their divergent energies into a compendium of human knowledge representing an impressive attempt to give a rational explanation to the universe.

The *philosophes* were attacked from many sides, especially by the Jesuits, the Jansenists, and the *Parlement* of Paris. Their works were publicly burnt and many *philosophes* were imprisoned for the expression of their views. But their official opponents were divided among themselves and many were won over to the views of the *philosophes*, including Malesherbes, the director of literary censorship at the critical period. The doctrines of the *philosophes* gradually established themselves and, by discrediting the Government, the judiciary, and the Church, they contributed to the French Revolution even though the great majority of the *philosophes* desired peaceful reforms, not a violent social upheaval. (See Peter Gay's remarks on the term *philosophe* appearing in the *Introduction* to this book).

CHAPTER 3, PP. 50–67

1. ROUSSEAU, JEAN-BAPTISTE. See Chapter 1, note 4.

2. LEIBNITZ, GOTTFRIED WILHELM VON (1646–1716). German philosopher and mathematician, inventor (shortly before Newton) of differential and integral calculus. He developed an immense philosophical system incorporating the theory of innate ideas and a doctrine of preestablished harmony in the universe, popularly interpreted as an optimistic philosophy: "All is for the best in this best of all possible worlds"—an attitude mercilessly ridiculed by Voltaire in *Candide*. Voltaire was equally scornful of Leibnitz' concept of "monads," self-contained indestructible souls, each reflecting the universe in varying degrees, existing in a hierarchy of ascending order, the supreme monad being God. According to Leibnitz, God allows free will yet shapes the world in accordance with a preestablished plan, making man tend in a certain direction without forcing him.

3. LOCKE, JOHN. See Chapter 1, note 36.

4. COLLINS, ANTHONY (1676–1729). English theologian; friend of John Locke. Collins set forth the position of the deists and defended the cause of rational theology. His *Discourse on Free Thinking* (1713) was answered by many clergymen and was satirized by Jonathan Swift. His *Inquiry Concerning Human Freedom* (1715) is regarded as an admirable statement of the necessitarian standpoint.

5. SHAFTESBURY, ANTHONY ASHLEY COOPER, 3RD EARL OF (1671–1713). English philosopher educated by John Locke; contributed to the field of moral philosophy. Shaftesbury reacted against individualism in ethics and found true morality in a balance between egoism and altruism, based on the idea of a harmony between society and the individual, making the general welfare identical with individual happiness. He believed man to be innately equipped

with spontaneous instincts or affections to promote this harmony. He called this the moral sense in the ethical field and was the first to use this term. His influence was considerable.

6. MONADS. See note 2 on Leibnitz.

7. BUFFON, GEORGES-LOUIS LECLERC, COMTE DE (1717–1788). French naturalist, famed for his *Histoire Naturelle* (1749–1804, 44 vols.; first three volumes including *Théorie de la Terre* and general views on generation of life appeared in 1749). Buffon's famous *Epoques de la Nature* (1779) marked important beginnings in geological study. He was the first modern writer to translate facts of nature into a history of nature with a method scientific in intention. His impatience with slow methods of science often led him to propound theories inadequately substantiated and often later disproved, but his hypotheses and theories of geographical zoology and geological periods pointed the way to Lamarck and Darwin. Theologians of the Sorbonne condemned his theory of the history of the earth (1751), and Buffon signed an abjuration of anything that might be construed as contrary to the narrative of Moses. Not hostile to religion, he sought to avoid theological controversy and kept the spheres of faith and reason separate.

8. CONDORCET, ANTOINE-NICOLAS DE (1743–94). French mathematician and philosopher and later politician; named perpetual secretary of the *Académie des Sciences*. A friend of D'Alembert, Turgot, and Voltaire, he wrote biographies of the last two. He shared Voltaire's antipathy to the Church and Turgot's ardor for social improvement. As an author he is remembered chiefly for his *Tableau historique des progrès de l'esprit humain* (1793–4). He was an ardent partisan of the French Revolution, and was a member of the Legislative Assembly and the Convention, but under proscription as a Girondin; this more moderate party incurred the hostility of such extremists as Danton, Marat, and Robespierre. He took poison to avoid the guillotine.

CHAPTER 4, PP. 68–74

1. POMPADOUR, ANTOINETTE POISSON, MARQUISE DE (1721–1764). A woman of the upper middle class, mistress of Louis XV. She was an intelligent patroness of literature and art but exercised unfortunate influence over politics, especially in matters of war and foreign affairs, for some twenty years.

2. MAINE, LOUISE DE BOURBON, DUCHESSE DU (1676–1753). Granddaughter of *Le Grand Condé* and wife of the duc du Maine, an elder son of Louis XIV by Louis' mistress Mme de Montespan. The duke was

declared heir to the crown in default of princes of the blood by royal decree of 1714 but lost his commanding position during the Regency (see Chapter 1, note 16). The duchesse du Maine took part in a conspiracy against the Regent (1718) and was temporarily imprisoned. She was famous for her literary and political salon maintained at Sceaux from 1700 to 1750.

3. MAUPERTUIS, PIERRE-LOUIS MOREAU (1698–1759). French scientist; first member of the *Académie des Sciences* to defend the principles of Newton and first Frenchman to be made a member of the Royal Society of London; member of a mission sent in 1736 to measure a degree of the meridian in Lapland, thus verifying the earth's shape as indicated by Newton. In 1740 Frederick II appointed him director of the Academy of Science of Berlin. A worthy man of no great scientific ability, he quarreled with Voltaire while the latter was residing in Berlin and was the subject of Voltaire's lampoon entitled *Diatribe du Docteur Akakia*, on the occasion of a scientific dispute between Maupertuis and the German mathematician Koenig.

4. LA METTRIE, JULIEN OFFROY DE (1709–1751). French physicist and materialist philosopher; author of *Histoire naturelle de l'âme* ("Natural History of the Soul") (1745), a work which excited violent hostility as being subversive of religious belief. He took refuge in Holland but had to flee that country after expressing even more dangerously materialistic views. Frederick II invited him to Berlin, where he died.

CHAPTER 5, PP. 75–92

1. VAUVENARGUES, LUC DE CLAPIERS, MARQUIS DE (1715–1747). Ethical writer, devoted to literature; a man of high and generous character whose virtue and sincerity won the affectation even of such skeptics as Voltaire. His *Introduction à la connaissance de l'esprit humain suivie de réflexions et maximes* (1746) attracted little attention until the 19th century. It consisted of three books dealing with the mind, the passions, and vices and virtues. He discerned both good and evil in man; refused to denigrate human nature as La Rochefoucauld had done; regarded the heart rather than the reason as the true source of best thought and actions. His writings breathe a serene and sympathetic spirit.

2. THE QUARREL OF THE ANCIENTS AND THE MODERNS. *La Querelle des Anciens et des Modernes* was a dispute which developed in the latter part of the 17th century between the advocates of imitation of the literature of classical antiquity and the champions of

progress, new ideas, and self-sufficiency. Charles Perrault, Fontenelle, Desmarets and others maintained the superiority of modern writers as representatives of the maturity of the human intellect. La Fontaine, La Bruyère, and Boileau held the opposite view. The dispute died down, and Boileau, in a letter to Perrault (1700), recognized, within certain limits, the equality in literary merit of the 17th century to any period of antiquity.

3. MIRABEAU, HONORÉ-GABRIEL DE RIQUETTI, COMTE DE (1749–1791). One of the great Revolutionary statesmen and orators. As a youth he led a violent, undisciplined life, and was several times imprisoned. Involved with the young wife of a septuagenarian marquis (1775) he fled with her to Holland. The lovers were arrested in 1777, he being sent to the prison of Vincennes and she to a convent; he wrote to her daily from prison and studied prodigiously, writing numerous essays on politics and finance. He began his public career in May 1789 as Deputy for the Third Estate for Aix-en-Provence; immediately distinguished himself by his powers of oratory, political genius, and a gift for clarifying the most complicated situation in a few words; held definite views on the need for a constitutional government with rights of the people guaranteed but with the king at its head; president of the Jacobin Club in 1790 and of the National Assembly in 1791. He died a natural death from excesses in work and pleasure.

4. CHATEAUBRIAND, VICOMTE FRANCOIS-RENÉ DE (1768–1848). Outstanding French literary genius of the early 19th century; spent a lonely childhood at the parental château of Combourg in Brittany; went to Paris in 1788 with an army commission. His career was interrupted by the Revolution, he went to America (1791) allegedly intent on discovering the Northwest Passage; his American travels were not too extensive, but were intellectually fruitful. He returned to France in 1792 on learning of the fall of the monarchy; fought with the *Armée des émigrés,* was wounded, and escaped to England (1793). He returned to France in 1800; made a sudden literary reputation with *Atala* (1801) and gained resounding fame with *Le Génie du Christianisme,* a work of Christian apologetics begun in London and opportunely finished at the moment when Roman Catholicism was about to be reinstated as the official religion of France. At first in favor with Napoleon, he became increasingly hostile to the Empire. He had a political career after Napoleon's downfall.

Chateaubriand was a lifelong frequenter of Mme Récamier's salon. By all accounts he was a sublime "poseur," egotist, and daydreamer. His writings were infused with an imaginative melancholy, frustrated yearnings for the infinite, and a poetic beauty exemplified in his famous tale *René*, which incarnates all the vague, unsatisfied longings, world-weariness, and a passion for nature in its most melancholy and terrifying aspects, typifying the early phases of Romanticism. He introduced *le mal du siècle* ("the sickness of the age") into French literature, much as Goethe had done for German literature with *The Sufferings of Young Werther* (1774). His emotional appeal and poetic style exercised a lasting influence on French writers.

5. HAMILTON, ANTHONY (ANTOINE) (1646?–1720). Scottish author of the French *Mémoires du comte de Grammont*; fought in the Dutch wars for Louis XIV; visited France during the first exile of the Stuarts (1649–60) and settled there after 1688. He fought for James II at the Battle of the Boyne (1690) and accompanied the defeated king to his exile in France at Saint-Germain-en-Laye. Hamilton was a master of French and wrote much, including verses and witty fairy tales.

6. LA FARE. See Chapter 1, note 24.

7. THE DRAME. The term *le drame* (literally: "the drama") was used in a specialized sense to designate a class of dramatic works intermediate between tragedy and comedy. Its theory was developed by Diderot (see Chapter 8, note 1) in discourses attached to his plays *Le Fils naturel* and *Le Père de famille*. According to Diderot's conception, they were to be serious dramas dealing with the domestic problems of middle-class life. It was not until the mid-19th century, in plays of writers like Augier and Dumas *fils,* that this theory of drama achieved its effective development and expression.

8. MALHERBE, FRANCOIS DE (1555–1628). Court poet, especially known as censor of earlier poets and the school of Ronsard. A purist in style, stressing strength and conciseness of diction, sobriety and clearness, and avoidance of mere ornament, he stood for intellectual as opposed to emotional poetry. He approved rigid rules for verse, restricted the poetic vocabulary, and prescribed accurate grammatical constructions in the interest of clarity and precision but at the expense of many useful terms and happy, if irregular, turns of phrase. He wrote comparatively little, mainly on high political themes and paraphrases of the Psalms. His verses follow his rules but generally lack inspiration.

9. AUBIGNÉ, AGRIPPA D' (1552–1630). Poet and ardent Protestant who

served Henri de Navarre as soldier, diplomat, and councillor; settled at Geneva after death of Henri IV. His chief poem, *Les Tragiques* (published 1616), in 9000 Alexandrine verses, has been described as the epic of Calvinism. It contains a fierce denunciation of the evils of the religious wars and of the enemies of the Reformation.

10. RÉGNIER, MATHURIN (1573–1613). Satirist. An interest in manners and characters led him to write his *Satires*, poems after the manner of Horace and Juvenal; which describe with vigorous and amusing traits the poet, the physician, the hypocrite, the Gascon adventurer, etc. He revolted against the reforms of Malherbe and the purists; believed, with Montaigne, that everything varies with the individual's point of view and that each should follow his own reason or inclination; he enjoyed high literary esteem. His satires prepared the way for Molière.

11. BOILEAU. See Chapter 1, note 3.

12. MAROT, CLÉMENT (1496–1544). A poet of the transition from the medieval tradition of allegorical didactic verse to the new spirit of the Renaissance, he wrote a great variety of poems, some lengthy like *Le Temple de Cupidon,* an allegory, but the great majority shorter pieces: epistles, eclogues, *rondeaux, chansons,* elegies, ballads, and some 300 epigrams plus translations of the Psalms. He was essentially a court poet, light, subtle, graceful, and amusing. He had a mordant wit which he directed against the theologians of the Sorbonne, the papacy, and the friars. He influenced the English poet Spenser.

13. VOITURE, VINCENT (1598–1648). Poet and letter writer. A man of brilliant social gifts covering more serious qualities of intellect, he is remembered as one of the principal habitués of the Hôtel de Rambouillet (intellectual center of Parisian society in the first half of the 17th century) where he was esteemed for his wit and amusing conversation.

14. LAMARTINE, ALPHONSE-MARIE-LOUISE DE PRAT DE (1790–1869). One of the great poets of the Romantic Movement; a man of action, statesman, and orator as well as a creative writer. His *Méditations Poétiques* (1820) introduced into French poetry a lyricism that had been lost for centuries. He expressed a poet's appreciation of Nature as a reflection of his own moods; and put into poetic terms *le mal du siècle* of Chateaubriand's prose (see note 4). He was a kindred spirit with the English poet Byron. As a politician, a member of the Chamber of Deputies, he delivered many impas-

sioned speeches on humanitarian themes that captured public opinion; a popular idol during the 1848 Revolution, he fell from favor thereafter and retired to private life.

15. CRÉBILLION, PROSPER JOLVET, SIEUR DE (1674–1762). Tragic dramatist whose literary activity extended over some fifty years. His plays abound in violent episodes and romantic complication rather than development of character or truth to life. His melodramas, of a highly tragic character, attempted, as he said, to evoke pity by terror. His masterpiece is *Rhadamiste et zénobie* (1711). Greatly esteemed in his day, he was used by the enemies of Voltaire to oust the latter from favor at court.

16. TARTUFFE. Famous character in Molière's comedy of the same name (1664–69). Tartuffe personifies the religious hypocrite. He professes extreme piety and makes a great public display of devout practices and seeming humility, but hoodwinks a gullible benefactor, takes control of his household, acquires title to his property, and is unmasked only when he tries to seduce his benefactor's wife while the husband is hidden in the room.

17. HERNANI. A poetic drama by Victor Hugo (1830); an epoch-making event in the Romantic Movement marking a deliberate break with classical tradition in subject, treatment, and versification. Its first two performances at the Comédie Française count among the great battles of the Romantics. The theater was packed with partisans. Below, in the expensive seats, were the traditionalists, determined to crush the play and with it the dangerous innovations of the new school. Above were the hordes of Hugo's admirers, young writers, artists, and musicians, led by poet Théophile Gautier wearing a cherry-colored satin doublet which became legendary. At both performances they outclapped, outshouted, and generally outdid the occupants of the boxes and orchestra seats with such effect that the success of the play and of the Romantic Movement was thenceforth assured.

18. CHÉNIER, ANDRÉ (1762–1794). Generally regarded as the greatest French poet of the 18th century. He was active in the early Revolutionary movement but protested against its later excesses, was imprisoned during the Reign of Terror and executed two days before the fall of Robespierre. His eclogues, idylls, odes, and elegies show intense devotion to ancient classical literature, especially the Greek elegiac poets, and gave expression to his love of nature, youth, and beauty. The lyrical satires written during his imprisonment reveal his disgust and despair at the atrocities of the

Terror. He restored to French versification a harmony and suppleness which had disappeared during the 18th century. His life
inspired the opera *Andrea Chénier* by Giordano (1896).

19. LA FONTAINE, JEAN DE (1621–1695). Poet and fabulist, born at
Château-Thierry in Champagne. Together with his friend Molière,
La Fontaine is probably the best known and best loved of all
French writers. His fame rests almost entirely on his *Fables,* some
230 of them appearing in 12 collections published from 1668 to
1694. Many of these are known to and relished by Frenchmen
of all ages, who have usually memorized a number of the most
familiar ones. They have always been extremely popular. There
were 37 editions before La Fontaine's death and they have frequently been translated into English. Besides his fables, La Fontaine
wrote light society verse, short stories, imitations of Boccaccio
and Ariosto, poems on classical themes, and a beautiful *Elégie aux
Nymphes de Vaux* (1671), a lament over the fall from royal favor
of his wealthy friend and patron, Nicholas Fouquet. But none of
these are so well known today as the *Fables.*

What we popularly call "Æsop's Fables" are frequently translations or adaptations of La Fontaine's fables. The French writer
transformed the fables of the ancient authors (Æsop included) into
little dramas, little pictures of life, vivid with details drawn from
his own keen observations of nature and society. Sometimes called
"a Moliére in miniature," he wrote dramatic poems usually so
effective that, unlike his predecessors, he had little need to propound the moral. It is often implied or expressed in one or two brief
lines that have passed into the language as proverbs. There is
action and dialogue. The characters are usually animals symboliz-
ing men of all classes yet frequently retaining their own animal
traits. (La Fontaine was one of the few writers in the 17th century
to study nature and to observe the habits and habitat of wildlife.
He spent much of his childhood out of doors while his father held
a post in the administration of forests and natural resources.)

La Fontaine led a rather vagabond existence as a parasite and
pensioner of wealthy patrons. His tastes were epicurean. The
morals of his fables generally reflect his own philosophy: a kindly,
easy-going indulgence for man's foibles marked by astute observations on human selfishness, vanity, stupidity, cruelty, and cynicism, viewed in a manner that can be both sad and amusing at the
same time. Among his best-known fables are: *La Cigale et la
Fourmi* ("The Ant and the Grasshopper"); *Le Corbeau et le
Renard* ("The Fox and the Crow"); *Le Loup et l'Agneau* ("The

Wolf and the Lamb"); *Le Loup et le Chien* ("The Wolf and the Dog"); *La Laitière et le Pot au Lait* ("The Milk-maid and the Pot of Milk"); and (one of his greatest): *Les Animaux malades de la Peste* ("The Animals Sick with the Plague").

CHAPTER 6, PP. 93–112

1. BOSSUET, JACQUES-BÉNIGNE (1627–1704). An eminent Catholic bishop, famed for his sermons and funeral orations as well as his educational and polemical works. His funeral orations combine the characteristics of a panegyric and a sermon and contain some of his most famous oratory. As tutor to the Dauphin, he wrote a *Discours sur l'histoire universelle* ("Discourse on Universal History") (1681), a chronological abstract of the history of the world, followed by a commentary showing (a) the development of religion, and (b) the causes of the rise and fall of empires (a vindication of Providence). He also wrote an exposition of the doctrine of the divine right of kings and their duties to their subjects. Bossuet championed the Gallican standpoint in the conflict between Louis XIV and the papacy. Eminent as a theologian, moralist, and orator, and a staunch defender of the traditional Catholic faith, he was called "the last of the Fathers of the Church" by his contemporary, La Bruyère. Because of a strong lyrical element in his writing, Lanson has elsewhere referred to him as "the great lyrical poet of the 17th century."

2. SAINT BARTHOLOMEW'S DAY MASSACRE. A slaughter of French Protestants (Huguenots) carried out in Paris on the festival of St. Bartholomew, August 24, 1572. The massacre was instigated by the queen mother, Catherine de' Medici, abetted by the duc d'Anjou (later King Henry III), Henri, 3rd duc de Guise, and the reluctant King Charles IX. It was planned to coincide with the appearance in Paris of numerous Huguenot leaders attending the wedding of Henry of Navarre (later Henry IV) to Marguerite de Valois, the sister of Charles IX. Under relentless pressure from his mother, Catherine de' Medici, the king is reported to have said: "Is that what you want? Then let them be killed. But make certain they're all killed!"

The order was given during the night of August 23rd. The slaughter began with the pealing of church bells in Paris and spread into other sections of France. The first victim was the Huguenot leader Coligny, a distinguished general, admiral of France, and adviser to the king. His death was followed by the murder of minor leaders and all Huguenots within reach of the soldiery and the mob. It is said that 30,000 persons perished in the massacre. Its immediate consequence was the outbreak of the fifth religious war in France.

Henry of Navarre (1553–1610), who had been raised as a Calvinist and sided with the Huguenots, escaped the massacre and, on the death of Henry III, became King of France (1589). He formally renounced Protestanism in 1593 and promulgated the Edict of Nantes (1598) granting religious toleration and certain civil rights to the Huguenots. This, the first example in the western world of a legal declaration of religious tolerance, terminated the religious wars in France.

3. TORCY, JEAN-BAPTISTE COLBERT, MARQUIS DE (1666–1746). French statesman and diplomat (nephew of Louis XIV's finance minister Colbert); played a prominent role in the War of the Spanish Succession and its conclusion, the Peace of Utrecht (1713–14).

4. DANGEAU, PHILIPPE, MARQUIS DE (1638–1720). An assiduous courtier who daily for thirty years from 1684 recorded in his *Journal* minute incidents of the court of Louis XIV; not esteemed for literary merit but of considerable historical value. Saint-Simon made extensive use of the *Journal* in the composition of his *Mémoires*.

5. VILLARS. See Chapter 1, note 17.

6. LOUVOIS, MICHEL LE TELLIER, MARQUIS DE (1641–1691). War minister of Louis XIV and remarkable administrator who reorganized the French army. He exerted a pernicious political influence by encouraging the king's inclination for war and by instigating religious persecution; his policies conflicted with those of Colbert. Louvois was largely responsible for the devastation of the Palatinate in 1689.

7. COLBERT, JEAN-BAPTISTE (1619–1685). Great finance minister of Louis XIV; *intendant des finances* from 1661 and *contrôleur des finances* from 1665. As minister of marine he built a powerful French navy and introduced important reforms in the financial system. He was inclined to excessive protection and regulation of industry, but aimed to make France great through general prosperity and reduced taxation. His aims were thwarted by the king's costly wars and the prodigal expenditures of the court. He created the *canal du Midi* connecting the Mediterranean with the Atlantic; founded academies of science, architecture, and inscriptions; reorganized the royal library; and protected men of erudition.

8. DESMARETS DE SAINT-SORLIN, JEAN (1596–1676). Poet; friend of Cardinal Richelieu; holder of high administrative office and an original member of the French Academy; adversary of Boileau in literary disputes and of the Jansenists in religious conflicts. He was the author of several epic poems, a romance, and comedies (best known: *Les Visionnaires,* 1637), a study of characters in which various extravagant types in polished society are ridiculed. Molière drew on this comedy for *Les Femmes Savantes* (1672).

9. SAINTE-BEUVE, CHARLES-AUGUSTIN (1804–1869). Famed French literary critic. He first studied medicine, but from 1827 on literature claimed him altogether. He engaged in literary journalism for the *Globe* and encouraged the Romantic Movement and its young authors. He formed a friendship with Victor Hugo and Hugo's wife Adèle which ended when his relationship with Adèle turned to passion. He was tormented for years thereafter by emotional stress and spiritual disquiet; took an interest in the history of Jansenism (see Chapt. 1, note 9) and lectured for a year on Port-Royal. The book form of these lectures is a masterpiece of re-creative literary criticism. He wrote for the *Revue de Paris* and the *Revue des Deux Mondes;* over a twenty-year period he wrote weekly essays of a critical and biographical nature, published on Mondays; hence the subsequent book form took the title *Causeries du Lundi* (1851–62, 15 vols.). Sainte-Beuve is regarded as "the father of modern criticism"; he was largely responsible for making professional criticism a major form of literary art.

10. MAINTENON, FRANCOISE D'AUBIGNÉ, MARQUISE DE (1635–1719). Widow of the poet Scarron, who became the mistress of Louis XIV and was secretly married to the king (about 1684). She was a modest, discreet, intelligent woman, capable of great self-control and inclined to piety, who appears not to have tried to influence the king in matters of policy. She founded Saint-Cyr as a convent school for the daughters of impoverished noblemen. Her letters reveal the good qualities of her character and a knowledge of human nature.

11. EDICT OF NANTES. The Edict of Nantes was promulgated by Henry IV on 13 April 1598, granting Protestants liberty of conscience, the right of public worship according to their tenets in certain localities outside Paris, and admissibility to all offices, together with some safeguards: certain towns, for instance, such as La Rochelle, Montauban, and Cognac were constituted *places de sûreté* ("places of safety"). This legal declaration of religious

tolerance was revoked by Louis XIV in 1685, leading to an exodus from France of thousands of Protestants.

12. THIERRY, AUGUSTIN (1795–1856). Historian who did much to stimulate research in history. He wrote vivid, picturesque narrative, enlivened by anecdote and local color. His two principal works are: *L'Histoire de la conquête de l'Angleterre par les Normands* (1823), whose theme is the Anglo-Saxon spirit of liberty surviving invasion, and *Récits des temps mérovingiens,* a vivid retelling of stories from the Chronicle of Gregory of Tours, preceded by *Considérations sur l'histoire de France* (1840).

13. HERDER, JOHANN GOTTFRIED VON (1744–1803). German philosopher, poet, and critic; leader in *Sturm und Drang* (Storm and Stress) movement (an intellectual reawakening in Germany closely allied with Romanticism). A student of theology, he was influenced by Kant. He contributed to philosophy, comparative religion, and mythology. His *Outlines of the Philosophy of Man* (1784–91) developed an evolutionary approach to history.

14. MICHELET, JULES (1798–1874). Historian, author of *L'Histoire de France* (1833–43), the most famous example of the 19th-century romantic narrative history. This book is a resuscitation of the past, picturesque, subjective, declamatory at times, but of high literary value. It contains a brilliant evocation of the Middle Ages and a moving study of Joan of Arc. He was a man of liberal, democratic sympathies and wrote seven-volume history of *La Révolution francaise* (1847–53). He refused to swear allegiance to Napoleon III and lost his post at the National Archives and Collège de France; lived quietly thereafter completing his history of France and other historical writings. Michelet is regarded by many as the greatest of French historians.

15. GUIZOT, FRANCOIS (1787–1874). Historian and statesman; a Protestant brought up in Geneva; Professor of Modern History at the Sorbonne (1812–30). He wrote numerous historical works dealing chiefly with England (particularly the development of its constitutional monarchy) and France. His *Histoire générale de la civilisation en Europe* (1828) and his *Histoire de la civilisation en France* (1829–32) are deemed fine examples of methodical, solidly documented work and lucid historical narrative. He stressed the rise of the middle class as the most decisive element in French history for maintaining a balance between absolutism and democracy; he favored constitutional monarchy. He had a political career as ambassador to London, foreign minister, and prime

minister until the Revolution of 1848, after which he lived in retirement devoting himself to historical studies.

16. HETTNER, HERMANN THEODOR (1821–1882). German man of letters; professor of Esthetics at Heidelberg University. He was the author of *History of Literature in the 18th Century* (1856–64), which is still regarded as authoritative.

CHAPTER 7, PP. 113–124

1. BYNG, JOHN (1704–1757). A British admiral, son of George Byng, Viscount Torrington. Sent to relieve the British garrison at Minorca (1756), he was defeated by the French and abandoned his task. He was court-martialed, convicted of dereliction of duty, and shot aboard his ship, March 14, 1757. The severe, though lawful, sentence aroused public indignation. Voltaire, who had known Byng in his youth, tried in vain to save him through humanitarian appeals. The event occasioned one of Voltaire's memorable *mots* in *Candide* (1759). When the ingenuous Candide asks why the admiral is being shot, he is told that "in this country it is good to kill an admiral from time to time to encourage the others." (Chapt. 23).

2. D'ALEMBERT, JEAN LE ROND (1717–1783). Philosopher and mathematician; collaborated in preparation of the *Encyclopédie* as Diderot's principal assistant until 1758; famed for his remarkable *Discours préliminaire* to the *Encyclopédie* and his article *Genève* (1757) which created a storm by its praise of the doctrines and practices of Genevan pastors. He was a religious skeptic, hostile to the priesthood. An influential member of the French Academy, he frequented literary salons and enjoyed a European reputation.

3. ROUSSEAU, JEAN-JACQUES (1712–1778). Famed philosopher. Born in Geneva, he had little formal education. He left Geneva in 1728 to become a wanderer. He found a protectress for 12 years in Mme de Warens; converted to Catholicism and reverted to Protestantism; acquired a taste for music and supported himself as a musical copyist; wrote a successful operetta, *Le Devin du Village* ("The Village Soothsayer") in 1752. He formed a lifelong liaison with a servant girl, Thérèse Levasseur.

Rousseau acquired literary prominence with two *Discours* on themes propounded by the Academy of Dijon. These discourses formed an intellectual and moral crisis in his life confirming him in the conviction that man is by nature virtuous, free, and happy but corrupted by society, the source of property, inequality, and despotism. He advocated returning to nature insofar as practicable.

He disapproved of the theater as fostering the vices of society. This view, and his criticism of Voltaire's pessimistic doctrine in the latter's poem on the Lisbon earthquake (1755), marked the beginning of a long quarrel between the two. His novel *La Nouvelle Héloïse* (1761) reconciled natural relations of man and woman with the social order. In *Emile* (1762) he expounded a theory of natural education and the idea of a natural religion. His famed *Du Contrat Social* ("The Social Contract") (1762) set forth a theory of the social state that Rousseau believed consonant with the state of nature: man is born free and force cannot be the source of right; government must be based on a compact; the principal objects of legislation are liberty and equality. While the treatise tends to disregard facts of history and the complexity of human affairs, it made itself felt, especially after 1789, contributing to the growth of new ideas by enforcing the principle of the sovereignty of the people. The opening words: "Man is born free, and everywhere he is in chains" struck a note which resounded far. His temperament was at variance with that of most 18th-century *philosophes*. His highly developed sensibility, emotionalism, feeling for nature, melancholy reveries, and lyrical utterances made him a precursor of the Romantic Movement.

4. TURGOT, ANNE-ROBERT-JACQUES (1727–1781). Famed economist and administrator. As finance minister under Louis XVI (1774–76) he tried to effect reforms in trade policies and remedy fiscal abuses but was opposed and toppled by hostile groups. He shared the economic views of the physiocrats; published many treaties, pamphlets, and articles; and was a friend of the *philosophes* and esteemed by Voltaire.

5. L'ENCYCLOPÉDIE. One of the great literary monuments of the 18th century, an encyclopedic dictionary of the knowledge of the day, including the arts, sciences, and trades; originally suggested by the *Cyclopaedia* of Ephraim Chambers (1728). Diderot persuaded the translators of Chambers' work to give it ampler scope and systematic classification of knowledge on Baconian lines. 17 volumes were published between 1751 and 1772. It embodies the philosophic spirit of the 18th century, attempting to give a rational explanation of the universe. It is marked by concern for truth and contempt for superstition. Publication was twice prohibited through Jesuit influence, but the government was half-hearted in its condemnation. The principal director of the enterprise was Diderot, assisted by D'Alembert. The work has little present-day value owing to the progress of knowledge, but it propagated the

scientific spirit and assigned to science its practical purpose. In addition to Diderot other famous contributors were Montesquieu, Turgot, Voltaire, Rousseau, and Buffon.

6. JANSENISTS. See Chapter 1, note 9.

7. PHILOSOPHE. See Chapter 2, note 10.

CHAPTER 8, PP. 125–136

1. DIDEROT, DENIS (1713–1784). A philosopher, encyclopedist, novelist, dramatist, art critic, and ardent disseminator of the philosophical ideas of his time, Diderot is regarded by many as the most profound and original mind in 18th-century France. Educated by the Jesuits, he devoted himself to literature and became a profound student of the natural sciences, which he made the basis of his philosophy. He undertook the direction of the *Encyclopédie* in 1745 (see Chapter 7, note 5), his most notable contribution to the advancement of knowledge. His *Pensées philosophiques* (1746) showed an attitude of skepticism towards religion but did not yet reflect his later atheism. A friend of Rousseau, he encouraged the latter to write his memorable discourse denouncing the evils of civilization.

He is regarded as the founder of art criticism in France. For the theater he wrote two prose dramas illustrating his theory that there is an interval between comedy and tragedy for plays that are neither one nor the other but deal seriously with problems of middle-class life (see Chapter 5, note 7). Diderot held the dubious view he could make drama a moral influence by having his characters sermonize with moral exhortations. Of special interest to contemporary existentialist thought is his *Le Neveu de Rameau* ("Rameau's Nephew"), a character sketch in the form of a dialogue: a pitiless examination of human nature stressing man's depravity and inevitable capitulation to social prejudices, conventions, authority, and the power of money. In philosophy he was a determinist and experimental materialist. He anticipated modern evolutionary ideas by arguing, from the facts of natural science, an imperceptible transition from inert to living matter. Like Rousseau, he regarded human nature as naturally inclined to virtue but perverted by society. In politics he was a moderate and pratical reformer, not a violent revolutionary. Diderot is regarded as superior to Voltaire and Rousseau in his scientific approach to philosophical problems.

2. HAMILTON. See Chapter 5, note 5.

3. DUCLOS, CHARLES PINOT (1704–1772). Historian, moralist, novelist,

noted for his witty conversation, energy, and practical sense rather than unusual talent. He was a friend of Voltaire and Rousseau and supporter of the *philosophes* and the *Encyclopédie*.

4. CYRANO DE BERGERAC, SAVINIEN (1619–1655). Parisian writer of fantastic and burlesque romances; freethinker, soldier, and duellist, of grotesque appearance (his long nose was celebrated). A studious and original thinker, he wrote a play in which the author visits the moon and sun, describing their inhabitants and institutions in a spirit of social and political satire. He inspired the heroic comedy of *Cyrano de Bergerac* (1897) by Edmond Rostand.

5. FONTENELLE. See Chapter 1, note 37.

6. ROUSSEAU, JEAN-JACQUES. See Chapter 7, note 3.

7. LEIBNITZ. See Chapter 3, note 2.

8. MONTESQUIEU. See Chapter 1, note 51.

9. LES WELCHES. *Les Welches* or *les Velches,* from the German *waelsch* meaning Italian or French, used contemptuously as signifying "ignorant," "barbarians"; a word Voltaire was fond of employing to designate his contemporaries of the 18th century, which he regarded as a period of literary decadence.

10. JOURNAL DE TRÉVOUX. See Chapter 2, note 6.

CHAPTER 9, PP. 137–160

1. CAPANEUS. In Greek mythology, one of the *Seven Against Thebes* (a tragedy by Aeschylus). Capaneus defied Zeus to prevent him from scaling the wall of the city and Zeus killed him with a bolt of lightning.

2. BASILOI. Larcher evidently accused Voltaire of writing (or speaking) French like a German-speaking native of Basel, Switzerland. The spelling *Basiloi* illustrates the point since it is a bastardized word, part German, part French. The French word for an inhabitant of Bâle is a *Bâlois*. The German word for the city is *Basel,* and a resident thereof is a *Basler*. The term *Basiloi,* denoting an impure French, is still used to describe certain people whose French is faulty. (It is perhaps unnecessary to remind the reader that Voltaire's French has long been admired for its linguistic clarity, purity, and natural vivacity).

3. NINON DE LENCLOS. See Chapter 1, note 11.

4. HARNACK, ADOLF (1851–1930). Director of the *Theologische Literatur-zeitung* (from 1881). He wrote many historical works on Christianity and biblical criticism; leader of a rational and critical school

of religious historians. In 1905 he was made head of the Royal Library in Berlin.

5. LOISY, ABBÉ ALFRED-FIRMIN (1857–1940). Modernist theologian and exegetist; dismissed from the professorial staff of the Institut Catholique de Paris in 1894 because of unorthodox views. From 1909 to 1932 he held the chair of History of Religions at the Collège de France. Besides *L'Evangile et l'Eglise* ("The Gospel and the Church") (1902) his most notable works include: *Etudes bibliques* (1901), *Le Quatrième Evangile* ("The Fourth Gospel") (1903), *Les Evangiles synoptiques* (1907–8), and *La Religion* (1917).

6. BOSSUET. See Chapter 6, note 1.

7. HERDER. See Chapter 6, note 13.

8. NIEBUHR, BERTHOLD-GEORG (1776–1831). German historian and diplomat, author of *Roman History* (1810–12). He was one of the first truly scientific historians, particularly in the area of ancient history.

9. MICHELET. See Chapter 6, note 14.

10. QUINET, EDGAR (1803–1875). Poet, historian, and politician. He wrote important works on Germany and Prussian politics. As professor at the Collège de France, he provoked Jesuit opposition and was relieved of his post. He was elected a deputy of the left in 1848 and exiled the same year. He then settled in Brussels and wrote a great variety of historical works including *La Création,* inspired by Darwin. He was reelected a deputy to the National Assembly in 1870, but, like Hugo, he exiled himself from France during the régime of Napoleon III. He was an idealistic patriot and fundamentally religious for all his anticlericalism; author of many historical, philosophical, and religious writings.

11. RENAN, ERNEST (1823–1892). Historian, Hebrew scholar, philologist, and critic. He was educated for the priesthood, but his philological and critical study of Semitic languages and biblical texts led him to question the divine inspiration of the Bible and, from that, the fundamental doctrines of orthodox revealed religion. Unable to take his vow, he left the seminary (Saint-Sulpice). After studies in Rome and archeological expeditions in the Middle East, he was made Professor of Hebrew at the Collège de France (1862), but his lectures were considered unorthodox and were suspended by government order. His chair itself was suppressed after publication of the *Vie de Jésus* (1863), first volume of his long-projected work *Les Origines du Christianisme* (which took 25 years to write). The value of this work has been disputed but it caused a sensation,

particularly the *Life of Jesus;* for beneath the enchanting, lyrical picture of the carpenter's son growing to maturity amid the flowers of the Galilean countryside lay a rationalization of the fundamental belief in the divinity of Christ. Reinstated at the Collège de France in 1870, he became its head in 1883. He is regarded as one of the foremost representatives of French thought during later years of the Second Empire.

12. DOM CALMET (1672–1757). An erudite Benedictine whose works include a commentary on the Old and New Testament.

13. BAYLE. See Chapter 1, note 43.

14. SPINOZA. See Chapter 1, note 38.

15. HOLBACH, PAUL THIRY BARON D' (1723–1789). German-born materialist and atheist philosopher. A man of wide erudition, he spent most of his life in France; wealthy and generous, he offered his houses in Paris and the country to the company of *encyclopédistes*. He wrote numerous tracts and pamphlets to the discredit of religion. His chief work, *Système de la Nature* (1770), is a treatise in defense of the materialist and determinist standpoint in philosophy and a culmination, in literary form, of the revolt against existing political and religious institutions.

16. MALEBRANCHE. See Chapter 1, note 39.

17. SPINOZA. See Chapter 1, note 38.

18. SHAFTESBURY. See Chapter 3, note 5.

19. THE FARM SYSTEM OF TAXATION. Under the Old Régime the task of collecting certain indirect taxes was farmed out, or leased for fixed periods, to private individuals. The system implied the right of exploitation. The tax collectors, known as *fermiers généraux* (farmers general), paid highly in the first instance for the privilege since they were able to amass very large fortunes from the post. Indirect taxes included the salt tax (*la gabelle*), customs duties at the frontiers of provinces as well as of the State, excise taxes, and tolls. The system dated from the 13th century and was so much abused that it became a powerful factor in the economic discontent of the pre-Revolutionary era.

Under the French monarchy the principal source of revenue was *la taille*, a direct tax levied on either real or personal property. The nobility and the clergy were exempt from this tax, as were a number of judicial, fiscal, and municipal officials. Its inequities also contributed to bring about the Revolution.

A celebrated comedy by René Lesage (*Turcaret:* 1709) vigorously satirized the type of unscrupulous tax collector (*fermier général*) who is indifferent to everything except financial profits and an ostentatious display of wealth, used to further social and amorous ambitions.

20. PARLEMENTS. See Chapter 1, note 48.

21. TURGOT. See Chapter 7, note 4.

CHAPTER 10, PP. 161–168

1. TRUDAINE, DANIEL-CHARLES (1703–1769). Economist, administrator, counsellor of the *Parlement* of Paris, counsellor of state (1734) and superintendent of finances and of bridges and highways (1744). He formed a school of engineers, who began the construction of French royal highways and was a member of the Academy of Sciences.

2. DUPONT DE NEMOURS, PIERRE-SAMUEL (1739–1817). Political economist and politician; one of the physiocrats who regarded land as the only source of wealth and the increase of products of the soil as the only means to property; friend of finance minister Turgot. He was a deputy to the States General in 1789. His hostility to the *Directoire* led to his voluntary emigration to America. (His son Eleuthère-Irénée founded the famous firm bearing the family name.)

3. LECOUVREUR. See Chapter 2, note 4.

CHAPTER 11, PP. 169–183

1. MAISTRE, JOSEPH DE (1753–1821). Moralist and Christian philosopher. His works, clear and vivacious in style, embody the Catholic reaction against the doctrines of the *philosophes*. He championed the nationalist and monarchical views of the *ultras* and opposed the progress of the physical sciences; he affirmed the divine right of the monarch, his absolute sovereignty, and the duty to support Papal supremacy. It was he who wrote: "Every nation has the government it deserves."

2. CHATEAUBRIAND. See Chapter 5, note 4.

3. THIERS, ADOLPHE (1797–1877). Statesman and historian, famed for two works: *Histoire de la Révolution française* (1823–7) and *Histoire du consulat et de l'empire* (1845–62). Models of clear-flowing narrative, they are among the standard histories of the Revolutionary and immediate post-Revolutionary eras.

4. RUHLIÈRE, CLAUDE DE (c. 1735–1791). Historian and writer of light verse. He is remembered for his account of the troubles in Poland in the late 1760's, published by Napoleon in 1806 as *Histoire de*

l'anarchie de Pologne et du démembrement de cette république ("History of the Anarchy in Poland and the Dismemberment of the Polish Republic"). He also wrote an important historical work on the causes of the revocation of the Edict of Nantes. His verse epistle on *Les Disputes* was inserted by Voltaire in his *Dictionnaire philosophique*.

5. ANQUETIL-DUPERRON, ABRAHAM-HYACINTHE (1731–1803). French orientalist. He went to India at age 23 in search of the sacred writings of the Parsees. He returned to Paris in 1762 with a priceless collection of manuscripts and spent the remainder of his life deciphering, commenting, and translating these. His translation of the *Zend Avesta* (1771) opened a new era in oriental studies.

6. DAUNO, PIERRE-CLAUDE-FRANCOIS (1761–1840). An ordained priest who welcomed the Revolution and was active in Revolutionary politics. He edited the *Journal des Savants* (1816–38) and lectured on history at the Collège de France, where he attached great importance to methods of research and documentation of sources. He published *Cours d'études historiques*, 1842–6, in 20 vols.

7. DARU, COMTE PIERRE-ANTOINE-NOËL-BRUNO (1767–1829). The *Intendant général* of Napoleon's *grande armée*, supplying its forces on several campaigns, notably in Russia; also a man of letters whose most noted and solid work was his *L'Histoire de la République de Venise* ("History of the Republic of Venice") (1819). He was a cousin of Stendhal, who often refers to him in his writings.

8. MICHELET. See Chapter 6, note 14.

9. SAND, GEORGE. Pen name of Lucile Aurore Dupin, baronne Dudevant (1804–1876). Novelist, fervent admirer of the Romanticists. *Indiana* (1831) was the first of many successful novels, tales, and essays produced in rapid procession for some forty years. A person of many enthusiasms, her literary output usually echoed whatever men or ideas were foremost in her personal life; had a passionate love affair with the poet Alfred de Musset and a nine-year liaison with the composer Frédéric Chopin, the first stage of which she describes in *Un Hiver à Majorque* ("A Winter in Majorca") (1841).

10. BALZAC, HONORÉ "DE" (1799–1850). One of the great novelists of all literature; author of *La Comédie humaine* (1842–8), the collective title of his many novels and tales affording a panorama of French society during the Consulate, the Empire, the Restoration, and the July Monarchy. More than 2000 characters appear and reappear. The framework is genealogical, geographical, and even geological, including all strata of society and its professions. The

underlying theme is that money can do everything and that self-interest is the supreme motive of human conduct. Among his most famous studies of Parisian and provincial life are: *Eugénie Grandet, La Cousine Bette, Le Cousin Pons,* and *Le Père Goriot.* Balzac had a dynamic, unflagging creative vigor, a superabundant imagination allied to remarkable powers of realistic observation and delineation of character. His style has been criticized for lacking the limpidity, harmony, or rhythm of the great French stylists, but it hammers its way to comprehensive impression through the vast resources of Balzac's thought and imagination. Certain characters he created are often discussed and used as types for comparison as if they had actually existed.

11. STENDHAL. Pseudonym of Henri Beyle (1783–1842). Novelist and critic; went to Milan with an army commission (1800) and recognized in Italy his spiritual home. After service with Napoleon's armies he returned to Italy for seven years, absorbed by art, music, literature, society, and an unrequited love he never forgot. His enduring fame rests on two novels: *Le Rouge et le Noir* ("The Red and the Black") (1830) and *La Chartreuse de Parme* ("The Charterhouse of Parma") (1839). In an age of Romanticism he was a forerunner of the modern psychological novelists, remarkable for his penetrating analyses of the motives for human behavior, always traceable to self-interest; was allied to the Romantics in his worship of unbounded, irrepressible energy in the pursuit of happiness, whether happiness was identified with love or power. His contemporaries, more concerned with describing the delights than analyzing the causes of sensibility, found little appeal in his attitude or writings. Appreciation came toward the end of the century, thus fulfilling a prophecy of his own. Other well-known works are *De l'amour* (1822), a study of love; and *Racine et Shakespeare* (1823–25), essentially a definition and defense of Romanticism in literature.

12. LACLOS, PIERRE CHODERLOS DE (1741–1803). Remembered as the author of *Les Liaisons dangereuses* (1782), a psychological analysis of the professional seducer and his victims in the higher echelons of society.

13. DUCLOS. See Chapter 8, note 3.

14. MÉRIMÉE, PROSPER (1803–1870). Novelist, archeologist, and historian. He wrote *Chronique du Règne de Charles IX* (1829), one of the early French historical novels inspired by Scott, and became one of the great French masters of the short story. Among the best

known are *Mateo Falcone, Tamango, L'Enlèvement de la Redoute, Colomba,* and *Carmen* (1847), this last the basis for Bizet's opera of the same name (1875). Mérimée also had an important political career: senator during the Second Empire and prominent at the court of the Empress Eugénie.

15. GIRARDIN, MME EMILE DE (1804–1855). Poet, newspaper columnist, and novelist. A beautiful and vivacious woman, she was the adored queen of the coteries which formed around the early leaders of the Romantic Movement.

16. TILLIER, CLAUDE (1792–1854). Pamphleteer and novelist; best known for *Mon Oncle Benjamin* (1841), a novel of provincial life and manners. He is noted for his verve and remarkable purity of style.

17. ABOUT, EDMOND (1828–1885). Novelist and brilliant journalist; founded and edited *Le XIXᵉ Siècle* ("The 19th Century") (1871), one of the most widely read conservative dailies during the early years of the Third Republic.

18. SARCEY, FRANCISQUE (1827–1899). Gave up teaching for journalism and became one of the best-known and soundest drama critics of the second half of the 19th century; contributed a weekly column for over thirty years to *Le Temps* (collected in *Quarante ans de théâtre,* 1900–02). He was not considered a profound critic, but his good sense, independent judgment, and understanding of the theater were renowned.

19. FRANCE, ANATOLE (1844–1924). Novelist, critic, and man of letters. He won fame with the novel *Le Crime de Sylvestre Bonnard* (1881). He was literary editor of *Le Temps,* a leading daily, and dominated contemporary letters by 1897. He was awarded the Nobel Prize for Literature in 1921. His other well-known novels include: *Thaïs* (1890), *La Rôtisserie de la Reine Pédauque* (1893), *Le Lys Rouge* (1894), and *L'Histoire Contemporaine* (1896–1901), a satire on French life, politics, religion, militarism, and anti-Semitism (with the Dreyfus case in vol. 4). He was famed for his charm as a writer; for his graceful erudition; and for his love of beauty, pagan antiquity, and 18th-century French classicism. His writings are characterized by subtle and biting irony, clarity of thought, and an elegant, melodious style.

20. VEBER, PIERRE (1869–1942). Writer of plays and novels who worked for various periodicals and newspapers including *The New York Herald;* author of humorous short stories employing tongue-in-cheek irony. Among his many novels are: *Les enfants s'amusent* (1894); *Vous m'en direz tant!* (with Tristan Bernard, 1894); *Chez*

les Snobs (1896); *Amour! Amour!* (1900). He also wrote numerous plays alone or in collaboration.

21. HERMANT, ABEL (1862–1950). Novelist. At first influenced by several literary schools, he eventually became most adept as an ironical chronicler of contemporary society. His works include a long series of novels entitled *Mémoires pour servir à l'histoire de la société* (1895–1913) and *Le Cycle de lord Chelsea* (1923–26). A purist in style, he was known for his satirical verve, sharp observations, and intellectual curiosity.

22. BEAUNIER, ANDRÉ (1869–1923). Critic and novelist; drama critic for *L'Echo de Paris* and literary critic for the *Revue des deux Mondes*. He wrote many novels, including *Dupont-Leterrier* (1900), *L'Homme qui a perdu son moi* (1911), *La Révolte* (1914), *La Folle Jeune Fille* (1923), numerous essays; and historical works. He was noted for refinement of style and sharp, penetrating literary criticisms.

23. COURIER, PAUL-LOUIS (1772–1825). Pamphleteer and scholar. He served in Italy where he indulged his passion for classical study. In his many pamphlets and letters to newspapers he upheld the rights of the peasants against oppression by the clergy and local government officials; also wrote much interesting correspondence to family and friends: *Lettres écrites de France et d'Italie* from 1787 to 1812.

24. PRÉVOST-PARADOL, LUCIEN-ANATOLE (1829–1870). Celebrated journalist of the Second Empire; wrote for the *Journal des Débats* and founded a weekly, the *Courrier du Dimanche*, which was suppressed for hostility to the Government. His attitude softened when Second Empire policies became more liberal. Ambassador to the United States in 1870, he suffered political disillusionment and committed suicide after the outbreak of the Franco-Prussian war.

25. ROCHEFORT, HENRI DE (1830–1913). Political journalist; contributed to *Le Nain jaune* and *Le Figaro* and founded the weekly *La Lanterne* in 1868, criticizing with wit and venom the government and person of Napoleon III. He held political office after the September Revolution of 1870 and founded two other newspapers: *La Marseillaise* (1869) and *L'Intransigeant* (1880).

26. BRUNETIÈRE. See Chapter 1, note 30.

27. CHERBULIEZ, VICTOR (1829–1899). Novelist of Swiss origin; wrote successful novels of manners in which sensational happenings were often placed against an historical or archeological background.

28. BOISSIER, GASTON (1823–1908). For a long time one of the best-known

historians of Latin antiquity, e.g., *Cicéron et ses amis* (1865), *La Religion romaine d'Auguste aux Antonins* (1874), *La Fin du paganisme en occident* (1891).

29. LEMAITRE, JULES (1853–1914). Drama critic for many years of the *Journal des Débats*. He is celebrated for his brilliant, impressionistic, often ironical articles, published in collected form as *Les Contemporains* (8 vols.) and *Impressions du théâtre* (11 vols.). He also wrote moderately successful plays and collections of short stories.

30. FAGUET, EMILE (1847–1916). Literary historian and critic. He was an indefatigable writer of widely ranging interests, though his favorite period was the 17th century. His criticism is seldom deemed profound but is stimulating by reason of his interest in men and ideas and his lively treatment. He wrote works of literary history and was drama critic for 20 years on the *Journal des Débats*.

31. FLAUBERT, GUSTAVE (1821–1880). Novelist; author of *Madame Bovary* (1857), celebrated novel of provincial life. He led a hermit-like existence at his country home near Rouen. In his correspondence he depicted himself as an extravagant Romantic who would go through life detesting all that is *bourgeois*, petty-respectable, platitudinous, and self-satisfied. He is often classed as a realist novelist because his aim was to achieve a rigidly objective and impersonal work of art, presented in the most perfect form. He imposed the severest restraint on the romantic, exuberant side of his nature, and his letters record the tortures his writing entailed. Other works include: *Salammbô* (1862), *L'Education sentimentale* (1869), *La Tentation de Saint Antoine* (1874), *Trois Contes* (1877), *Bouvard et Pécuchet* (1881).

32. CHATEAUBRIAND. See Chapter 5, note 4.

33. HUGO, VICTOR-MARIE (1802–1885). Generally regarded as the greatest poet of 19th-century France, perhaps of all French literature; also novelist, dramatist, and grand figure of the Romantic Movement. He exiled himself from France during the dictatorship of Napoleon III (1852–70), returning after the disastrous Franco-Prussian War. He had a political career as Senator of the Third Republic. His battles for liberty of the people and the arts alike made him a national idol. He is doubtless best known in the English-speaking world for his novels, notably *Notre-Dame de Paris* ("The Hunchback of Notre Dame") (1831), a vivid evocation of Paris in the Middle Ages; *Les Misérables* (1862), and *Les Travailleurs de la Mer* ("Toilers of the Sea") (1866). As a dramatist Hugo waged war

against classical conventions, beginning with *Cromwell* (1827) and *Hernani* (1830) (see Chapter 5, note 17). In the poems entitled *Les Châtiments* (1853) he denounced Napoleon III as the betrayer of his country in powerful and moving satirical verse.

34. RENAN. See Chapter 9, note 11.

35. MONTESQUIEU. See Chapter 1, note 51.

36. ROUSSEAU, JEAN-JACQUES. See Chapter 7, note 3.

37. BUFFON. See Chapter 3, note 7.

38. DIDEROT. See Chapter 8, note 1.

39. BACHAUMONT, LOUIS PETIT DE (1690–1771). Writer of memoirs (*Mémoires secrets*) which he began in 1762 and were continued by others. They constitute an important document in the history of ideas during the reign of Louis XV, dealing with politics, art, literature, theater, etc. He had a skeptical, epicurean mind of wide intellectual curiosity. He was an habitué of the salon of Mme Doublet.

40. UNIGENITUS DEI FILIUS. Title of the papal Bull of 1713 condemning one hundred and one propositions in the *Réflexions morales* of the Jansenist Quesnel. (See also Chapter 1, notes 8 and 9.)

41. THE DECLARATION OF THE RIGHTS OF MAN. A declaration voted by the Constituent Assembly August 27, 1789, setting forth the guiding principles of the French Revolution. It was modeled on the American Declaration of Independence.

Article XVI, in which Lanson observes the presence of Montesquieu, states: "Any society in which the guarantee of rights is not assured or the separation of powers not determined has no constitution."

The Articles in which Lanson finds "objectives most strongly advocated by Voltaire" read as follows:

VII. No man may be indicted, arrested, or detained except in cases determined by law and according to the forms which it has prescribed. Those who instigate, expedite, execute, or cause to be executed arbitrary orders should be punished; but any citizen summoned or seized by virtue of the law should obey instantly, and renders himself guilty by resistance.

IX. Every man being presumed innocent until judged guilty; if it is deemed indispensable to keep him under arrest, all rigor not necessary to secure his person should be severely repressed by law.

X. No one may be disturbed for his opinions, even in religion, provided that their manifestation does not trouble public order as established by law.

XI. Free communication of thought and opinion is one of the most precious of the rights of man. Every citizen may therefore speak, write, and print freely, on his own responsibility for abuse of this liberty in cases determined by law.

42. PREFECT. An important civil office created by Napoleon in 1800 as part of his reorganization of local government in France. The Prefect (*le Préfet*) is the executive head of a *département*, which is the principal administrative and electoral division established during the French Revolution to replace the former French provinces (Normandy, Brittany, Burgundy, etc.). There were 83 *départements* to begin with. By 1965 the number was 87. *Départements* are subdivided into *arrondissements, cantons,* and *communes,* roughly administrative or electoral rather than territorial subdivisions.

A Prefect is directly appointed by and responsible to the central government. He has an elected body, *le conseil général* ("the general council"), to assist him. The Prefect of a *département* has police powers except in Paris, where there is a special office of *Préfet de police.*

43. CONCORDAT. In general, an agreement between the Roman See and a secular government on matters that concern both. The Concordat of 1801, ratified by law in 1802, between Pius VII and the First Consul Bonaparte, reestablished Roman Catholicism and its free practice as the religion of the majority of Frenchmen; defined the relations between France and the Holy See; and demarcated the temporal and spiritual powers of the Church (e.g., as regarded the nomination, institution, and payment of the clergy, and claims to Church property). This settlement between Church and State lasted until 1905 when the Roman Catholic Church was disestablished in France and disendowed.

44. THE FALLOUX LAW. Regarding the Falloux Law, *Education in France* (a bulletin issued in 1963 by the Office of Education, U.S. Dept. of Health, Education, and Welfare) makes the following observations:

"Louis Napoleon had been elected president of the Second Republic by universal suffrage which was newly established in 1848. The eligible voters had (greatly) increased . . . and the power of the Catholics was thereby strengthened. . . . In the field of education there followed the Falloux Law of 1850 under (which) bishops were made members of the committee which appointed the heads (rectors) of each of the major administrative units for education, which were called academies. Moreover, the bishops were given prominent places on the councils in each of the academies, and it became easier for members of the clergy to teach in public schools. At the same time, liberal teachers were hunted down and accused of being revolutionaries. . . . The Falloux Law intensified the conflict between Church and State. For more than half a century to follow, small French communities were split, with the priest as symbolic head of one side and the village public school teacher as head of the other. . . ." (Chapt. II)

45. WIELAND, CHRISTOPH-MARTIN (1733–1813). German poet and writer who became famous as a satirist and was called "the German Voltaire."

46. GORANI, COUNT JOSEPH (1744–1819). Italian publicist born in Milan; member of the literary society of *Il Caffè*. His *Treatise on Despotism* (1770) placed him in the ranks of the *philosophes;* he was an ardent supporter of the French Revolution.

47. BECCARIA, CESARE BONESANA, MARQUIS DE (1738–1794). Italian publicist; student of the French economists and encyclopedists; famed as an advocate of reforms in the penal code. His *Essay on Crimes and Punishments* (Engl. tr. 1767) is one of the first arguments against capital punishment and inhuman treatment of criminals. His writings on economic theory anticipated the wage and labor theories of Adam Smith.

48. VERRI, PIETRO, COUNT (1728–1797). Italian writer; founded, with his brother Alessandro and friends, the liberal journal *Il Caffè*; economist, philosopher, and statesman; published many articles and essays on current political and social themes.

49. FOSCOLO, UGO (1778–1827). Italian writer of an ardent, passionate temperament; dedicated to liberal ideas; served as an officer in Napoleon's armies. He is one of the first outstanding writers of modern Italy. His writings include sonnets, odes, tragedies, and literary appreciations of Petrarch, Dante, and Boccaccio.

50. MONTI, VINCENZO (1754–1828). Italian poet; uncontested head of the neoclassical movement. Anticlerical, he admired Napoleon, who named him a professor at the University of Pavia and historiographer of the kingdom of Italy. He later rallied to Austria after Napoleon's downfall.

51. LARRA, MARIANO-JOSÉ DE (1809–1837). Spanish author whose father was a medical officer in Napoleon's armies; wrote numerous satirical articles for various newspapers which (collected and published 1835–7) constitute a complete satire on Spanish manners and morals

of the period; wrote a play *Macías* (1834) and a long novel dealing with the same character. His promising literary career was cut short by suicide.

52. HEINE, HEINRICH (1797–1856). German poet, famous for his lyrics and his wit and irony. Born of Jewish parentage, he was baptized a Christian (1825) and lived in Paris after 1830. Politically he was a radical who hoped to see a liberal government established in Germany. He wrote many songs and poems, a number of which were set to music by Schubert, Schumann, and others. The most famous of these is *Die Lorelei*. He also wrote travel sketches and literary criticism in both French and German.

A SELECTED BIBLIOGRAPHY

NOTE

This bibliography consists solely of works written in English, or available in English translation.

GENERAL WORKS ON THE EIGHTEENTH CENTURY

Becker, Carl, *The Heavenly City of the Eighteenth Century Philosophers*. New Haven, Conn., Yale University Press, 1955.

Beljame, Alexandre, *Men of Letters and the English Public in the Eighteenth Century, 1660–1744: Dryden, Addison, Pope,* edited with an Introduction and Notes by Bonamy Dobrée (translated by E. O. Lorimer), London, Kegan Paul, Trench, Trubner & Co., 1948.

Berlin, Isaiah, *The Age of Enlightenment, The 18th Century Philosophers,* New York, Mentor Books, New American Library, 1956.

Cassirer, Ernst, *The Philosophy of the Enlightenment,* Princeton, N.J., Princeton University Press, 1951.

Dunham, Barrows, *Heroes and Heretics: A Political History of Western Thought,* New York, Alfred A. Knopf, 1963.

Gay, Peter, *The Party of Humanity: Essays in the French Enlightenment,* New York, Alfred A. Knopf, 1963.

Havens, George R., *The Age of Ideas,* New York, Holt, Rinehart and Winston, 1955 (also available in paperback, New York, Collier Books, 1962).

Hazard, Paul, *The European Mind: The Critical Years,* New Haven, Conn., Yale University Press, 1953.

Manuel, Frank E., *The Eighteenth Century Confronts the Gods,* Cambridge, Mass., Harvard University Press, 1959.

Mowat, Robert B., *The Age of Reason,* London, Harrap & Co., 1934.

Nicolson, Harold, *The Age of Reason: The Eighteenth Century,* Garden City, N.Y., Doubleday and Co., 1961.

WORKS BY OR ABOUT VOLTAIRE

Bottiglia, William F., *Voltaire's Candide, Analysis of a Classic,* Geneva, Droz, 1959.

Brailsford, Henry N., *Voltaire and Reform in the Light of the French Revolution,* Geneva and Paris, 1959.

Brumfitt, John Henry, *Voltaire, Historian,* New York, Oxford University Press, 1958.

Durant, Will and Ariel, *The Age of Voltaire*, Vol. 9 in *The Story of Civilization*, New York, Simon and Schuster, 1965.

Foster, Milton P., ed., *Candide and the Critics*, Wadsworth Guides to Literary Studies, Belmont, Calif., Wadsworth, 1963.

Gay, Peter, *Voltaire's Politics: The Poet as Realist*, Princeton, N.J., Princeton University Press, 1959.

Maurois, André, *Voltaire, Living Thoughts Presented by André Maurois*, New York, Longmans, Green, and Co., 1939.

Meyer, Adolph, *Voltaire, Man of Justice*, New York, Howell, Soskin, 1945.

Mitford, Nancy, *Voltaire in Love*, Harper and Row, New York, 1957.

Morley, John, *Voltaire*, London, Macmillan, 1913.

Nixon, E., *Voltaire and the Calas Case*, New York, Vanguard, 1963.

Redman, Ben Ray, ed., *The Portable Voltaire*, New York, Viking Press, 1949.

Torrey, Norman, *The Spririt of Voltaire*, Old Marston, Oxford, Marston Press, 1963 (repr. of 1st ed.).

Voltaire, *The Age of Louis XIV* (translated by Martin P. Pollack), Everyman's Library, New York, E. P. Dutton and Co., 1926.

Voltaire, *Candide* (a bilingual edition, translated and edited by Peter Gay), New York, St. Martin's Press, 1963.

Wade, Ira O., *Voltaire and "Candide": A Study in the Fusion of History, Art, and Philosophy*, Princeton, N.J., Princeton University Press, 1959.

Wade, Ira O., *Voltaire and Mme. du Châtelet*, Princeton, N.J., Princeton University Press, 1941.

INDEX

This index (not provided in the French edition) refers both to Lanson's biography and Pomeau's *Commentary*. It does not include any references to Peter Gay's *Introduction*. (R.A.W.)

249